WITHDRAWN

STUDIES IN EVANGELICALISM
edited by
Kenneth E. Rowe &
Donald W. Dayton

1. Melvin E. Dieter. *The Holiness Revival of the Nineteenth Century.* 1980.

2. Lawrence T. Lesick. *The Lane Rebels: Evangelicalism and Antislavery in Antebellum America.* 1980.

3. Edward H. Madden and James E. Hamilton. *Freedom and Grace: The Life of Asa Mahan.* 1982.

4. Roger H. Martin. *Evangelicals United: Ecumenical Stirrings in Pre-Victorian Britain, 1795-1830.* 1983.

5. Donald W. Dayton. *Theological Roots of Pentecostalism.* 1987.

6. David L. Weddle. *The Law as Gospel: Revival and Reform in the Theology of Charles G. Finney.* 1985.

7. Darius L. Salter. *Spirit and Intellect: Thomas Upham's Holiness Theology.* 1986.

8. Wayne E. Warner. *The Woman Evangelist: The Life and Times of Charismatic Evangelist Maria B. Woodworth-Etter.* 1986.

9. Darrel M. Robertson. *The Chicago Revival, 1876: Society and Revivalism in a Nineteenth-Century City.* 1989.

THE CHICAGO REVIVAL, 1876:

Society and Revivalism in a Nineteenth-Century City

by

DARREL M. ROBERTSON

Studies in Evangelicalism, No. 9

The Scarecrow Press, Inc.
Metuchen, N.J., & London
1989

British Library Cataloguing-in-Publication data available

Library of Congress Cataloging-in-Publication Data

Robertson, Darrel M., 1950-
    The Chicago revival, 1876 : society and revivalism in a nine-
teenth-century city / Darrel M. Robertson.
        p.   cm. -- (Studies in evangelicalism ; no. 9)
    Bibliography: p.
    Includes index.
    ISBN 0-8108-2181-8
    1. Revivals--Illinois--Chicago--History--19th century. 2. Moody,
Dwight Lyman, 1837-1899. 3. Sankey, Ira David, 1840-1908. 4.
Chicago (Ill.)--Church history--19th century. I. Title. II.
Series.
BV3775.C5R6   1989
269'.24'0977311--dc19
                                                        88-34865

To My Parents

Marvin and Gladys Robertson

TABLE OF CONTENTS

ACKNOWLEDGMENTS

I am indebted to many people for their help in the development of this study. Dr. Garth Rosell first instilled in me a
fascination with American religious history. His interest in
the history of revivalism proved especially contagious, and
his encouragement and friendship continue to be a source of
inspiration. Dr. T. Dwight Bozeman provided stimulating
counsel throughout the writing of the manuscript. He and
Dr. Malcolm Rohrbough of the University of Iowa History
Department offered editorial suggestions and searching criticisms that proved always helpful as I struggled to rewrite
and reword the materials. Dr. Jeffery Cox also read the
manuscript and provided both encouragement and constructive
criticism.

For their courtesy and expert archival advice, I also
wish to thank the library staffs at the Moody Museum in Northfield, Massachusetts; McCormick Theological Seminary; Garrett
Theological Seminary; Chicago Theological Seminary; Newberry
Library; Chicago Historical Society Library; and the Presbyterian Historical Society Library. A special word of gratitude
is due to the staff of the University of Iowa Library and to
Walter Osborn at the Moody Bible Institute.

Except for the love, patience, and encouragement of
my best friend and partner in life, Patricia K. Robertson,
this book would never have been initiated, let alone completed.
For her and my two children, Andrea and Garth, who always
make coming home the highlight of the day, I am most thank-
ful. To my parents, Marvin and Gladys Robertson, who
taught me the meaning of love and faith, it is my greatest
joy to be able to dedicate this volume.

EDITORS' FOREWORD

The current resurgence of Evangelical religion has highlighted
the important role of this force in the formation of American
and British culture. This series will explore its roots in the
Evangelical revival and awakening of the eighteenth century,
its nineteenth-century blossoming in revivalism and social
reform, and its twentieth-century developments in both sectarian and "mainline" churches. Diversity within Evangelicalism will be highlighted--the search for holiness, the Mil-
lennial traditions, Fundamentalism, and Pentecostalism. We
are pleased to publish Darrel M. Robertson's study of post-
Civil War revivalism's urban context: The Chicago Revival,
1876: Society and Revivalism in a Nineteenth-Century City.

Mr. Robertson is pastor of the United Presbyterian
Church and First Congregational Church in Ashland, Wisconsin. After completing undergraduate studies at Moorhead
State University, Mr. Robertson studied theology at Bethel
Theological Seminary in St. Paul and took the M.A. and Ph.D.
in history at the University of Iowa. He has taught both
at Bethel Theological Seminary and at the University of Iowa
and is the author of several scholarly articles on American
church history.

Donald W. Dayton   Kenneth E. Rowe
Northern Baptist Theological   Drew University
   Seminary   Madison, NJ
Lombard, IL

LIST OF TABLES

Chapter I

INTRODUCTION

In October 1876, Dwight L. Moody and Ira D. Sankey embarked on a three-month revival campaign in Chicago, Illinois. Their highly organized effort was a marvelous success in the eyes of many contemporary observers. The newly erected Tabernacle, seating eight thousand and designed specifically for the Moody meetings, was filled repeatedly to overflowing. Even cold winter weather and a hotly contested presidential election campaign did not diminish interest in the revival. Descriptions of the event were front-page material in Chicago's leading newspapers, which also reprinted Moody's sermons, often verbatim, the day following their delivery.[1] Special streetcar lines were set up to facilitate travel to the Tabernacle. Cumulative attendance at the nightly sessions was estimated as high as nine hundred thousand persons in a city whose total population in 1876 numbered about four hundred thousand.[2] Several thousand ministers and church leaders invaded Chicago from the outstate area for a three-day Christian Convention held at the midpoint of the meetings. As they departed they took with them revival excitement to every part of the state. At the conclusion of the meetings more than six thousand names were listed at a session of converts.[3] During the revival and in the months immediately thereafter, large numbers of new members were added to those city's churches which had actively supported Moody's and Sankey's efforts.

The religious fervor which Moody and Sankey generated in Chicago in 1876 was part of a broader phenomenon extending to other major urban centers in America. From 1875 to 1877, Moody and Sankey conducted revival campaigns in New York, Philadelphia, Brooklyn, and Boston. Thousands crowded the meeting places wherever they went. Collections of Moody's

1

sermons and Sankey's gospel hymns were printed and became
overnight best sellers. Moody and Sankey became household
names among both the churched and the unchurched. Cities
across America vied for the honor of hosting a Moody and
Sankey meeting in their community. Revival was anticipated
and seemingly achieved wherever the two evangelists chose
to conduct services. The religious excitement that followed
Moody and Sankey in the mid-1870s was not equaled in the
remainder of the nineteenth century.

A Moody and Sankey revival was a religious and social
event of large significance for many urban dwellers in nineteenth-century America. Denominational distinctions were
set aside, and thousands of evangelical Christians came together to work as one for the revivalists.[4] Religious experience and theological questions were, at least temporarily,
established as topics of central importance to large numbers
of the public. Lethargic churches were enlivened and membership in many increased dramatically. Leading businessmen
financed the venture, encouraging their employees to attend
the meetings. Marshall Field, the prominent Chicago dry-
goods merchant, went so far as to arrange a special service
for his workers presided over by Moody and Sankey. Most
important for the purposes of this study, the revival promoted
certain religious and social values to which large numbers of
people allied themselves by various means--conversion, the
joining of Moody-supporting churches, active labor on behalf
of the evangelists, and the expression of fervent vocal sympathy or financial assistance for the cause.

Two questions arise at the outset of this exercise. Why
the need for a full-length, intensive examination of a Moody
campaign in a single city? And why Chicago? A cogent answer to the former question must point to the significance of
the evangelist and to the large numbers of people who were
affected by his crusades. In a preface to his recent study
of Moody's theology, Stanley N. Gundry calculates that Moody
brought the Gospel message by voice or pen to the attention
of at least 100 million people.[5] In light of such numbers it
is probably true that Moody "could plausibly have been called
Mr. Revivalist and perhaps Mr. Protestant" in the latter decades of the nineteenth century, and it was the great urban
revivals of the 1870s that thrust him into these positions of
influence.[6] Moody's understanding of the Christian Gospel
became a kind of standard for orthodoxy among many evangelical

Protestants. Moody himself became a figure around whom
conservative Protestants rallied. Numerous institutions which
he helped to found--the Student Volunteer Movement, Summer
Bible Conferences, and the various educational institutions--
became bastions of evangelical activism in the latter decades
of the nineteenth century and the early years of the twen-
tieth century. Only recently, however, has the historical
guild shown much interest in or appreciation for the significance of Moody. James F. Findlay's 1969 biography, Dwight
L. Moody: American Evangelist, 1837-1899, remains the best
full-scale, scholarly assessment of the revivalist.[7]

The aim of the present work is two-fold: first, to
provide a general exposition of events constituting the Chicago revival; second, to analyze the manner in which revivalism functioned socially in 1876 Chicago. The following
two chapters acquaint the reader with the city and explore
selected sources of social stress among Chicagoans. Chapters
Four and Five chronicle the events of the revival months and
examine closely Moody's and Sankey's evangelistic techniques.
Chapters Six, Seven, and Eight analyze the appeal of the revival to a select group of respondents. The concluding chapter explores the ecclesiastical and social results of the revival
in Chicago. The book proceeds on the assumption that social
conditions within Chicago worked to make segments of the
city's population especially receptive to revival and, in particular, to the rhetoric of Moody's sermons. Those sermons,
selected socioeconomic and political aspects of the city, and
the people who joined "revival churches" in the immediate
aftermath of the Moody campaign are, therefore, examined
intensively.[8]

Why Chicago? Perhaps the best reason for selecting
Chicago is the abundance of extant primary and secondary
materials pertaining to the social, economic, political, and
religious development of the city. The half-dozen newspapers
that chronicled Moody's three months in Chicago are readily
available in the city's many excellent public and private li-
braries. Located there also are the numerous Chicago-based
religious periodicals which took particular interest in the
Chicago meetings. These local magazines also reveal much
about prevailing attitudes and opinions among leading evangelicals in Chicago in the 1870s.[9] Several excellent histories
of the city shed much light on the socioeconomic and political
development of Chicago in the late nineteenth century. The

most important of these is Bessie L. Pierce's detailed, three-
volume study, A History of Chicago.[10] Curiously, the city's
religious history generally has been neglected by historians.
The few studies to address religious concerns and development have focused very narrowly on the Social Gospel movement or specific religious reformers.[11]

Aside from the obvious benefits of supplementing existing knowledge about the city's history, there is yet another
reason for selecting Chicago. It is my contention that the
conclusions drawn here may be suggestive of what happened
in other American urban centers which hosted Moody revivals,
because Chicago in the mid-1870s was in many important respects like New York, Brooklyn, Philadelphia, and Boston.
All, for example, struggled with the problems of industrialization and urbanization. Inadequate housing and transportation, poverty, labor unrest, sewage disposal, increasing crime,
and so on were concerns shared by all large American cities.
Massive immigration and a swelling Roman Catholic and foreign-
born population were altering significantly the social and religious compositions of these large urban metropolises.

There were differences, to be sure. Chicago, along
with New York City, had an unusually large number of foreign-
born people;[12] but it had achieved its position of metropolitan
eminence much later than New York, Brooklyn, Philadelphia,
or Boston. Social and cultural forms were, therefore, perhaps entrenched less firmly in Chicago than in its Eastern
counterparts. The lingering effects of the depression of 1873
were less serious in Chicago than in the Eastern metropolises
even though Chicago's economy in the mid-1870s was far from
healthy. Chicago had experienced a devastating fire in 1871
which required the complete rebuilding of the downtown commercial area, but the city had recovered fully by the time
the depression occurred in 1873. By and large, then, the
cities Moody visited from 1875 to 1877 when his revival meetings were a focus of national interest shared similar characteristics and faced common problems. The differences that
existed were of degree, not of kind.

Any study that proposes to inquire into the origins and
function of a religious revival must proceed with great caution.
It is doubtful that any revival can be explained wholly. The
motivations of individuals embracing a revival are too varied,
complex, and personal to be embraced within a monocausal

assessment. Historic American revivals functioned at a variety
of levels for participants including that of personal religious
experience. As sociologist William Tremmel has noted, religion
itself is "an experience of great satisfaction and immense
personal worth. [It] is not only something for people (func-
tional) but is something to people (an experience, even an
ecstasy)."[13] Such ecstatic or mystical experience is beyond
historical analysis. But the testimony of those who claimed
such experience is an important part of the story to be told.

The Moody and Sankey revival was a profoundly personal religious experience for those who attended the Tabernacle meetings and came away somehow comforted or enlivened
in their faith. Their words, chronicled in diaries and journals, testify to that fact. This book seeks neither to ap-
plaud nor to dismiss the reality of what they perceived as
happening to themselves. To do either would be a rather
foolhardy act of speculation. However, it is both feasible
and appropriate to offer certain careful generalizations about
revivals and revivalistic phenomena within a particular social
setting when the evidence one has begins to suggest a certain
picture. This work is an attempt to describe just such a
picture.

Chapter II

THE CITY

It surprised almost no one when Dwight L. Moody in the summer of 1876 selected Chicago as the fourth of five major cities
from which to launch his massive and ambitious program to
revive and evangelize America. Lauded by contemporaries as
the Empire City of the West, Gem of the Prairies, and Queen
of the Lakes, Chicago was well on its way to achieving the
lofty status of America's second greatest city. By the mid-
1870s, the Midwestern metropolis was firmly entrenched as
the preeminent trade center of the West and the axis for the
nation's greatest railroad network.[1]

Chicago had always been enterprising. When it was
scarcely three decades old and had only one hundred thousand
residents, it had attracted the Republican nominating convention of 1860 away from the larger urban centers of the East.
Ten years later, the population had tripled to almost three
hundred thousand inhabitants, and by the time of the Moody
meetings in 1876 another hundred thousand persons called
Chicago home.[2] Its superb location for rail and water transport attracted to the city the greatest portion of the agricultural and mining produce of the central and western regions. Chicagoans boasted about the massive waterworks
which drew drinking water through a two-mile-long tunnel
into the city's reservoirs. In the 1860s and early 1870s, new
industries joined the already flourishing lumberyards, meatpacking plants, stockyards, distilleries, and dry-goods manufacture to pump fresh blood into the economic life of the rapidly expanding city. Elegant hotels, like the Grand Pacific
and the renowned Palmer House, entertained distinguished
guests of Chicago, while lesser establishments catered to a
steady stream of transients. Indeed, so great was the city's
reputation worldwide that Otto von Bismarck told a visitor

from the United States in 1870, "I wish I could go to America
if only to see that Chicago."[3]

The Great Fire of October 1871 nearly doomed the city's
aspirations. It began about 9:00 p.m. on Sunday evening,
October 8, in the barn of Mr. and Mrs. Patrick O'Leary on
the near West Side of the city. An unusually hot, dry summer combined with the wood-frame construction of most houses
and buildings to make the city especially vulnerable to the
flames. Nevertheless, when the fire bells rang at 9:30 p.m.,
few Chicagoans were seriously worried about their safety.
This time, however, there was good reason for concern. The
fire department was misdirected and rushed to a spot about
a mile away from the fire. By the time they reached the correct location, the inferno was totally out of control. Fanned
by gusting southwesterly winds, the flames jumped the Chicago
River and roared through the heart of the city. Although,
by a strange quirk of fate, the O'Leary home itself was un-
harmed, when the fire was finally put out by a light rain on
Tuesday, an area of three and a half square miles and buildings valued at $196 million had been destroyed.[4] Most of
Chicago's most famous stores, churches, and buildings were
gone. Nearly one hundred thousand persons were left home-
less.[5]

Chicago was down but not out. The smoke had not yet
cleared when the Tribune announced that "the people of this
once beautiful city have resolved that CHICAGO SHALL RISE
AGAIN." A day after the fire, a fruit and cider stand set
up shop in the rubble of Clark Street. Two days later, W. D.
Kerfoot, a real estate broker, announced that he was reopen-
ing with "all gone but wife, children and energy." Splashed
across papers nationwide, the picture of Kerfoot standing in
front of his ramshackle office against the background of the
charred city testified to the determination of Chicagoans to
rebuild.[6] Within a week, temporary housing had been erected
for more than five thousand persons, and construction had
commenced on two hundred permanent business structures.
The Relief and Aid Society took charge of the distribution of
food and clothing for the needy. Reconstruction offered immediate employment to thousands of workers in desperate need
of income. Less than a month after the fire, Field, Leiter &
Company were selling dry goods in a temporary structure
near the river while hundreds of workers were busy rebuilding their downtown store, bigger and better than before. On

the first anniversary of the fire, Chicago's volume of trade
actually exceeded that of October 1871. Within three years
a visitor to the city was pressed to find any evidence of the
burning. The Saturday Review of London, impressed by
Chicago's incredible recovery and boundless enterprise, decided that the city must be the "concentrated essence of
Americanism."[7]

The day after the fire, John S. Wright, a well-known
Chicago booster, predicted that "Chicago will have more men,
more money, more business within five years than she would
have had without this fire."[8] Though few people believed
him on that October day, Wright was correct. The new factories and stores were both larger and better equipped than
the old. The brick and iron which replaced wood as the pre-
dominant material for construction downtown was safer and
offered significantly better architectural possibilities for the
builders. The city skyline rose several stories higher in the
rebuilding of Chicago. At the same time, workers resumed
the rush to the city in ever greater numbers to aid in the
process of reconstruction. Despite the panic of 1873, Chicago's economy continued to grow. In 1874 the stockyards
received a record 843,966 cattle, 333,655 sheep, and 4,758,379
hogs. Dry-goods sales, the press announced proudly, totaled
more than $50 million, and the trade in boots and shoes almost
$12 million. The dramatic recovery from the disaster of 1871,
the swelling population of the city, and the annual increase
in economic output in spite of depression caused one leading
Chicago booster, Deacon Bross, to proclaim loudly that it was
the city's "manifest destiny" to become one of the great urban
centers of America, perhaps even of the world.[9]

By the summer of 1876, Chicago had gathered to itself
a population just in excess of four hundred thousand persons.[10] The residents of the city were almost equally divided
between foreign-born and native Americans. Slightly more
than half of the native population were lifelong inhabitants of
the city, and the largest portion of the remainder had their
roots in the Old Northwest. In 1880 only 2.5 percent of the
native-born population of Chicago originated in the South.
Bessie Pierce, who perhaps understood the city better than
any other historian, noted that it was the regional social patterns of the North, largely inherited from New England, that
predominated in the city.[11]

Germans, Irish, and Scandinavians formed the largest portion of the foreign-born population living in Chicago in the 1870s.[12] Generally speaking, the newly arrived immigrants found employment at the lowest remunerative levels in the city's occupational scale. Germans frequently provided the labor force in breweries, distilleries, and factories. Large numbers of the Irish were engaged in the labor of rebuilding the city. The lumberyards and stockyards also employed many Irishmen, and the Democratic party in Chicago provided jobs for others. Scandinavians often found work at the shipyards, in domestic service, and in manufacturing. They constituted the largest portion of the city's tailors, dressmakers, and milliners. All three ethnic groups had been preceded by immigrants of like nationality who frequently had found success and prosperity in Chicago. The newly arrived foreign-born fully expected to emulate their former countrymen's social and economic achievements.[13]

Chicago's foreign-born tended to cluster together into distinctive ethnic concentrations. Within these enclaves they found customs that were familiar, a language they understood, and friends and family members to help in the search for jobs and generally to ease their adjustment to life in Chicago. Germans flocked to the near North Side, establishing their beer gardens and naming the streets and businesses after Germans of renown. The Irish located themselves in large numbers in the area southwest from downtown near the stockyards and lumberyards where many were employed. Irish pubs, the tall spires of massive Roman Catholic cathedrals, and the astounding festivities which occurred there on St. Patrick's Day helped to identify the distinctively Irish presence in that section of the city. Scandinavians were more dispersed throughout the city than were the Germans or Irish but still predominated in certain wards in the near North Side and in the northwest.[14]

The immigrant presence contributed significantly to the cosmopolitan character of the city. Germans, Irish, and Scandinavians each had their respective daily newspapers, societies, and even theatre groups. Each sought consciously, though in varying degrees, to preserve distinctive national customs and, in the case of the Germans, to retain the use of their language. Scandinavians tended to sympathize with the Republican party, Germans were a mixed group politically, and the Irish, almost to a man, were fervent Democrats.

Differences in custom and religion separated the Germans and
Irish especially from the heavily Protestant, evangelically
oriented, native-born majority. Scandinavians, on the other
hand, more readily were accepted and assimilated by the native Chicagoans, perhaps because of the hearty confidence
of the Norsemen in the process of Americanization and their
remarkable propensity toward the Protestant virtues of frugality, hard work, and peaceful living.[15]

The foreign-born population provided the largest share
of the labor force which rebuilt Chicago and, in a sometimes
tense alliance with the city's commercial leadership, propelled
Chicago toward a position of industrial preeminence in the
West. It was during the 1870s that Chicago became, in Sandburg's memorable lines, "Hog butcher for the World, Tool
maker, stacker of wheat, Player with railroads and the nation's freight handler."[16]

By good fortune or providence, the meatpacking industry had been spared the ravages of the Great Fire. At the
mile-square Union Stockyards, established in 1865 southwest
of the city limits, much of the country's livestock was slaugh-
tered and prepared for market. Under the innovative genius
of Chicago's "Big Three" in meatpacking--Philip D. Armour,
Gustavus Swift, and Nelson Morris--the industry applied the
technology and science of the new age in order to expand
the market and maximize profits. Refrigerator cars were built
by the packers themselves and employed to ship fresh meat
nationwide. Waste products of the slaughter were channeled
into such marketable items as glue, fertilizer, and soap. By
the mid-1870s Chicago was the unquestioned meatpacking capital of the world.[17]

In her roles as "tool maker" and "stacker of wheat,"
the city profited from her ready access by rail and sea to
the rich mineral resources and agricultural produce of the
Midwest. Iron ore and soft coal found their way to huge
blast furnaces located on the south branch of the Chicago
River and on the Calumet River. The steel produced there
fed innumerable local manufactures. Among the most pros-
perous and expanding of these was Cyrus McCormick's reaper
plant and the Crane Brothers' Manufacturing Company. Each
employed hundreds of workers. Corn and barley found their
way to the large distilleries and breweries located on the North
Side. Wheat was hauled into Chicago and ground into flour

at the city's mills. Industrial expansion throughout the 1870s
made Chicago a national center of manufacture as well as a
center of commerce. [18]

Nowhere was the genius of Chicago's entrepreneurs more
evident than in the merchandising business. The unchallenged
leader was Marshall Field. Together with his financially astute
partner, Levi Leiter, Field erected a fabulous dry-goods business which enjoyed retail and wholesale sales of more than
$13 million in 1871. The fire was only a temporary setback
for the well-insured Field. Field, Leiter & Company immediately restocked its merchandise, rebuilt the downtown store,
and by 1881 had doubled its sales to $24 million. While Mar-
shall Field led the way, Chicago merchants John V. Farwell,
the Mandel brothers, and Montgomery Ward built sizable fortunes in the dry-goods business. In 1872 Ward opened his
wholesale house of merchandise for "farmers and mechanics
throughout the Northwest." The first of the nationwide mail-
order companies, Ward typified the sophistication and expansion of Chicago's commercial leadership in the Midwest. [19]

Marshall Field was just one of many Chicago business
giants who had risen from lowly beginnings--a clerkship pay-
ing $400 a year in 1856--to the head of a large and prosperous
company and, in the process, amassed a considerable personal
fortune. Gustavus Swift, Philip Armour, and Nelson Morris,
the last a German-born immigrant, could have related similar
rags-to-riches stories. Less spectacular, but more common,
was the general success story of middle-class Chicagoans,
many of whom had arrived with little or nothing in the 1850s
and had carved out a respectable niche in the commercial and
social structure of the city. These citizens owned decent
homes, lived comfortable if modestly, and held jobs somewhere
in the middle to upper rungs of the economic ladder. Under-
standably, their experiences and the visible evidence of their
prosperity raised the expectations for similar success and
rapid advancement among newly arrived city dwellers. [20]

In reality, however, life in Chicago in the mid-1870s
was a series of sharp contrasts and paradoxes with the chasm
between the wealthy and the newly arrived laborer virtually
uncrossable. The city's elite segregated themselves in exclusive residential districts. The most fashionable area in 1876
was on the South Side in the area of Prairie Avenue. The
migration of the socially prominent southward had been initiated

by the Marshall Fields who in 1873 moved into a $175,000 mansion designed by Richard Hunt Morris. The Philip Armours and the George Pullmans soon joined the Prairie Avenue set, as did W. W. Kimball of piano fame and his wife. Within an area of five blocks, forty of the sixty members of the exclusive Commercial Club had their homes. The wealthy few who shied away from the South Side, whether by personal preference or because of the outrageous price of land, settled for "Millionaire's Row" along lower Michigan Avenue or "McCormicksville" on the North Side.[21]

Regardless of the location of their residence, Chicago's well-to-do and socially elite lived similarly. Fine carriages and horses waited to carry them to any desired destination. Butlers, maids, and house servants greeted callers and catered to the needs of the house. Immaculate ballrooms were the sites of dances, and ornately furnished parlors served for more personal teas and house calls. Before calling on friends, the socially astute lady scanned carefully the Bon Ton Directory, giving the "names in Alphabetical order, Addresses and Hours of Reception of the Most Prominent and Fashionable Ladies Residing in Chicago and Its Suburbs." Attendance at theatres, operas, and concerts was expected and, perhaps, enjoyed by most. An invitation to the Potter Palmers or the Cyrus McCormicks signified one's acceptance by the socially elite. Men and women of social prominence found companionship and status in exclusive clubs like the Fortnightly Club for women and the Chicago and Commercial Clubs for gentlemen.[22]

Less than a mile west of Prairie Avenue there existed a world totally foreign to the experience of the Pullmans or Armours. Clustered together in the vicinity of the stockyards to the southwest was the largest concentration of Irish laborers in the city.[23] Most lived in simple, wood-frame cottages, sometimes erected on both the front and rear of lots and situated on streets with few sewers and practically no pavements. The most densely populated district was just north of the south branch of the Chicago River nearest the downtown area. In 1873 a writer for the Tribune described the conditions of living on one of the worst spots in this area, Maxwell Street near Halstead Street.

The street may be singled out of a thousand by the peculiar, intensive stench that arises from pools of

> thick and inky compound which in many cases is
> several feet deep and occasionally expands to the
> width of a small lake. Almost at every step a dead
> dog, cat or rat may be seen. These usually saga-
> cious animals had mistaken this for a respectable street
> because it is very broad and tried to pass through,
> but with their lives had to pay for their reckless-
> ness and foolhardiness. The poor creatures un-
> doubtedly died of asphyxiation.[24]

Admittedly, conditions on Maxwell Street were unusually bad.
But poor and overcrowded housing, inadequate sanitation,
and muddy streets were common throughout the city's working-
class districts.[25]

Almost invariably, the lowest-paid workers (usually the
latest group of immigrants) were forced to endure crowded,
dark, unsanitary conditions of living, places one health in-
spector in 1881 termed "unfit for habitation by a civilized
people." Disease was a chronic problem in these ramshackle
buildings. Reports on mortality in the various wards of the
city showed a close correlation between poor housing and poor
health. In 1881 fully half of the children of Chicago died before reaching five years of age, and the next year a study
by the Department of Health revealed that deaths in the tene-
ment wards outnumbered those in other city wards almost
three to one.[26]

During the 1870s a kind of informal segregation based
upon housing began to take form in the middle- and working-
class residential areas of Chicago. The poorest immigrants
tended to cluster in a broad band of older homes and hastily
constructed tenements stretched around the central business
district. Unable to afford either the costs of transportation
to and from work or the better built, but higher priced,
housing farther away from the downtown area, these Chicagoans often crowded three or more families into a poorly constructed, poorly ventilated home. An attached shed in the
rear of the home facing the alley sometimes housed yet another family--an attempt by the owner of the home to supple-
ment his meager income. In 1881 in the predominantly German Fourteenth Ward, 1,107 buildings housed 18,976 persons.
Every building in the district housed at least three families,
and 174 structures provided shelter for five or more families.[27]

From these increasingly congested, poverty-stricken
areas the more successful inhabitants moved away at the first
opportunity. Most often, they occupied newer homes constructed at a distance from the business district, thus forming a second band of residences--this time composed of middle-
class citizens. These families still lived modestly but were
less crowded and more comfortable. Their distant location
from downtown employment was ameliorated by transportation
improvements that made commuting feasible.[28]

Thus the pattern of residential living in Chicago was
affected directly in the 1870s by the continual influx of immigrants. Arriving with few resources and no income, these
folk took whatever shelter was available, often in vacant
houses, rear-lot tenements, or congested flats in the old
areas near downtown. Conditions were scarcely tolerable.
Yet, those who survived often prospered sufficiently to climb
out of the worst areas into more pleasant neighborhoods
nearby and, in time, to the newly constructed areas on the
fringes of the city. It was, indeed, not unreasonable to
hope that some second- or third-generation son might one day
build by the lake and find a niche in the Commercial Club
downtown.

Despite lingering economic troubles due to the depression of 1873 and the very real social ills among the city's
poor, Chicago's social and commercial leaders chose to emphasize their city's accomplishments and its promise of a splendid
future. They took pride in a public school system which en-
rolled 51,128 pupils in 1876. Their sons and daughters received advanced instruction at increasingly prestigious schools
like the University of Chicago, Lake Forest College, and Northwestern University. The Philosophical Society and the Literary Club offered further intellectual stimulus to interested
Chicagoans. The most elaborate cuisine of the day was available at the restaurants of the Grand Pacific Hotel or Palmer
House--the latter, revolutionary for its time with large rooms,
a dining hall of magnificent proportions, and a barbership
famed equally for its service and for the silver dollars im-
bedded in the floor. Wealthy Chicagoans doubtless enjoyed
taking guests to these extravagant hotels, whose size was described as "monstrous" even by Pierce, a well-traveled newspaper publisher who visited the city in 1876. For entertainment,
cultured citizens had their choice of plays, concerts, and
operas presented at McVicker's Theatre, Hooley's Theatre,

and the Academy of Music. In 1873 P. T. Barnum brought
his fabled "Greatest Show on Earth" to the city for those
whose tastes were less sophisticated. In the same year civic
pride was boosted by the erection of the Inter-State Industrial Exposition Building, a gaudy structure of glass and iron
which extolled Chicago's achievements in trade and industry.
"This is a peerless metropolis," exulted Andrew Schuman in
the Lakeside Monthly, asserting that Chicago had proved itself such "in its indomitability of spirit, in its solidity of
structure, in its imposing architecture, in its development of
a sleepless vitality, an unaltering faith and an irrepressible
progressive impulse."[29]

    Religion was also a significant part of the experience
of many Chicagoans in the 1870s. The Standard, a Chicago-
based Baptist weekly, reported in 1876 that 218 functioning
churches were located in the city. Of this number, about 100
congregations represented the mainline evangelical Protestant
denominations, another 33 were Roman Catholic churches, the
various Lutheran congregations totaled 25 in number, and 17
Episcopalian churches were listed.[30] The Catholic and Lutheran churches profited most from the continuous influx of
foreign-born immigrants to the city. By 1876 only the Methodists were able to match the number of Roman Catholic churches
in Chicago, and by the close of the 1880s Lutheran membership in the city exceeded that of all other Protestant denominations.[31]

    The more established citizenry tended to flock to the
sanctuaries of large Methodist, Presbyterian, Congregational,
and Baptist churches located most often in the residential
areas of the middle and upper classes.[32] In many cases the
parishioners of these congregations worshiped in imposing
edifices, paid sizable pew rents, and listened to well-educated,
articulate clergymen.[33] A visitor to Chicago in 1875 was duly
impressed by the sophistication of the city's leading ministers.

> Chicago is no place for weakness. Nor can medio-
> crity in the scholastic attainments of clergymen find
> much favor here. Chicago pays good salaries for
> teachers of Divine truths, and is able to command
> them. The poor preacher, that is, the man who
> preaches poorly can hardly find much comfort here.
> He must soon become conscious that he is not up to
> the Chicago standard.... The apostle of to-day is

a scholar and an orator, a man of intellectual ability,
and qualified in all respects to minister to the spiritual wants of a metropolitan flock.[34]

Some lamented the elegance and imposing respectability of
such churches, arguing that such features alienated the working classes and poor. Generalizing about Protestant churches
nationwide, the Nation in 1875 observed that "to become a
pew holder in all the leading churches ... is to become a
stock holder in a wealthy and flourishing corporation, and
the more powerful the preacher, the more it costs to hear
him." Christianity, except in the Roman Catholic churches,
it concluded, had "become the religion of the comfortable and
well-to-do."[35]

Protestants in Chicago, however, had not given up on
efforts to convert the city's poor and unchurched. Mission
societies of every denomination were active in the city, and
numerous individual congregations supported mission chapels
erected at strategic locations in working districts.[36] Sunday
schools, both those associated with the missions in the city
and those connected with the established churches, continued
to propagate the Gospel among the young. At least five Sunday schools in Chicago regularly greeted more than one thousand students each Lord's Day morning. A survey of the
Congregational, Methodist, and Presbyterian churches in the
city shows that thirty of these congregations cared for a
Sunday school of at least three hundred students.[37] Another effective means of evangelical outreach was afforded
the Protestant churches by the Young Men's Christian Association. Chartered in 1858, the Chicago YMCA had grown to
more than a thousand members by 1873. Its newspaper, Every-
body's Paper, published in the city, circulated a satisfying
sixty thousand copies a month. Offering recreation, Gospel
meetings, entertainment, warm meals, and shelter, the YMCA
sought to usher newly arrived young men into the membership of the supporting denominations and to expand the moral
influence of Protestant Christianity throughout society.[38]

Chicago was not the outwardly religious town in 1876
that it had appeared to be in the mid-1850s when a visitor
remarked that the Sabbath there was "more respected than
in any town of 20,000 inhabitants or upwards, south of Philadelphia."[39] Now beer gardens and pubs were filled on Sundays, horsecars carried attenders to the theatre or out to

dinner, and Sunday newspapers were delivered at many door-steps. The reading of Scripture in the Chicago public schools had been abolished by law in 1875. And only about one in twenty-two Chicagoans in 1872 held membership in a Baptist, Presbyterian, Congregational, or Methodist church.[40] The Presbyterian Interior in the year of the Moody revival estimated that half the city population was "unchurched" or "heathen."[41] Gambling thrived and brothels offered their wares without hindrance. Barrel houses and concert saloons were spread throughout the city. Miss Addie Ballou, a noted Boston re-former, arrived to speak at Farwell Hall in September 1871, after spending two weeks investigating vice and crime in the city. Her comments shocked the moral sensibilities of Chicago Christians. "It is a deplorable fact that Chicago is an evil place," she declared.

> The city fathers and clergymen countenance not only three hundred and fifty brothels, but hundreds more places of assignation. I have personally seen city of-ficials and ministers in the brothels. Your taxes are going to the support of harlots. It is not only the criminals who maintain vice, but the elite of this city, which has become a modern Sodom that must perish if it does not change its ways.[42]

Still, the churches and their lay and clerical leadership continued to exert a powerful influence upon the city. Per-sistent, and sometimes effective, pressure was directed against Sabbath breakers and the whiskey trade. The city's two greatest merchants, Marshall Field and John V. Farwell, mem-bers respectively of the First and Second Presbyterian churches, refused to hire men who drank alcohol and would not advertise in the Sunday newspapers.[43] The YMCA received generous support in its effort to direct the paths of young men toward righteous living.[44] And religious newspapers like the Congre-gational Advance, the Presbyterian Interior, the Baptist Standard, and the Methodist Northwestern Christian Advocate had large circulations and gave a distinct moral tone to Chi-cago's and the nation's news.[45] Chicago's Protestants had certainly lost the hegemony in morals and religious outlook they had once enjoyed in the city. But the battle, they be-lieved, was far from over and their resources were still im-pressive.

The religious inclinations of many leading Chicagoans

caused them to read with interest the astounding reports of
revivals in Scotland and England. Revivals were familiar to
these folk. Some, in fact, remembered fondly the religious
excitement that had swept the city in 1857 and 1858.[46] Others
attended regularly the annual camp meetings conducted by
the Methodists near the lake. The English revivals were especially fascinating to Chicago readers, however, because the
central figure in the crusades was Dwight L. Moody. Moody
was an adopted son of Chicago whose labors for the local YMCA
were well remembered. A Sunday school and independent
church founded by the revival preacher still flourished on
the city's North Side.[47] Curious Chicagoans wondered if the
local evangelist could possibly match his successes overseas
in his home town.

But Moody was not the only newsworthy item that caught
the attention and interest of Chicagoans in 1876. The revela-
tion of the evils of the Tweed Ring in New York City combined
with reports of fraud and corruption in government at the
national level caused many Chicagoans to shake their heads
in dismay. The more censorious citizens of Chicago frowned
upon reading the daily accounts of Henry Ward Beecher's alleged promiscuity with the wife of one of his parishioners.
Equally newsworthy were reports of events farther West.
Battles with Indians always made colorful reading, and the
city's newspapers in 1876 did not disappoint their readers.
Reports of continuing Indian troubles climaxed with dramatic
front-page accounts of Custer's massacre. Almost as eye-
catching was the account of the bank robbery in Northfield,
Minnesota, and the subsequent capture of some members of
the notorious James and Younger gangs. The death of wealthy
Cornelius Vanderbilt provided a moral lesson for some that
virtue was ultimately more important than was the accumulation
of great wealth. The Civil War continued to weigh upon the
minds of Chicagoans in the 1870s. Reminiscences of great
battles and the horrors of the prison camp at Andersonville
reminded readers of the evils of the South. Throughout the
year, politically active Chicagoans riveted their attention on
the upcoming presidential elections scheduled for November
1876.

It was, of course, the literate middle and upper classes
who formed the largest portion of the readership of Chicago's
leading newspapers and magazines. For numerous others in
the city the daily quest for mere survival probably consumed

all their time and energy. Those who had little yearned for something better. Increasingly, they expressed their frustrations, sometimes violently. On the other hand, those who had secured a niche in the city's social and economic structure sought to maintain what they had achieved. The tensions between groups in these situations distressed some Chicagoans and aroused fears in the hearts of others. The world of Chicago was undergoing massive alterations in the 1870s due to immigration, urbanization, and industrialization. These changes heightened the levels of stress and strain for many Chicagoans. Increasingly, economic troubles, social unrest, and political controversies were debated against a background of ethnic and religious distrust. When Moody at last returned to the city in 1876, some Chicagoans were ready to promote revival as an antidote for the city's ills.

Chapter III

IMMIGRANT AND CATHOLIC: THE
SOURCES OF STRESS AND STRAIN

On Christmas Day of 1875, the Reverend A. E. Kittridge,
pastor of the large and prestigious Third Presbyterian Church
of Chicago, summarized for his congregation the general de-
moralization he perceived in local and national life.

> Our own city is but a picture of all our large cities,
> and you well know how mighty are the waves of ini-
> quity in Chicago, how the law has quailed before
> the power of the gambling community, and has con-
> fessed its helplessness to execute its penalties; how,
> in defiance of law, houses of shame line our most
> beautiful streets and avenues; how the majority of
> our rulers are men without principle, using their
> official power for self-aggrandisement; how the open
> drinking saloon, from the fashionable resort of busi-
> ness men and clerks to the lowest bar-room, are
> making drunkards by the thousands and breaking
> tens of thousands of loving hearts, and yet sustained
> by the law; how infidelity has grown bolder than
> ever before, and Sabbath-breaking is on the in-
> crease.[1]

A growing "foreign" influence in Chicago and "Romish attacks"
upon the city's institutions, he declared, was in large part
responsible for the present moral debacle.

Kittridge's pained outcry typified the response of many
Protestants in Chicago to the severe economic and social alterations resulting from rapid urbanization and industrialization. Life in the city seemed suddenly out of control and
disorderly. Traditional values and cultural mores appeared

in jeopardy. Economic woes and repeated political and social
crises in the 1870s further exacerbated tensions. Kittridge
and other Protestant leaders like him who attempted to assess
the problems and identify their causes did not, however, often
comprehend the complexity of the social and economic transformation which so disturbed their living. Instead, they found
a more easily discernible, if simplistic, explanation for their
troubles in the large, newly arrived foreign-born and Roman
Catholic populations.[2] This development, and the series of
events and circumstances in Chicago which especially encouraged it, provided the crucial background for the revival of
1876.

Economic misfortunes troubled Chicago throughout the
1870s. In February 1876 the Tribune commented that "dull-
ness and depression are terms that imperfectly indicate the
disastrous character of the year just ended to every form of
American industry and enterprise. Prostration and exhaus-
tion are words that come much nearer the real state of the
case."[3] The number of business failures in the first nine
months of 1876 was the largest of any comparable period since
the onset of the panic.[4] The Western Manufacturer complained
in early 1877 that for "more than three years ... we have
been passing through the valley, with the waves of adversity
rising gradually higher and higher, and ever and anon carrying off some new victim into the slough of bankruptcy."[5] As
the Moody and Sankey Tabernacle neared completion in late
September, many Chicagoans longed for better times, but the
outlook was dim.

The depression hit hardest among the working classes.
After the Great Fire the work of rebuilding the city had made
jobs plentiful and wages high. Attracted by promises of sure
prosperity and unlimited work, laborers, both native and
foreign-born, flocked to Chicago.[6] But the exhilaration over
plentiful work was short-lived, for in another year panic rav-
aged the country and spread unemployment and suffering
throughout Chicago. Appeals for assistance in finding jobs
poured into the city's Employment Bureau. Thousands of
workers lost their jobs; where employees were retained, reductions in wages often were imposed.[7]

In the winter of 1873, anxious and frustrated working
men had begun to organize to protest the decreasing wages
and general lack of work. In late December ten thousand

angry workers marched on City Hall demanding that the city
council either initiate a program of public works or provide
direct relief. With the city's treasury near bankruptcy, the
council in desperation turned to other agencies for financial
relief. A meeting was quickly arranged between labor leaders
and the Relief and Aid Society which had in hand funds left
over from fire relief estimated at nearly $1 million. Despite
the workers' request that the funds be distributed immediately
among the poor and jobless, the Relief and Aid Society promised only to care for the truly "destitute." To its credit the
society did distribute as much as $4,000 in a single day in
the long, cruel winter of suffering which followed.[8]

For the next few years hardship continued unabated,
nurturing resentment and despair. Even where wages were
not actually decreased, frequent layoffs and rumors of pay
cuts generated anxiety among workers. Strikes were common-
place, often accompanied by violence. Radical speakers, ignored in better times, gained large audiences and numerous
converts among the ranks of those worried about tomorrow's
bread. On June 13, 1875, a mass meeting of workers in
Turner Hall listened avidly to the prophecy of socialist John
Simmins that "proletarian revolution within a few decades"
with all its attendant terrors would come to Chicago "if the
ruling classes threaten to suffocate the labor movement."[9]
Filled with anger and growing frustration, some workers expressed their passions violently. When August Hielank, a
Bohemian laborer involved in a bloody strike of lumber shovers
in May 1876, committed suicide, the Evening Journal reported
the incident with icy succinctness. "No cause, except despon-
dency, caused by poverty, is assigned. The Coroner was
notified."[10]

The angry rhetoric and the violence of strikers and
the ever-increasing tension between labor and capital roused
the concern of many Chicagoans. As early as 1874, the Tribune had predicted that

> the growing gulf between rich and poor, the sharply-
> marked division between the two in a country in
> which cash and caste are apt to be cause and effect--
> this is creating a social stratification in which the
> lowest stratum is volcanic, is boiling over with hate
> of its condition and rage at those above it. When
> this is the case look out for an explosion.[11]

In particular, those citizens who had secured a stable position in the city's economic and social structure and whose present well-being and future opportunities were tied to the perpetuation and good health of those structures saw in the labor turmoil a serious threat to their welfare. While these mostly lower-middle and middle-class Chicagoans often expressed sympathy for the dilemma of the common laborer, they abhorred the violence which accompanied labor protest and condemned strikers who forcibly excluded from jobs others willing to work for less. Such actions threatened to undermine the economic stability of the city and posed a more serious threat to their security than did the depression itself.

As economic troubles lingered and labor violence worsened, the rhetoric surrounding the controversy between labor and capital increasingly took on a distinct religious and ethnic tone. Evangelical Protestant magazines in Chicago, like the Standard and the Northwestern Christian Advocate, identified the strikers as "ignorant foreigners," mostly Catholic, who were being misled by "a parcel of blatant Communist demagogues" acting "in behalf of the Commune."[12] Numerous of Chicago's evangelical ministers issued fervent denunciations of the actions of the protesting workers as "Wholly un-Christian" and the visible result of "the growing power of the Romanists."[13] An ethnic bias similarly tinged reports of labor unrest in the middle-class, Protestant, and Republican-oriented Tribune. On May 9, 1876, the paper described some three thousand lumber mill workers on strike in protest of pay cuts as "a mostly queer gang. A mass of ignorant Bohemians, Poles, Germans, 'Low Dutch' and Irish who could speak little except their own language."[14] By the summer of 1877 when the "Great Strikes" broke out nationwide, some evangelicals in Chicago showed no hesitation whatsoever in attributing the widespread turmoil as much to a Romish and foreign plot against American institutions as to the severe economic difficulties faced by workers.[15]

If some Chicago evangelicals blamed immigrants and Catholics for the labor troubles of the 1870s, many also tended to identify them with a perceived rise in crime, drunkenness, Sabbath breaking, and general immorality. The vote of the Irish population, the Tribune reported in 1876, was responsible for keeping the saloons of Chicago open during Sunday worship hours. The popular Harper's Weekly blamed on the Roman Catholic Irish the "rapid growth of crime and pauperism;

the corruption of the young; the decay of education." And
Charles Brace's Dangerous Classes of New York, a study re-
viewed favorably in several Chicago newspapers, concluded
that "an immense proportion of our ignorant and criminal
classes are foreign-born." "Intemperance," he asserted, "was
the major cause of crime ... and the Irish are the worst of-
fenders."[16]

Not suprisingly, then, the movement for temperance
reform gained new vitality in Chicago in the mid-1870s. Both
Protestants and Roman Catholics pledged support for the
crusade, hoping, as the Western Catholic of Chicago put it,
to rout forever "that accursed hireling of Satan--King Alcohol."[17] The numerous temperance societies organized in the
city directed their attention particularly to the inhabitants of
the densely populated Irish sections with reports of some success.[18] The pledge of the League of the Cross, became a
sign of respectability. Temperance lectures were advertised
widely and offered on a regular basis. Religious magazines
published frequent stories depicting, sometimes extravagantly,
the evil effects of alcohol on the home and family. Typical
was the attitude of the Advance.

> A drunkard in his cups cannot conveive of a pure
> woman. He forgets his mother and sister. His mind
> revels in the scenes of the low theatre or the brothel.
> What, when sober, he would have abhorred, he now
> delights in. His filthy stories, his profane oaths,
> his irascible temper and impudent words are the
> legitimate fruits of the drink devil that is in him.
> Hence it becomes easy for some, thus crazed, to
> strike or murder, or commit unmentionable crimes
> against social purity.[19]

The temperance crusade blossomed in 1874 when thousands of women across the nation flooded into the ranks of
active reformers. In February of that year, groups of pious
women invaded saloons in various locations in Chicago. Following the example set in other places, they knelt in prayer
and sang the hymns they believed might save their listeners
from a drunkard's grave. Sit-ins of this sort continued well
into March. Other women canvassed the city urging men and
women to sign the "Home Pledge," promising thereby that no
intoxicating liquor would be used in the home as a beverage
or for cooking and that adherents would also discourage its

manufacture and sale for such purposes. On March 16, 1874, some two thousand women met in the Clark Street Methodist Church and prayerfully drew up a statement protesting the opening of saloons on the Sabbath. A petition was circulated obtaining more than fourteen thousand signatures and was presented to the city council by a delegation of sixty crusading ladies.[20]

The aims of the Chicago reformers fell short of the desired mark, for they were unable to prevent passage of the ordinance permitting the sale of liquor on Sundays. Instead, the council, as a mild gesture of appeasement, ordered all saloons so engaged to close and curtain all doors and windows opening on the street. But the lack of immediate success did not finally discourage the temperance advocates. By November, women across the nation had organized themselves as the Women's Christian Temperance Union, and to the crucial post of corresponding secretary they elected Chicago's own Frances Willard.[21]

Under the leadership of Willard, the WCTU became, in Chicago and nationally, the largest and most influential of the temperance organizations. A fervent Methodist and active worker under Moody in the Chicago revival, she also moved the organization in the direction of evangelicalism. The activities of the union were reported regularly in the city's leading evangelical magazines. Women from evangelical churches assumed positions of local leadership. The special temperance meetings which Moody held in 1876 were conducted jointly by Moody's staff and by the WCTU. In 1877 Willard temporarily resigned her post with the union to work full-time with Moody, to return as the president of the WCTU in 1881. When Moody arrived in Chicago in the fall of 1876, temperance and revival (Moody style) moved in common directions.[22]

Evangelicals entering the temperance cause probably anticipated that the objects of their concern resided largely among the same "dangerous classes" with whom they associated labor unrest and other social turmoil.[23] The Germans and Irish were most commonly identified with the saloon and the bottle. Germans were notorious for keeping their beer gardens open on Sunday regardless of Sunday closing laws.[24] And the Irish admitted to their excessive use of alcohol. "Were I asked to say what I believed to be the most serious obstacle

to the advancement of the Irish in America," wrote John Francis Maguire,

> I would unhesitatingly answer--Drink.... Almost
> invariably the lowest class of groggery or liquor-
> store--that which supplies the most villainous and
> destructive mixtures to its unfortunate customers--
> is planted right in the centre of the densely-crowded
> Irish quarter of a great city.[25]

Evangelical Protestants saw in temperance not only a
means of social improvement but also a possible way to restrain the alien elements in society and cause them to conform
more closely to approved modes of behavior. It was, moreover, a standard evangelical opinion that reform from drink,
to be effective, must occur within the context of religious
conversion. "The only hope for rum-sellers and drunkards
is Jesus Christ of Nazareth," reasoned the Presbyterian Interior. "We don't believe in reforms. They are well enough
in their place, but we believe in nothing but regeneration."[26]
And regeneration, evangelicals understood, meant a turning
of one's life away from old values and practices and the embracing of a godly life. Evangelical activists in the temperance movement saw in the crusade not only a means to elimin-
ate "demon rum," but the promise of an end to such widespread social ills as crime, poverty, labor unrest, divorce,
and the general disintegration of the American family.[27]

Evangelical Chicagoans in the 1870s were also disturbed
by the growing neglect of Sabbath observance. Like abuse
of alcohol, Sabbath breaking was blamed most frequently on
immigrants. "Nearly all the Presbyterial Narratives speak of
the frightful prevalence of Sabbath desecration," declared
the first "Annual Narrative of the State of Religion" to be
produced by the recently reunited Presbyterian Church in
the United States of America in 1870. "This vice grows with
the growth of immigration from the nations of Europe."[28] What
the Presbyterians found to be true nationally was true also
of Chicago. By 1876 Sabbatarian laws in Chicago clearly were
breaking down. Sunday beer gardens flourished in the German sections and pubs were full in the Irish quarters. The
Baptist Standard typified Protestant anxieties in the city when
it condemned the German population for its "crusade against
our Sabbath and all of its sacred institutions."[29]

The hyperreaction of certain evangelicals to Sabbath
breaking must be placed in juxtaposition to the elevated place
which Sunday observance had attained in evangelical thought.
James Findlay observes correctly that "reserving Sunday
solely for rest and the exercise of the common religious activities of the community had become a seemingly immutable
principle that was the sheet anchor of an orderly, respectable, and law-abiding society." As a spokesman at the 1876
General Assembly of the Presbyterian Church in the United
States of America expressed it, "Observance of the Sabbath
day is identified with good order and public prosperity."
Chicago's Baptist weekly, the Standard, espoused similar sentiments. The Sabbath, it declared, "is one of the great foundations out of which has come our national character; the religious spirit, the love of education, the reverence for law
and order which have been our distinguishing characteristics
from the beginning."30 The very foundations of America's
greatness and prosperity, these evangelical spokesmen believed, were endangered by the immigrant abuse of the Sabbath.

It is observable, then, that several important issues
which raised Protestant apprehensions in the 1870s in Chicago
had as their common denominator the foreign and Catholic
population of the city. Immigrants and Catholics were perceived as prone to alcoholism and labor unrest. Frequently,
they were labeled as Sabbath breakers. In every instance,
the foreign and Catholic presence in the city seemed inimical
to prevailing Protestant cultural mores and a barrier to evangelical efforts to Christianize America.31 By their sheer numbers, these foreign-born shook the Protestant domination of
American culture.

Two issues, however, raised Protestant sensibilities in
Chicago to a fever pitch. The first was an alleged "Romish"
plot to subvert and eventually to control the public school
system. The second and related issue identified Catholics
and foreigners generally in a supposed scheme to undermine
the democratic system and wrest political control of the city
and nation.

Protestants had long understood public education as a
counter to the project of that "old deluder Satan" to keep
people from a knowledge of Scripture.32 And, as Winthrop
Hudson expresses it, the "little red schoolhouse" was regarded,

along with motherhood and the home, as one of the most
cherished institutions of American life.[33] In this kind of
emotionally charged atmosphere, Catholic demands that private
schools receive tax support equivalent to that underwriting
the Protestant-oriented public schools gained little headway.
Frustrated and angry, certain Catholic spokesman responded
with harsh and bitter condemnations of American public education. Bishop Bernard McQuaid in 1876 called the school
system "a huge conspiracy against religion, individual liberty,
and enterprise." Several years previous, Father Michael
Mueller, in a popular tract entitled Public School Education,
argued that public education in America was a disease which
would "break up and destroy the Christian family" and described the public schools as "hotbeds of immorality" where
"courtesans have disguised themselves as school-girls in order
the more surely to ply their foul vocation."[34]

     Such rhetoric did not encourage already suspicious
Protestants to lend an understanding ear to Catholic requests
for public funding of their schools or to Catholic complaints
about the reading of the Protestant (King James Version)
Bible in the public schools. Indeed, Protestants generally
came to see both developments as symptomatic of a new, aggressive attempt by the Catholic church to subvert the existing social order which, in so many ways, embodied the ideals
and moral values of evangelical Protestantism. Tax support
of parochial schools, in the minds of Protestants, amounted
to support for an education whose sole purpose was to proga-
gate error and win converts from among Protestants. The ultimate goal of the scheme, said the Methodist Quarterly Review, "is the substitution in the public schools place of a
more intensely sectarian system, an ecclesiastically controlled
system, a Papal system." Furthermore, schools without Bibles,
according to popular Protestant belief, would rear a nation of
amoral, godless voters. Chicago's Presbyterian magazine, the
Interior, identified the deeper principle at stake in the Bible
question. The reading of Scripture in the schools, it argued,
was a necessary "public recognition of God" which "brings our
consciences in daily contact with His law." Returning to the
subject several months later, the Interior delineated the consequences for the nation should the reading of Scripture be
removed from public institutions like the schools.

          Let religion, the pure and simple Christianity of
          the New Testament, desert the oaths, the seats of

justice, the halls of legislation, the temples of learn-
ing, the marts of commerce, the sanctuaries of worship, and all the high places of trust and power; it
will require no sage's counsel or prophet's foresight,
to tell in what direction we are drifting, or what
destiny lies before us.[35]

In pulpit and with pen, Protestant clergymen urged their
countrymen to hold fast on the "Bible question." Much more
was at stake, they argued, than simply the reading of several
Bible verses in the public schools. The Catholics "mean the
spiritual and temporal and ecclesiastical domination of America,"
wrote Chicago Methodist Gilbert Haven. "The surrender of
the Bible is the beginning of the end."[36]

In Chicago Protestant fears of a Catholic plot to seize
control of the schools crystallized with the murder of Francis
Hanford on August 6, 1876. A devout Methodist and former
assistant superintendent of schools, Hanford had provided
information to the city council alleging "that a corrupt ring
existed in the Board of Education." Hanford further alleged
that "the instigator and engineer-in-chief of all [this] devilry"
was Mrs. Alexander Sullivan, an Irish Roman Catholic and
wife of the secretary of the Board of Public Works. According to Hanford, Mrs. Sullivan, in collusion with the Catholic
clergy and the city's Democratic mayor, Harvey Colvin, had
engineered successfully the scheme to remove the Bible from
the public schools by manipulating nominations for the Board
of Education.[37] Mayor Colvin, suggested Hanford, had agreed
with Mrs. Sullivan to place in nomination before the council
only the names of men who were Roman Catholic or susceptible
to control by Sullivan. In turn, the Catholic clergy pledged
the Catholic vote to Mayor Colvin.[38]

When the city council met on the evening of August 6,
1876, to deal with Mayor Colvin's latest nominations to the
Board of Education, Hanford's list of accusations was in the
possession of the Committee on Schools. After some disagreement over the propriety of reading the letter in public because of the specific nature of the charges, the aldermen took
action to make the letter part of the public record. Hanford's
letter was read in the presence of a large number of reporters,
and the committee went on to report against the nominations
because, it concluded, the men were nothing more than "political aspirants," ill-chosen, unqualified and might, indeed,

be susceptible to manipulation. While noting that three of
the nominees were men of the Catholic religion and the other
two were "nobodies," the Committee ended its report by in-
sisting that its recommendations were not a "question of
nationality or religion," but of concern that the "best men"
receive the positions. [39]

    Toward the end of the heated session, Alexander Sulli-
van entered the council chambers. He remained for only a
short period but long enough to hear the accusations made
against his wife and to learn that, according to Hanford, his
own job as secretary of the Board of Public Works was due
solely to his wife's influence upon the mayor. An angry Sullivan hurried home, piled his wife and brother into a carriage,
and drove the few blocks from his home to the Hanford residence. Upon reaching his accuser's home, he confronted Hanford with the matter. In the confused moments which followed,
Sullivan demanded a retraction which Hanford refused to give.
The two men fell to brawling on the front lawn. A friend of
Hanford pulled Sullivan away, whereupon the enraged Sullivan
drew a pistol and shot Hanford in the chest, killing him in-
stantly. [40]

    Protestants did not hesitate to call attention to the nu-
merous lessons the public might learn from the sad affair.
The Northwestern Christian Advocate remarked that Sullivan
was Irish, and by his actions he, "like his race in general ...
proved his lack of balance." The Advance blamed the tragedy
in part on Mrs. Sullivan's indiscretion in "entering the arena
where men contend."

> It is the illogical theory that Mrs. Sullivan could
> pursue the gains of politics without its necessary
> cost in scandal, misrepresentation, and heartburn;
> that she could enjoy all the exemptions which are
> due to women of the chivalric pattern, that has re-
> sulted in desolating two houses, placing a corpse in
> one and a felon in the other. [41]

Many Protestants attributed the tragedy in part to vola-
tile Irish tempers and in part to a woman who took the ill-
conceived action of removing herself from woman's proper
sphere; they also understood the sinister force behind the
whole affair to be the Roman Catholic church. In the weeks
that followed the murder, several prominent Chicago evangelicals

railed against the Catholic church. "This is the real spirit
of Rome today in Chicago," said one. "She has drawn the
Word of God out of our schools. Next she will destroy as
godless our public schools; then a censorship over all teach-
ing and publishing will follow, as fast as power shall be secured." James McLaughlin, a Chicago Presbyterian, specula-
ted that Hanford's accusations were grounded in fact and suggested that he was murdered "lest he might unearth something
startling." McLaughlin went on to condemn the "Romaniza-
tion" of the schools and of American institutions in general.
"I am no advocate of bigotry," he declared,

> but, on the other hand, I would be just as unwilling
> to allow an imported population to become masters of
> the land and interfere with the characteristics and
> institutions of the Commonwealth.... Give Catholics
> the control of your School Board and what is the re-
> sult? They will aim at effecting every change that
> will abolish the very semblance of every sentiment
> and principle and book that is not in accord with
> their religious feelings.

Catholics should not be on the Board of Education, he bluntly
concluded. Their "intense sectarianism" is a "self-disqualifica-
tion" for the office. [42]

The religious press reacted with equal fervor to the
Hanford murder. An editor for the Congregationalist organ
of Chicago, the Advance, condemned outright "a movement
which begins with excluding the Bible from the schools and
ends with violent denunciations of a highly respected teacher
by a Catholic woman and the summary killing of this teacher,
at his own peaceful threshold, by her husband." The Presbyterian Interior saw in the incident "a threat ... against every
other citizen who does his duty in protecting the schools from
an influence which is universally regarded as a dangerous
one." Like McLaughlin, the Advance called upon Protestants
to act in concert against the perceived Catholic threat.

> There are now seven millions of Catholics in this
> country.... The other thirty-three millions of our
> population had better take the trouble to decide some
> things while they can; or otherwise, if we commit a
> blunder, like that of our fathers in their compromise
> with the slave power, and consent that all the children

of the land may grow up without moral and spiritual
enlightenment, we shall wake up at last to find a ...
power worse than slavery fastened upon our vitals....
The duty of Chicago is clear--to put out of the
School Board, and keep out, such members as lack
either the moral perception or intelligence to appreci-
ate this question with its far reaching consequences.[43]

The intense furor in Chicago over the school question reflected how deep-seated was the conviction of certain Protestants that Catholicism posed a serious threat to cherished
American values and institutions.

Equally vitriolic and significant was the Protestant response to the pervasive corruption of government at both the
local and the national level. Again both Catholics and immigrants seemed to certain observers a likely cause of the
problem. Both groups, Protestants assumed, were especially
susceptible to political manipulation. All of the issues discussed to this point were politicized to varying degrees in
the elections of 1875 and 1876, but the concern for purifica-
tion of government predominated in the rhetoric of politicians.
Cries for "reform" and "moral purity" in government resounded
from all sides. Within the city itself, political furor centered
around the controversial administration of Mayor Harvey D.
Colvin.

Harvey Colvin was elected mayor of Chicago in the fall
of 1873. His supporters, the newly organized People's party,
were composed largely of German and Irish voters who found
common ground in opposing Sunday closing laws and the alleged inequities of "Puritan rule." Colvin handily defeated
the candidate of the Law and Order party and, on March 16,
1874, much to the dismay of evangelical Protestants, the Colvin-
dominated council repealed the ordinances for Sunday closing.[44]

In the years that followed, the People's party fell quickly
into disrepute due to a record of corrupt administration, in-
ternal dissension, and tickets of unqualified candidates--
groups of men whom the Chicago Times described as "black-
legs, pimps, grogshop loafers, communist lazzaroni, and other
political dead-beats."[45] The party's ultimate downfall came,
however, in connection with a piece of crafty political maneu-
vering aimed at retaining power. In October 1874, opponents
of the Colvin administration succeeded in obtaining the necessary

ten thousand signatures to force the Common Council to call
a popular referendum on the question of city reorganization.
The intent of the action was to shorten Mayor Colvin's term
of office. At the mayor's direction, the council set April 23
as the time to vote on a new charter. Bessie Pierce explains
the reasoning behind the choice of dates.

> The choice of this date was astute, for the incorpora-
> tion act provided that a city election should take
> place, instead of in the autumn, on the third Tues-
> day of April after the bill was accepted by the people.
> Since the third Tuesday in April fell on the twentieth,
> the Council's action lengthened the official lives of
> incumbents from November, 1875 to April, 1876; and
> because the Mayor was to be chosen in an odd year
> it extended Colvin's term to April, 1877. On the
> twenty-third, the voters in a close election accepted
> the new charter, though the outcome was inconclusive
> until the courts decided in its favor. [46]

The blatant political manipulation engineered by Colvin
and his supporters roused the ire of many Chicagoans. Typical was the indignation expressed by the Tribune.

> Corruption stalks through the Council Chamber with-
> out disguise.... The price of legislation is marked
> in plain figures, and the aldermen are "runners"
> intently hunting up trade. Everything is for sale,
> from a contract to a franchise.... Offices are created
> that they may be sold to the highest bidder, and
> never, even in the history of New York, was there
> a Government so rotten, criminal, and corrupt as
> that which has fastened itself on Chicago. [47]

From the pulpits, too, issued protests against the corruption so evident in government. Protestant clergymen exhorted their congregations to return to an "old-fashioned
faith in God" and prayed for a revival of the "old-fashioned
virtues of integrity, honesty, economy, and simplicity of
character." "If the buyers and sellers of votes, if the men
who make merchandise of souls, or are themselves the merchandise, have made [government] a den of thieves," cried
one minister, "let us drive them out by the lash of a just
and overpowering public sentiment. Faith in God, faith in
honor, in chastity, in temperance, in frugality, this is the

faith we need. With it we shall live. Without, we shall
die."[48]

Public indignation at Colvin's actions and a subsequent
demand for reform manifested itself in the election of aldermen in April 1876, the first municipal election under the new
charter. On the Sunday before the election, Protestant voices
rang loud and clear as to the duty of Christian voters in
Chicago. The Reverend Arthur Mitchell, pastor of the First
Presbyterian Church of Chicago, addressed the "Duties of
Christian Citizens in the Present Crisis." Mitchell called upon
Chicagoans to elect men of "integrity." "There was a work
to be done by Christians next Tuesday," he exhorted, "to
rescue the government of the city from the hands of thieves,
and place it in the hands of decent men." A Methodist clergyman, the Reverend T. P. Marsh, remarked that in recent city
elections, citizens had complacently "let the devil carry off
the ballot-box, announce the results of elections, and set his
minions enacting and executing laws." In light of the present
trouble, he thought it the responsibility of Chicago's Christians to become politically active, "rescue the ballot-box,"
and stop Colvin. The Reverend J. H. Walker of Reunion
Presbyterian Church spoke in more subdued and sober tones,
instructing his parishioners to vote only for those candidates
"who are known to be honest, able and reliable." However,
it was doubtless very obvious to most in the pews that the
majority of the candidates so described must be Protestant,
Republican, and fervently anti-Colvin.[49]

When the votes were counted on April 18, the old Law
and Order party, now under the Republican banner, had
soundly defeated the Democratic ticket, comprised of Colvin
supporters and members of the disbanded People's party. But
the drama was not yet complete. In an effort to rid themselves immediately of Colvin, thousands of voters wrote in
the name of Thomas Hoyne, an independent, for mayor.
Hoyne's election was illegal since the mayor's term was not
up for another year. Nonetheless, the new council, now
composed of a majority of Colvin's enemies, declared Hoyne
to be mayor. Chicago now had two mayors. Again the courts
intervened and declared Hoyne's election to be invalid, but
permitted the new council to call a special election for mayor.
As a result, Monroe Heath, a Republican, was elected mayor
of Chicago, and Harvey Colvin was swept from office.[50]

At the very time that Chicago's Protestants were strug-
gling to save their city from corrupt administrations and supposed Catholic conspiracies, their moral sensibilities were disturbed further by revelations of a nationwide Whiskey Ring
in which Chicago politicians played a conspicuous part, helping to defraud the government of full payment of the excise
tax on liquor. On May 10, 1875, federal agents carrying out
raids simultaneously in Chicago, Milwaukee, and St. Louis
found evidence of large-scale fraud in all of these cities. In
Chicago three distilleries and four rectifying establishments
were seized, and in October a grand jury returned indict-
ments against several wealthy Chicago brewers and noted public officials.[51]

The unfolding story of fraud and collusion on the part
of politicians and those involved in the whiskey trade had at
least two significant results. First, it provided yet another
link in what appeared to many Protestants to be a carefully
designed plot to use the Catholic and foreign-born vote, and
the capital of wealthy German and Irish brewers, to control
the city's government for their own ends. The evidence
available to Chicagoans appeared to give credence to the
theory. The Germans and Irish had given their votes to
Colvin in return for his promise to repudiate the Sunday closing law. Colvin had been faithful to his word, and the foreign-
born voters remained the power behind the corrupt administration of the Democratic mayor. In office, Colvin catered further to the immigrant and Catholic element in the city by ap-
pointing Roman Catholics to the school board and the city
council. Keeping favor with the large foreign-born voting
blocs, the mayor and his administration then proceeded to
fleece the pockets of local government by selling offices, auc-
tioning franchises, and allying with "whiskey" to share in the
profits of unpaid federal taxes.

James McLaughlin, the Presbyterian minister, put the
pieces of the puzzle together nicely in a sermon, "Political
Misrule," preached in Chicago in September 1876. After expressing some reluctance to tackle political issues from the
pulpit, McLaughlin sallied forth to do verbal battle with the
evil forces at work in his city. He lamented the surrender
of the government to a "saloon Democracy--a gambling, reckless, thieving mob, and all because the good, honest man had
refrained from participating in the selection of the lawmakers."
He thought that this was especially the case in Chicago, and
the result was to be seen in a "depleted treasury and

the enormity of taxation." He urged the "better classes" of
Chicago to become politically active and to end the reign of
"five-year citizens and knaves." "The fact that the lower
classes had grown into a control of the City Government,"
he continued, "was illustrated by the Bible being driven from
the public schools." However, it was not the Romanists alone
in the board who threw it out, "but the lowest, vilest, pot-
house politicians. They did it to please the Romans, and to
get the Roman vote, whereby to continue their hold on office
and their license to steal." Nonetheless, his parishioners had
best beware, he advised, for

> it was political corruption that upheld Rome.... It
> was seeking to plant its heel here, intolerant as it
> was and if unarrested would push its plans by in-
> trigue and the sword, if necessary, until Protestan-
> tism was driven from the land.[52]

The publicity surrounding the Whiskey Ring trials had
the second effect of asserting reform as a national issue, not
simply a local concern. Eighteen seventy-six was a presidential election year. Very early in the year, the Tribune prophesied correctly that the issue of chief priority to voters would
be "honest government." From one end of the land to the
other, the paper reported, "comes the demand for honesty in
politics.... The new year opens in the midst of a war upon
corruption."[53]

Rumors of whiskey rings, wine rings, and political rings
abounded in the local press. Reports of election frauds and
the stuffing of ballot boxes were common news items.[54] In
March it was disclosed that General William W. Belknap, the
secretary of war in the Grant administration, had accepted
kickbacks of more than $25,000 while supervising the Bureau
of Indian Affairs. This incident led two Chicago-based Protestant weeklies to engage in a lengthy and sometimes ridicu-
lous argument whether it was "wine" or "lace" (wealth) that
was at the root of the latest public scandal.[55] The Advance
reacted to the Belknap fraud with an article entitled "The
Nation Shamed." The sad affair, it believed, was "symptomatic of the existing political and social character of our time."
The Baptist Standard, the Presbyterian Interior, and the
Tribune printed similar contributions, each condemning the
event and deploring the "fearful decadence of morals" at every
level of society. As a solution to the widespread corruption
in government, the Tribune proposed that

the highest offices of the land should be filled from
the one hundred thousand persons in the country
who have fortunes so ample that they can support
the magnificence of living indulged in by Washington
society without stealing, taking bribes or the like.[56]

When Chicago Republicans learned that Benjamin Bristow was
responsible for exposing the whiskey fraud, they responded
by enthusiastically forming a Bristow Reform Club dedicated
to the great reformer's candidacy for president.[57]

The zeal of the secular and religious press in attacking
public corruption was matched by that which issued from the
Protestant churches of Chicago. The Tribune characterized
the tenor of the sermons on the Sunday after Belknap's demise
as a call for "a return to republican simplicity and old-fashioned
honesty." The Reverend David Burrill of Westminster Presbyterian Church lamented "the abuses of authority in every department of our public services" that "are being unearthed
as never before.... From the office of Chief Executive down
to the Mayorality of our own city, we look almost in vain for
any adequate sense of either dignity or duty." "Honest politicians," he concluded, "are met with as rarely as palm trees
in the desert." The Reverend J. H. Rowbridge, pastor of
the Chicago Riverside Chapel, drew similar conclusions. "The
righteousness of politics is an unknown quality," he observed,
"and is for the most part at the farthest possible remove from
purity or honesty." Rowbridge went on to cite hard money
and patronage of public office as responsible for much of the
dishonesty of government, and called Christian citizens to return to the "way of righteousness." "Honest men must combine to drive from place and power in our municipal affairs
the worthless characters that now disgrace and rob us," he
argued. "We are praying, my brethren, for a revival of religion. It is well. But let us pray for a 'rain of righteousness,' which should cleanse the fountains and fill the streams
of our national life."[58] Because Northern evangelicals and
the Protestant press in Chicago had long tended to associate
the Democratic party with the South, and more recently with
the villainies of Tammany Hall, the sentiments of Rowbridge
and other ministers probably worked further to entrench the
majority of the city's Protestants in the Republican camp.
By the fall of 1876, as both the Moody campaign and the November election drew near, many of Chicago's evangelicals
were firmly committed to work both for the success of the

evangelist and the election of the Republican ticket headed
by Rutherford B. Hayes.[59]

The choice of Hayes as the Republican standard-bearer
was received enthusiastically by many Chicago evangelicals.
The Tribune and Inter-Ocean, both avowedly Republican and
evangelically inclined newspapers, endorsed Hayes in the most
glowing terms. He was a man of integrity, the Tribune said,
who would bring to the nation "honest administration." Hayes
was a patriot. Unlike his Democratic opponent, he had fought
vigorously for the North in the recent war. Most importantly,
he was committed to "reform," and as governor of Ohio had
led an attack on corruption in public office.[60]

Even more fervent was the attack of the Republican
press on the Democratic party and its candidate, Samuel Tilden. Both the Tribune and the Inter-Ocean openly questioned
Tilden's loyalty to the Union, citing evidence repeatedly of his
alleged sympathies toward the Confederacy. The Tribune
went so far as to say that the effect of Tilden's election would
be to "reverse the judgment of the war." Both papers treated
charges of tax evasion against the Democratic candidate as
proven fact and alluded frequently to Tilden's alleged connections with the infamous Tweed Ring of New York. Furthermore, the Republican papers, anticipating the sympathies of
their readers, were careful to point up Tilden's support for
the "Grey Nun's Act" when governor of New York--an act
which exempted graduates of Catholic schools from being examined before school boards when applying for positions as
teachers in the public school system. Such a privilege, the
papers noted, was denied even to graduates of the most
prestigious Eastern schools and provided sufficient proof of
Tilden's sympathy toward the Roman Catholic population.[61]

Several Chicago evangelical magazines were equally vigorous both in their endorsement of the Republican nominees
and in their denunciation of the Democratic ticket. The
Methodist Northwestern Christian Advocate lauded Hayes as
a "plain, honest man, whose trust is in God." Of the Democrats it alleged that "specific bargains" had been made at the
convention with "papists" on the school issue. "And any
party pandering for the sake of papist votes deserves execra-
tion and overwhelming defeat." Similarly, the Congregational
Advance cited Hayes for "his burning loyalty and his personal
bravery during the war ... his successful gubernatorial

administration, [and] his manly tone as to the Bible and the schools." Hayes and his running mate, William Wheeler, the Advance observed in another editorial, were "active Christian men"--Hayes a good Methodist and Wheeler a faithful Congregationalist. Borrowing from the title of Sankey's popular gospel hymn, the Advance called upon Christian voters to "Hold the Fort" against the South, the Catholic church, and the Democrats. "It is not our purpose to make any personal assaults upon the Democratic candidates," the editors declared, "but it is evident that they do not represent the principles and aims to which our readers as Christian men, are intelligently committed." A vote for Tilden and Hendricks, they warned, would be a "vote contrary to their prayers." While other Protestant papers in Chicago, like the Standard and Interior, took less pointed stands than did the Advance, not one produced an editorial in support of the Democratic ticket. [62]

By the fall of 1876 the socioeconomic, political, religious, and ethnic strains present in Chicago were fostering a deep sense of distress and apprehension among many Chicago evangelicals. Generally stable economically and from middle-class backgrounds, many of these persons must have been troubled by the violence of labor agitation. [63] Their present jobs and their prospects for future prosperity were tied closely to the maintenance of the social and economic status quo. Strikes, and the material and economic devastation which they portended, threatened not only their financial ruin but the safety of their homes and families as well. These evangelical Protestant churchgoers were also in large proportion native-born citizens and often of Anglo-Saxon heritage. [64] The values they held dear were those traditionally cherished by Protestant America. Economically they embraced laissez faire capitalism. They tended to exude confidence that hard work by an honest Christian man would, in time, bring prosperity. In politics, most were zealous defenders of the democratic system. Religiously, they were convinced that the health of the nation in all of its facets was tied to its continued allegiance to Protestant ideals. [65]

However, the specter of an impending Catholic and foreign onslaught against those ideals, evidenced by the removal of Bibles from the schools, the repeal of Sabbath laws, and the flood of allegations about plots and conspiracies among politicians and papists seemed to imperil the cultural hegemony that middle-class Protestants enjoyed in Chicago. Increasingly, the immigrant and Catholic populations were seen as dangerous and subversive elements in the city. Irish and Germans by their abuse of the Sabbath, their love of drink, and their alien customs were perceived as un-American and their activities as a threat to the purity of home and hearth, that institution valued by most nineteenth-century evangelicals above all others. Democracy itself appeared endangered to some as these others either sold their votes or cast them as instructed. In response, many worried and frightened Protestant leaders condemned the sources of their anxiety and called their comrades in the pew to action.[66]

One way in which Protestants responded to the perceived danger was political activism. Typical of the exhortations issued in pulpit and press was the call of the Standard to its Chicago readers.

> It is the religious duty of every Christian man in America to attend the caucuses, primary meetings, and elections, and see to it that honest men are nominated, honest measures proposed, honest voting done, and dishonest men, arrested, tried, convicted and punished.

For many Protestants this entailed vigorous support for the Republican party and its candidates for the presidency in 1876. They identified the party of Lincoln as the standard-bearer of honesty, freedom, and the continuation of a "Christian civilization." Hayes was a Protestant and a "patriot." Protestant support for the Republican party further signaled opposition to the immigrant and Catholic population, which many associated immediately with the Democratic party.[67]

The polarization of religious and ethnic groups in the city along party lines was reflected in the rhetoric which Democratic leaders used to rouse their constituencies against Republicans. If Protestant Republicans applauded their Presidential candidate as a God-fearing reformer whose wife was active in the WCTU, Democrats expressed their abhorrence of the same qualities in such terms as "Sabbatarian," "Puritan," "Muckraker," and "Temperenzier." Hayes, they made clear, was a man for the Roman Catholic and immigrant voter to fear. Late in the campaign the Democratic press attacked Hayes alleging that he attended a meeting of the American

Alliance and approved a series of resolutions including opposition to the formation of Roman Catholic organizations in
America, the interference of Roman Catholics in the political
system, the preservation of the American school system, and
the reading of the King James Bible in the schools. The allegations were unfounded, but the content of the charges was
revealing. Even as Protestants organized in fear of the perceived Catholic threat, Catholics were being exhorted to stand
together against the Protestant onslaught.[68]

   A second way in which Protestants dealt with their
anxieties was to enlist themselves in the Moody and Sankey
campaign. Thousands of evangelical Christians in the city
gave their time and money to further Moody and Sankey's
effort to reach the unsaved with the Gospel of Jesus Christ.
Prayer vigils were initiated in churches throughout the
city. Ministers gathered to map a common strategy to bring
to all Chicago the news of Moody's coming. Thousands of
copies of the "Moody and Sankey Hymnal" were printed and
distributed. Newspapers carried daily reports of progress
in erecting the great Tabernacle. The topic of revival was
addressed in sermon after sermon. Through the labor of
Protestants of every denomination, the Moody and Sankey
meetings were brought to the very center of public attention.

   Why did the Moody campaign engender such an eager
response from the Protestants of Chicago? Moody was, of
course, a home-town boy returned as a hero. Old friends
and co-workers, YMCA members, and supportive businessmen
from days past paved the way for the world-renowned evangelist's triumphant homecoming. Churchmen longed for growth
in their congregations. The revivalist's successes elsewhere
promised large increases for the membership rolls of churches
active in the revival effort. Nor ought one to dismiss lightly
the proselytizing impulse inherent in traditional evangelical
Protestantism. Moody shared this vision. Yet interwoven
with these aspirations was another: the expectation--conscious
or unconscious--that a successful revival would diminish
Protestant troubles and fears. As Protestants viewed the
matter, a true revival in Chicago would entail the conversion
of large numbers of the unchurched poor and foreign-born.[69]
It would mean the firm reestablishment of the values and institutions Protestants held dear, thereby assuring the eventual
defeat of the "Romish" threat. Poverty would diminish as the
values of industry and frugality permeated every level of

society.[70] The conflict of labor and capital would harmonize through revival.[71] Revival could do wondrous things for Chicago. It could even direct politics to the channels Protestants understood to be right and good. The Inter-Ocean suggested as much when it predicted in September, "If Moody and Sankey have the success which good men pray for, the Democratic vote in Chicago will be next to nothing in November. For that matter it might be unanimous."[72]

Even as the stresses and strains of the first half decade of the 1870s predisposed certain Protestant Chicagoans to see a Moody and Sankey revival as a social cure, Moody himself was making careful preparations to ensure that his revivalistic foray into the city would meet with success. In the years since his departure from Chicago in 1873, Moody had become a peerless evangelist, expert in the strategy and techniques of effective religious revival. Immediately following his decision in the summer of 1876 to hold meetings in the city, Moody and his aides moved to implement that strategy in Chicago. Their labors provided an important link in the chain of factors contributing to the Chicago revival. That aspect of the story is discussed in the following chapter.

Chapter IV

ORGANIZING FOR REVIVAL: MOODY'S STRATEGY OF PREPARATION

In the hands of Moody and Sankey, revivalism was not a haphazard venture. Months before the evangelist strode to the Tabernacle pulpit for his first Chicago sermon, his personal lieutenants and Chicago supporters had begun orchestrating events designed to prepare the city for revival. The bringing together of thousands of evangelical Christians in the city was itself a significant social event. Moody sympathizers were organized and imbued with a sense of the ultimate importance of the work. The meetings fostered common goals, attitudes, and feelings among participants and with the revivalists. These processes, and Moody's skills in facilitating them, proved crucial both to the success of the Chicago meetings and to their ultimate social function.

To Chicagoans Moody was, of course, more than just an accomplished revival preacher. He was a home-town boy made good--a Marshall Field of evangelism so to speak. It was in the Windy City that the young Moody had first discovered and subsequently developed his gifts of soul winning. From the first tidings of his phenomenal successes in Great Britain to his triumphant homecoming in late 1875, many of the people of Chicago had followed with deep interest the rising star of Dwight L. Moody.[1]

Moody had come to Chicago in the late summer of 1856. From his very first days he was active in both business and evangelical concerns. Employed as a salesman in the boot and shoe industry, Moody's aggressiveness and devotion to his work resulted in large sales and early promotions. When customers did not readily appear in the store, he would stand outside and attempt to drum up business among passers by.

"I have a good position, and mean to work my cards to make
it better," he wrote his mother in 1858. "I have been very
successful so far, and if nothing happens I shall do well."[2]
Privately, he set a goal of $100,000 as the size of the fortune
he hoped eventually to accumulate. By 1860 Moody had saved
$7,000, his prospects for success in business were excellent,
and his confidence unbounded. "I can make money quicker
than anyone except Marshall Field," he wrote home.[3]

Moody's efforts in business were matched by his zeal
in religion. Immediately upon his arrival in Chicago he joined
the Mission Band, a group of young men from the First Methodist Church of Chicago who engaged in distributing religious
tracts and invitations to attend church and Sunday school.
He also rented pews in the Plymouth Congregational Church
and, as he expressed it, "I went out on the streets button-
holing every man that came along to get him into the church.
I filled one pew and then I got another and I filled three
pews."[4]

In 1857 Moody, along with Chicago and most of the nation, was swept up in a "great revival of religion." Moody
wrote home of his eager participation in the daily noon prayer
meetings which were the distinctive characteristic of the revival, but the revival services held nightly were equally attractive to the enthusiastic young Christian. "I go to meeting every night," he wrote. "Oh, how I do enjoy it. It
seems as if God was here himself." Equally important, the
revival drew Moody into the activities of the Chicago YMCA.
Moody's evangelistic and organizational labors for the YMCA
did much to develop the skills he later applied to revivalism.[5]

Stimulated by the revival, Moody started a mission Sunday school of his own in 1858. Located in a deserted saloon
on Chicago's North Side, the mission was situated in the
heart of one of the most dangerous sections of the city. Crime
and prostitution were rampant, housing was poor and overcrowded, and the area was well supplied with gambling houses
and saloons. Moody accepted the challenge enthusiastically.
The mission school grew rapidly and, by 1860, the average
attendance was more than a thousand students. Moody's zeal
and his unorthodox methods of recruiting children, expecially
among the poor, became a topic of conversation and sometimes
ridicule. A well-known caricature depicted Moody riding on
a pony through the slums followed by ragged children. Some
called him "Crazy Moody."[6]

Moody's success brought him important supporters--in particular, the friendship of John V. Farwell, the prominent dry-goods merchant.[7] So well known was the mission school that President-elect Lincoln took time to visit it while in Chicago in 1860. More important, the success of the venture convinced Moody to give up selling shoes and make "saving souls" his full-time business.[8]

From 1860 to 1873 Moody remained active in various religious enterprises in or near Chicago. During the war years he joined the United States Christian Commission, visiting hospitals, camps, and battlefields, aiding chaplains and holding special prayer meetings. At Camp Douglas near Chicago, Moody conducted revival meetings among Northern troops and Southern prisoners. At the same time he continued his Sunday school work in the city.[9] Moody suffered through this hectic schedule of activities in order to fulfill, as best he could, his mandate to save souls. A student of Moody's rhetorical talents and methods has described accurately the revivalist's approach to evangelism as the "personal type." Whether speaking to an audience of one or to a group of ten thousand, Moody aimed to focus his message upon the individual's need for salvation.[10]

At the war's end Moody focused his efforts once again upon the evangelization of Chicago. The YMCA and the Sunday school continued to be the two major vehicles through which he endeavored to reach the city for Christ. His diligent labors for the YMCA led to his election as president of the Chicago association in 1866. In the four years thereafter, Moody organized its charity work and promoted personal evangelism through the noon prayer meetings held daily at the YMCA headquarters. Moody took personal leadership of most of these services.[11]

At the same time, Moody's Sunday school was burgeoning and by 1864 had increased sufficiently to require a larger building. Upon its completion the Sunday school evolved into a church, which came into being officially as the Illinois Street Church on December 30, 1864.[12] Moody also involved himself more and more in the interdenominational conventions held for the promotion and improvement of Sunday schools. Because of the success of his own Sunday school, he was much in demand as a speaker. Moody's speaking talents were polished there. He also established important nationwide

connections on the convention tour which later aided him in
his urban campaigns. The conventions were to benefit him
in yet another way. At a session held in Indianapolis in
1870, Moody first heard Ira D. Sankey and soon after established what would be a permanent working relationship with
the singer.[13]

        In 1873 Moody decided to enter full-time evangelistic
work. Accompanied by Sankey, he left Chicago and sailed
for England.[14] From 1873 to 1875, the two evangelists criss-
crossed England, Scotland, and Ireland achieving spectacular
successes. Huge throngs filled the meeting halls to hear
Moody preach the Gospel and Sankey sing it. Clergymen expressed both surprise and delight over the religious excitement the evangelistic campaign engendered. Magazines and
newspapers, both British and American, reported on the happenings and attempted to assess critically the impact of the
revival in city after city. The British tour climaxed with
four months of meetings held in London in the spring of 1875.
Over twelve thousand people attended the first meeting in
Agricultural Hall. Total expenditures for the four months of
meetings amounted to more than $160,000. Committees of lay-
men and ministers orchestrated every aspect of the operation. The entire city was canvassed and personal invitations
extended to every citizen. A large choir was recruited and
participated in the services. At the conclusion of the London
meetings there was little doubt in anyone's mind that Moody
and Sankey were kings in the world of mass evangelism.[15]

        Evaluation of the results of the British meetings and
the factors producing whatever measure of success Moody
and Sankey enjoyed there are not a part of the purpose of
this investigation. However, the British experience did have
at least two important consequences that bear directly upon
Moody's later efforts in revivalism, including the Chicago meetings. First, the two years in Britain were the formative
stage in the development of the revival techniques and methods Moody would employ throughout his career. The format which evolved included one or two large meetings daily
coupled with after-meetings in the "inquiry room," and a host
of specialized gatherings such as visits to outlying areas,
and services exclusively for women, young men, Sabbath-
school teachers, children, or workers as need arose. The
structure of the Chicago meetings was little more than an expansion and modification of this early pattern. Second, and

perhaps more important, the British revivals brought to Moody and Sankey a degree of fame and notoriety previously unknown to them and doubtless far beyond their expectations. By the time the two evangelists returned to New York in 1875, public interest in their plans was at a high pitch, and requests for revival meetings poured in. Although they had never held a revival meeting in their home country, Moody and Sankey returned to America accepted as the world's greatest living evangelistic team. From this time on, Moody began his revivals with the advantage of being a well-known public figure. The curiosity that he and Sankey generated among the public probably caused as many people to attend their meetings as did honest religious enthusiasm.[16]

Almost immediately upon Moody's return to the United States, prominent evangelical leaders in Chicago organized themselves and issued a formal invitation to the evangelists to commence meetings in their city.[17] At first it appeared that the Windy City might be honored as the site of Moody's initial revival meetings--the evangelist expressing his intention to go to Chicago immediately after a period of rest at the family farm in Northfield, Massachusetts.[18] But other leading metropolises were also hot on Moody's trail. On September 14, 1875, Moody convened a meeting at Northfield, inviting two representatives each from four cities--Chicago, Philadelphia, New York City, and Brooklyn--to help him decide where to begin his American revivals.[19] Even this conference did not result in a final decision. For another month Moody pondered his choices, ultimately basing his decision upon criteria he had developed in Britain. Two indispensable conditions were set to determine whether he would enter a community to conduct revival meetings: first, evidence of united support from the evangelical churches of a city; and second, a guarantee of suitable facilities for the meetings. Chicago in 1875 failed both requirements. The city lacked a building adequate to Moody's needs, and its evangelical churches were still somewhat divided in their opinions about Moody.[20] Brooklyn gained the honor of hosting the first Moody revival meetings in the United States.

Moody's supporters in Chicago were saddened but not finally discouraged by the revivalist's decision. Moody reassured them of his desire to come to Chicago as soon as the way was properly prepared and certainly within the next two years. In the months that followed, their task was aided

considerably by the glowing reports of the evangelist's successes in New York and Philadelphia. Questions about
Moody's methods, training and theology receded in the face
of reports of thousands of converts and large gains in membership among churches that supported his work. By 1876
the evangelical ministers of Chicago stood virtually united
in their desire that Moody initiate meetings in their city.

Numerous businessmen in the city also rallied to the
Moody banner. Commercial giants, like the Fields, Armours,
John Farwell, Cyrus McCormick, and John Crerar, were among
those who offered generous financial backing for the revival
meetings.[21] Like most businessmen supportive of Moody,
they were staunch evangelical churchmen.[22] Some, like Farwell and T. W. Harvey, the lumber magnate, were counted
among Moody's most intimate friends. These men had aided
Moody financially in numerous earlier evangelistic ventures
and seem genuinely to have shared the revivalist's concern
for the spiritual welfare of their fellow men. But they were
also businessmen. Most probably recognized that money spent
on Moody's behalf might bring commercial as well as spiritual
return. In light of the labor unrest of the 1870s which
threatened their interests, many businessmen probably considered it a sound investment to support an evangelist whose
social and economic values coincided so closely with their
own--one, indeed, who had himself once been a successful
Chicago businessman. Moreover, if conversion at a Moody
meeting meant conversion to traditional Protestant ethics and
values (as most Protestants certainly understood it to mean),
then mass conversion was exactly what Chicago seemed to
need. As one Chicago minister rather bluntly put it, "When
Chicago has had a revival of religion she will be ripe for a
revival of business, and we would be able to give a fair show
both to God and mammon."[23] Not surprisingly, then, when
Moody arrived in the city in early June to participate in a
dedication service for the Chicago Avenue Church, a well-
organized and prepared group of eager clergymen and businessmen were on hand to greet him.[24]

Chicagoans gave Moody a "rousing" welcome at his June
visit. The Inter-Ocean reported that by 7:30 p.m. when the
meeting was scheduled to begin the church was full, "every
available foot of room was occupied: men and women stood
in the passageways and sat on the steps leading to the gallery."[25] Several days later a group of ministers met with

the evangelist "to ascertain whether Mr. Moody would not at
an early date hold a series of revival meetings in Chicago."
Moody informed them that his next campaign would commence
on October 1 but that he was as yet undecided whether the
site should be Chicago or Boston. During the summer months
ahead, he explained, he intended to rest and to "research
for fresh thoughts and ideas."[26] The meeting adjourned with
no decision on the minister's request.

In the weeks that followed, evangelical leaders in the
city took steps to convince Moody that Chicago was ready
for revival. On June 10, following the noon prayer meeting,
the ministers present resolved unanimously to hold special
evangelistic meetings each Monday at noon at Farwell Hall.
The revival services were to be accompanied by union prayer
meetings for revival, and a committee was appointed to conduct and advertise the special meetings. According to a reporter present at the session, "It [was] generally believed
that the amount of interest displayed at these preparatory
meetings [would] do much toward commending Mr. Moody as
to the advisability of spending a season here himself."[27]
The ministers further pledged their unity in the revival effort and offered Moody a promise of complete cooperation
should he decide to inaugurate meetings in Chicago. The
minister of the Plymouth Congregational Church was said to
have assured Moody that "there was no church in Chicago
but what would be controlled by Mr. Moody and do as he
wished during the meetings."[28]

The labors of the Chicago clergy impressed Moody sufficiently that he remained in the city in order to attend another meeting of evangelical leaders a week later. At this
session Moody made clear his expectations regarding facilities.
He observed that the Exposition building was large enough
but was located too far over on one side of the city. What
he desired was a new brick structure that would be centrally
located and seat about eight thousand persons. The money
necessary for the construction of such a building, he suggested, should be raised by the local businessmen. Their
willingness to enter into such a task, said Moody, would be
the determining factor in his coming to Chicago. After all,
the evangelist observed,

> other cities were willing to put up buildings, and
> take all trouble off his hands.... If the businessmen

thought the matter a bother, well and good; unless
the thing was done cheerfully they would not come.
If, on the other hand, it was carried out, he should
feel that the Lord called them that way.[29]

The following Monday in a meeting at Farwell Hall, businessmen sympathetic toward the proposed revival effort picked
up the gauntlet Moody had thrown down. A committee on
arrangements and finances was created which included such
merchants of stature as Henry Field, William Dering, and T.
W. Harvey. The businessmen estimated that a minimum of
$25,000 was needed to meet anticipated expenses. Before
the meeting ended they had collected more than $5,000 in
pledges among themselves.[30]

In the ensuing weeks the committee met regularly to
discuss the building Moody had requested. Progress on the
matter was hindered first by disagreement about Moody's request that the meetings be held at one central location,[31]
and later by the heavy costs of the proposed Tabernacle.
Finally, on August 12, 1876, a public announcement was issued that the Tabernacle would be erected on property owned
by John V. Farwell located on the corner of Monroe and
Franklin streets. Moody's wishes prevailed. The site was
centrally located, and all the meetings would be conducted
there.[32]

Construction of the Tabernacle was underway by mid-
August. Descriptions of the building indicate that its design
was intended to approximate Moody's wishes as nearly as possible. The brick structure was large--190 feet by 160 feet--
seating about eight thousand people. The bulk of the audience was expected to be seated at ground level--some 4,500
chairs being arranged on the bottom floor. Another 2,900
chairs were placed in the 40-foot-deep gallery which surrounded the hall on three sides. Underneath the sloping
floor of the gallery, rooms were sectioned off for use by committees and for "inquiry work." A large and "commodious
office" on one side of the hall was especially fitted for the
use of the press. Across the front of the Tabernacle extended the deep and broad platforms from which Moody and
Sankey would address the congregation. Space was provided
for Sankey's organ, a large choir, and several hundred "distinguished people." Scripture verses decorated the wall behind the evangelist, and commentators took special notice of

an illuminated cross with the words, "God Is Love," shining
along the crossbeam, and a star positioned at the head. The
building was lighted by gas and heated by steam. As one
impressed observer noted,

> Everything as far as it goes, is after the manner of
> a row of first class wholesale stores, and in the
> whole, it would seem to be impossible to construct a
> great auditorium in which convenience and security
> should be more perfectly attained. [33]

Even as workers labored to ready the Tabernacle for
an October 1 opening, other Chicagoans were hard at work
at a variety of tasks aimed at preparing the city for the arrival of the evangelists. The Farwell Hall noon meetings
soon were joined by nightly union revival prayer meetings.
In addition, special meetings for prayer and praise aimed to
prepare the city "for some near demonstration of Divine
Power" were announced and conducted at various Chicago
churches. [34] The prayer meetings climaxed on Thursday,
September 28, when evangelical clergymen proclaimed jointly
a citywide day of fasting and prayer for the coming revival
services. [35]

Other preparatory work was delegated by the executive
committee to subcommittees usually headed by one of its members. The subcommittees dealt with specialized concerns,
like advertising, visitation, and the solicitation of funds to
cover building and other costs. They typically accomplished
their tasks in a thorough and efficient manner. The city
was blitzed with news of the impending meetings. Posters
were printed and distributed among willing merchants and
shopkeepers, and posted on billboards and in streetcars,
Newspapers published daily advertisements and printed flyers
for public dispersal. Perhaps equally helpful was their regular coverage of Moody's whereabouts and of the activities of
his workers in the city. A systematic house-to-house visitation was conducted in an attempt to acquaint every resident
of Chicago with news of the coming revival services and to
extend a personal invitation. Workers left a handbill at every
household, containing a drawing of the interior of the Tabernacle with the hours of meetings and the address printed on
the back. The handbill also carried a personal word from
the evangelist:

"Behold, I bring you good tidings of great joy,
which shall be to all people." St. Luke 2:10.
   My Friend: I have come among you for the purpose of proclaiming the glad news of Christ's gospel.
And although many gather to hear the Word, they
form only a small proportion of the population.
   A large number of Christian friends have therefore agreed together to do what I am unable to ac-
complish, namely, to visit every home and family
with the good old story of God's great love in giving
His Son to die for us.
   The Lord Jesus Christ when he was on this earth,
knew well how the daily cares of life prevent men
from thinking about the world to come, and, therefore, He not only preached the gospel to multitudes
but often spoke to single individuals by the way-
side and in private houses; and His Apostle Paul
not only taught publicly, but from house to house,
and for three years in one city ceased not to warn
everyone night and day with tears.
   We need just the same warning, and the friends
who now visit you have come to remind you that
"God so loved the world that He gave His only be-
gotten Son that whosoever believeth in Him should
not perish but have everlasting life."36

The massive publicity campaign combined with the erection
of an impressive building and the large gifts of distinguished
citizens (made public knowledge in the local press) doubtless
impressed many Chicagoans and roused widespread curiosity.

   The selection and training of the choir, ushers, and
inquiry-room workers served further to identify sympathetic
evangelicals in Chicago with the revivalist and the goals he
set forth. A choir of more than six hundred voices was recruited from the ranks of the city's evangelical churchgoers
and placed under the direction of the well-known singer,
George Stebbins. Stebbins met regularly with the choir in
the later weeks of September and rehearsed the songs to be
used in the services.37 Special training was also provided
for the three hundred ushers required for the meetings. The
ushers were recruited three weeks in advance of the campaign
and instructed carefully how to deal with emergencies, large
crowds, and unruly persons in attendance. As in the case
of other revival workers, Moody stipulated to the committee

in charge of recruitment that the ushers be evangelical Christians.[38] Since converts were the prizes sought most zealously by the evangelists, it was only natural that the most careful preparations were made on their behalf. Inquiry rooms were spacious and placed at convenient locations where ministers and lay workers could provide spiritual counsel to interested persons. These workers were given lengthy training on techniques of person-to-person evangelism.[39]

Mass revivalism on the scale Moody envisioned it was an expensive undertaking. The costs of the Chicago meetings were estimated at $30,000.[40] The task of raising funds to cover the expenses was placed in the hands of the Executive Committee for Finances and Arrangements, composed of leading Chicago businessmen.[41] Moody himself felt no compunction to aid in the fund-raising efforts and, as has been noted, made the successful initiation of the task a requirement for his and Sankey's coming. Probably, Moody had few worries about the abilities or the willingness of the city's commercial leaders to fund his activities. He was well acquainted with many of them and had worked extensively with some when serving as president of the Chicago YMCA.[42] Concerned that collections might inhibit the attendance at the Tabernacle of potential converts, Moody refused to allow offerings to be solicited during the meetings, with the single exception of the concluding service when a special collection was taken to help alleviate the indebtedness of the local YMCA.[43] The expenses of the campaign, instead, were funded by contributions, large and small, collected privately outside of the actual Tabernacle services.[44]

Various auxiliary groups also engaged in the preparatory work of the crusade. One hundred policemen were on hand for the opening meetings, anticipating correctly the need for crowd control. Local streetcar companies made arrangements to serve the needs of those seeking transport to the meetings, and special trains were scheduled to run directly from the suburbs to the Tabernacle downtown. For those who lived at a distance from the city, eleven different railroad lines offered discounted excursion rates. The local light company went so far as to requisition locomotive headlights to better illuminate all the streets leading to the Tabernacle.[45]

Of all the techniques Moody employed to organize the

meetings the most controversial was the printing of admission
tickets. For the first weeks of meetings, persons holding
tickets were granted early admittance to the services. The
stated purpose of this practice was to give irregular churchgoers and the unchurched a better chance to see and hear
the revivalists. But the system did not function as intended.
Tickets were distributed at Farwell Hall and appear to have
been monopolized by evangelicals eager to see Moody and
Sankey. The poor and unchurched were, most often, not
sufficiently interested or motivated to make the necessary
effort to acquire tickets. Moreover, at the early meetings,
there were more tickets distributed than seats available,
which led to numerous well-justified complaints. The practice
alienated one Chicago observer completely.

> Modern evangelists, ensconced in a $20,000 temple,
> issue purple-tinted cards of admission to those whose
> self-righteousness is sufficient to embolden them to
> apply at the office of the YMCA for these certificates
> of good moral character.[46]

Moody wisely abandoned the use of general admission tickets
after the first few weeks of meetings. However, tickets of
admission to the platform continued to be issued for the duration of the meetings. Choir members, ministers, businessmen,
and other distinguished guests received admission cards, as
did newspapermen. Controversial though it was, the system
was consistent with Moody's strategy to stimulate interest in
the services. The sense of value and significance surrounding other programs to which admission was gained by ticket
was, thereby, transferred to the Moody services.

One can scarcely help but be impressed by the sheer
number of people Moody enlisted in the revival effort before
the meetings ever began--six hundred choir members, three
hundred ushers, an equal number of inquiry-room workers,
one hundred policemen, and hundreds more to carry on the
systematic visitation of households throughout the city and
to perform tasks assigned by the various committees. The
counting of revival workers suggests how preparation for
the campaign functioned to mobilize Chicago's evangelical
Protestants in support of Moody. Moreover, the techniques
that Moody employed in Chicago--the issuing of admission
tickets, the advertisement campaign, the erection of the
Tabernacle, the publication of the names of large donors to

the cause and the size of their contributions, the special arrangements for transportation--all imbued the meetings with
a heightened sense of significance and value and enhanced
the prestige of the revivalists. All of this worked to enliven
interest in the coming meetings.

Such devotion to systematic procedure reflected Moody's
businesslike approach to revivals. In the course of his YMCA
work and later in the British meetings, Moody had discovered
strategies which seemed to aid in the success of revival--
tactics which garnered for him the united support of local
evangelicals and attracted large crowds to the meeting places.
This is not to suggest, however, that Moody consciously
minimized the divine agency which evangelicals identified as
the center of a true revival. There is no reason to doubt
the revivalist's sincerity in his repeated assertions as to the
miraculous nature of the event. However, Moody also believed
that man was God's instrument in revival and that human actions were vital to the work of evangelism. Thus Moody developed his program for revival, employed it effectively, and
waited as God wrought his results. It was no surprise to
the revivalist when the Tabernacle was filled to capacity for
the opening service of the Chicago campaign.[47]

The engagement of a virtual armada of workers in various prerevival activities suggests also how widespread Moody's
support was in 1876 Chicago. A careful reading of contemporary comment on the revival reveals that of the major Protestant denominations represented in the city, only the Unitarian and Episcopalian churches responded unfavorably to
Moody and Sankey.[48] Moody posed formidable theological
problems for the Unitarians, and the evangelist's informal
style combined with his emphasis on personal conversion perhaps troubled High Church Episcopalians. Evangelical commentators complained frequently about the noninvolvement of
the Unitarians and Episcopalians in the revival work.[49]

But what impressed most observers was the broad base
of Moody's support.[50] In part this is explained by the widespread acceptance by the mainline Protestant denominations
of revivals as a means of periodic rejuvenation and growth.[51]
Moody's and Sankey's appeal, however, went beyond this.
They attracted support from liberals in the churches as well
as from conservatives, and even garnered sympathy with certain Roman Catholics.[52] Moody's wide-ranging appeal is best

explained as the result both of his naturally gregarious and
warm personality and of his desire to avoid sectarian entangle-
ments. Moody had a magnificent gift for conveying the genuineness and sincerity of his own personal Christian commitment to others in such a fashion that it drew them to him.[53]
The impression received by a contributor to the Congregationalist in 1875 upon hearing Moody was typical.

> He has humour, and he uses it; he has passion, and
> he uses it; he can tell racy anecdotes, and he tells
> them; he can make people cry as well as laugh and
> he does it. [Yet] to him nothing is common or un-
> clean. He has given himself to God, all that he
> has, all that he is, and he uses every faculty and
> resource of his nature to prevail upon men to hate
> sin and to trust and love Christ.[54]

Ultimately it was this ability to convey sincerity and concern
which enabled the evangelist to attract and hold undivided
the loyalties of people of varying theological opinions and of
different denominations.

At the same time, Moody was careful to avoid any form
of what he called "party spirit." Moody was not opposed to
denominationalism, but he was convinced that certain sectarian differences should be set aside in order best to carry
out the fundamental responsibility of all Christians to evangelize the world. Consequently, Moody avoided sermon topics
which might have divided evangelical supporters. Not once
in the Chicago meetings did he address the subjects of church
polity, the role of women in church worship, open and closed
communion, or baptism--all of which were matters of hot de-
bate in the contemporary religious press. Moody's potentially
controversial eschatological views were expressed only briefly
and in services held near the conclusion of the meetings.[55]
All this was consistent with Moody's understanding of his
function as an evangelist. His task was the proclamation of
the Gospel. Any topic, however important in its own right,
which might hinder the effective proclamation of that Gospel
was best left to others.[56] One perceptive observer summed
up well the ingredients of Moody and Sankey's approach to
evangelical Christians in Chicago.

> Standing aloof from even the shadow of sectarian
> propagandism or theological disputation, they enlisted

>the co-operation or, at least, the good will and God-
>speed of all denominations of Christians, and so con-
>ciliatory was their speech, and so rational their
>methods, in appealing to the irreligious or indifferent,
>that, unlike the experience which would probably
>have attended a different course, little if any time
>was lost in provoking criticism or combatting objec-
>tions.[57]

Moody's personality, his emphasis upon a simple Gospel composed of a core of central truths held in common by most
evangelicals, and his tact in dealing with denominational differences and clerical sensibilities combined to diminish possible sources of hostility toward the revivalist and to engender,
instead, a widespread sympathy for his labors.

This achievement was crucial to Moody's success in
several ways. Not only did it facilitate the cooperation necessary for urban revivalism, but it appeared to elevate the
goals of the revival above and beyond petty denominational
differences. Moody's revival meetings gained, thereby, a
degree of importance and standing which they likely would
have lacked had the evangelist been forced to cater to denominational prejudices. For the revival season, at least,
evangelical Protestants in Chicago were able to see themselves
as one body with shared values and common goals. While
the battle to evangelize Chicago would be waged during and
after the meetings, the preparatory labors already had gone
a significant way toward separating the city into two identi-
fiable camps--Moody's workers and Moody's potential converts.

Although sympathy toward the revival work was widespread in Chicago, numerous critics did raise their voices in
protest. The sharpest attacks before and during the revival
meetings came from a local Unitarian minister. On June 12,
1876, when Moody supporters were only beginning to organize
themselves in Chicago, the Reverend J. T. Sunderland wrote
a letter to the editor of the Inter-Ocean criticizing Moody's
and Sankey's reported successes in Great Britain. Citing
communications he had received from English ministers, Sunderland stated that interest in revival had ceased immediately
upon the departure of Moody and Sankey from London. There
were, he said, no lasting spiritual results. Indeed, the
large crowds at the Moody meetings resulted, he said, from
the "bewildering fascination" of Englishmen with the hymn

singing and the "shrewd business management of the meetings." Sunderland's observations were given an apparent
degree of legitimacy by a letter from England published in
the same issue of the Inter-Ocean. The letter, from a Mr.
Farrington, suggested that Moody's revivals were man-made
rather than God-made--a point where Moody seemed vulnerable. Farrington wrote:

> One command, "Do not sound a trumpet before thee!"
> is not enforced at his coming. For months before
> his advent [in Manchester] the trumpets blew daily.
> Ministers taught their flocks that the Lord was com-
> ing to do a great work here. Daily noon prayer
> meetings were organized, in which the prayers were
> advertisements of this Moody who should come, and
> in which the hymns were rehearsals of the choruses
> to which Sankey's solos should be sung. So it is
> everywhere ... the whole thing is worked up with
> all the system of a political campaign.... This is
> nothing against it but it explains the mystery of the
> eager anxious throng. Just a day or two ago this
> great evangelist who relies so much, not upon an
> arm of flesh, but upon the power of God refused to
> go to Sheffield because there had been a break in
> the ministerial organization which was there to work
> from house to house to make his path straight and
> his crowds great before him.58

The activities of preparation to which Farrington referred
were already familiar to many Chicagoans, and his remarks
may have troubled some would-be Moody supporters. Even
the revival-oriented Advance expressed some concern about
the real benefits to the local churches of massive urban revivals. "There is a common complaint," said the Advance,
"of the tremendous strain upon the strength of the brethren
assisting in the work, which quite forbids their continuing
their usual labors in their own churches." Revival meetings
in other large cities had bred discontent with the normal activities of the churches because they "lacked the excitement"
of the Moody services. The Advance also expressed its concern about the extravagant statements of some Moody converts. It reported the testimony of one such outspoken believer: "I was brought up in an Episcopal Church; but I
have found since I have become a Christian, that that is no
place for me!" One hardly needs wonder at the lack of

enthusiasm with which certain Episcopal churchmen greeted
the news of Moody's coming to their city.[59]

As October drew near, the enthusiasm of Moody's workers was paralleled by a quiet skepticism on the part of some
of those outside the evangelical churches. The Times predicted:

> Mr. Moody will find a field here rather different
> from those he has explored before, and it is fairly
> doubtful whether he can create the outburst of semi-
> religious fervor which has attended his ministrations
> elsewhere. The pulpits of this city have taught a
> great community in doctrine and morals to very great
> advantage for thirty years, and it is fairly doubtful
> if the teaching of the churches can be reconciled
> with the practice and preaching of this curious horta-
> tory evangel.[60]

David Swing's large independent and liberal-minded congregation meeting in McVicker's Theatre decided to decline active
participation in the Moody meetings but, significantly, their
liberal pastor felt comfortable enough to serve on several committees and sit on the platform on occasion behind the revivalist.[61] Local Catholic and Jewish leaders appear to have remained generally silent on the impending crusade in Chicago.
For those outside the evangelical churches of Chicago, an attitude of curious if humored interest tinged with a mild degree of outright skepticism seems to have prevailed. The
Times perhaps spoke for many of these when in late September it ran a front-page spread on Moody and the coming
meetings, proclaiming with tongue-in-cheek enthusiasm, "The
Salvation Shop--to be presided over by the ONLY Moody and
His Psalm-Singing Brethren."[62]

Even as Chicagoans witnessed the flurry of activities
in anticipation of Moody and Sankey's arrival, arrangements
were being made to carry the revival impulse from the city
to the entire Old Northwest. Never content to achieve anything less than maximum impact, Moody recognized that this
required the fullest use of revival personnel. His personal
philosophy, he once stated, was that he would rather "put
ten men to work than do the work of ten men."[63] His talents
as an administrator, organizer, and inspirer of men enabled
him to do just that. He first harnessed the energies of many

evangelical Protestants in Chicago. But making the most of
the endeavor, Moody determined that the excitement generated
in the large metropolis should be spread to encompass the
Midwest region. To achieve this goal Moody enlisted the aid
of other experts in revival. The foremost of these in the
Chicago campaign was Thomas Cree.

Cree had been a traveling secretary for the International Committee of the YMCA prior to his recruitment as
secretary of the executive committee in charge of arrangements for the Moody revivals. Arriving in Chicago several
days before the evangelist, Cree assumed supervision of the
day-to-day operation of the meetings. From his office in
Farwell Hall flowed a steady stream of printed information and
instructions. These materials covered a variety of concerns:
responsibilities of ushers and choir members, information for
ministers and dignitaries regarding seating procedures on the
platform, and the solicitation of money from interested persons
or groups in the city. All problems of an organizational nature came first to Cree's attention. His talents freed Moody
for the evangelistic work which Moody deemed his foremost
concern.[64]

Cree coordinated the effort to spread the revival from
Chicago to other Midwestern communities. He corresponded
regularly with out-of-town newspapers requesting coverage
of the Chicago meetings in their columns. He also communi-
cated with evangelical ministers located in these cities, in-
quiring often about the possibilities for local evangelistic work
in conjunction with the Chicago meetings. When cities of
sufficient size responded favorably, Cree made arrangements
for an evangelistic team (preacher and singer) to conduct
services of several weeks' duration. All told, five teams recruited by Moody toured the Midwest conducting revival services in Beloit, Wisconsin; Kalamazoo, Michigan; Peoria, Illinois; and numerous other locations. Reports of their successes were printed regularly in Chicago's newspapers and
read at the Tabernacle meetings.[65]

A list of people who worked with Moody in specialized
phases of his Chicago campaign or served on the evangelism
teams touring the Midwest is impressive. Revival preachers
included Henry Morehouse, George Needham, and J. R. (Major) Cole, all acclaimed English Preachers; D. W. Whittle and
W. J. Erdmann who, like Moody, were Chicago-based lay

evangelists; and Charles Morton, a spokesman for the YMCA.
Their musical partners included such singers and composers
as Philip Phillips, P. P. Bliss, George C. Stebbins, and
Moody's compatriot, Ira D. Sankey. The gospel songs of
these men were among the most popular sacred music of the
day. Among others assisting Moody in Chicago were two
women, Emma Dryer and Frances Willard, the latter being
head of the Women's Christian Temperance Union and a woman
recognized by one prominent historian as "the single most
impressive reformer to have worked within the context of
the evangelical churches."[66] The labors of this multitalented
group of highly regarded personalities in support of Moody
went far toward ensuring the success of the endeavor.[67]

    The presence of people like Cree, Morton, and Willard
indicated Moody's desire to employ in the revival effort the
personnel of existing organized evangelical groups within
Chicago. Both the YMCA and the WCTU played conspicuous
roles in the Chicago meetings. Because of their nondenominational status, the two groups served perfectly as neutral
bases from which the revivalist could direct his forces. They
also fitted well into Moody's scheme to emphasize evangelical,
but not denominational, concerns in the revival. The rooms
of Farwell Hall (the YMCA facility) were used extensively by
revival workers for planning sessions, preliminary services,
noon prayer meetings, and the regular Friday temperance
activities. Its large auditorium also served frequently to ac-
commodate overflow crowds at the Tabernacle. The WCTU
was involved especially in the Friday temperance work aiding
alcoholics converted at the Moody services. The members of
both groups, moreover, engaged in the house-to-house visitation program and made themselves available to the evangelist
as he required.

    By October 1 the orchestrated events of revival workers
over the previous four months effectively had prepared the
city for the arrival of the evangelists. Confidence and enthusiasm characterized Moody's supporters. "The success of
the scheme seems assured," boasted a reporter for the Chicago Daily News several days before a single meeting had
even been held. The Appeal, the Chicago organ of the Reformed Episcopal Church, anticipated "such a revival season
... as has never been witnessed in our midst before." A
reputedly "judicious" Methodist remarked, "If there are not
a hundred thousand souls converted in the Northwest this

season I shall be greatly disappointed."[68] The sense of ex-
pectancy that enveloped some in the city led one Chicagoan
in the direction of the inquiry room even before a sermon
was preached.

> When the Tabernacle was being built I was on hand
> every day, and when some of the workmen inquired
> what my business was, I told them I was the inspec-
> tor. I was hoping all the time, that, when the build-
> ing was finished, I might be the first one to be con-
> verted. I was not the first, but, glory to God! I
> was converted there.[69]

The excitement built up by weeks of preparation for the famed
evangelist's arrival had already begun to reap its dividends.

Many factors, then, coincided to prepare the way for
a successful revival season in Chicago. Certain religious and
ethnic tensions, as suggested earlier, disposed some Chicagoans to see revival as a possible solution to certain of the
anxieties they faced in 1876 and likely impelled them into the
revival work. Equally important was Moody's personal reputation as an evangelist. Moody's name drew the curious to
the meetings, and his reported successes in England and
America emboldened Chicago supporters. The revivalist's
organizational skills buttressed further the promise of effective revival. It has been shown that his workers engaged
in a lengthy, detailed program of activities which enhanced
the prestige of Moody and the meetings. The building of
the Tabernacle, the special prayer meetings, the mass of
revival-related church activities, and the massive publicity
campaign were among the factors which imbued the meetings
with a sense of the extraordinary. Something grand and
wonderful seemed about to occur. "We are together in the
ship, and Christ is standing on the shore, and telling us to
let down our nets for a draught," one confident and excited
minister related to a group of Moody workers.[70] But the
harvest was not one that should have surprised astute observers because of its sudden and unexpected arrival. The
strategem for revival had been executed carefully, and the
city was primed for the coming of the evangelists. As one
participant recalled the Chicago revival years later: "No
General ever planned a military campaign with more care and
precision than were the Tabernacle meetings.... It is not
strange that with such a prayerful preparation of fagots the
fire should commence to burn at the first meeting."[71]

Chapter V

MOODY AND SANKEY IN CHICAGO

On October 1, 1876, at precisely 3:30 p.m., Dwight L. Moody
ascended the stage of the great Chicago Tabernacle, completed only days earlier. He seated himself in a chair near
the railing of the platform and bowed his head in several
moments of prayerful meditation. As he lifted his eyes, his
gaze fell on more than eight thousand men, women, and
children crowded into the large building, their eyes fixed in
eager anticipation upon the famed evangelist and his singing
partner. As he looked to his left, Moody noted Sankey's
large organ situated prominently in the center of the stage.
Behind his organ stood the renowned singer. Turning around,
Moody observed another mass of humanity. Seated to the
rear across the entire platform were more than three hundred
local clergymen and distinguished citizens. And behind this
group on elevated levels sat the choir of six hundred voices
to lead in the congregational singing. Above the muffled
whispers of the audience, Moody distinguished loud voices
and shouts issuing from the mob that milled outside the Tabernacle. He winced at an obscenity or two offered by some in-
dignant persons unable to gain access to the packed auditorium. But the hurt passed quickly and was replaced by a
deep satisfaction at all that he saw. Months of hard work
and careful planning had brought this moment to reality.
Chicago, his adopted home, was ready for revival. The campaign for Christ and for right was about to begin.[1]

The Chicago revival encompassed three and one-half
months of meetings and unfolded in three distinct stages--an
initial period of intense prerevival preparation, followed by
the early weeks of meetings aimed to fire the spirits and
garner the support of the city's churchgoers, and, finally,
a ten-week evangelistic blitz of Chicago designed to reach
every class in the city and win new converts to the Gospel.

The initial stage of preparation was the subject of the preceding chapter. Ministerial organizations and business committees were formed to lay plans for the coming services. The Tabernacle was financed and erected. Choirs were organized. Ushers and policemen were recruited. Inquiry-room workers were trained. And an intense publicity campaign was launched. By October 1 the Moody and Sankey meetings were a matter of public knowledge among Chicagoans.

The advent of the meetings signaled the second stage in the strategy to evangelize the city. During the first two weeks of meetings, Moody and Sankey focused their efforts on the revival of Christians. At the initial prayer meeting in Farwell Hall, Moody stated bluntly the order of priorities to be upheld if Chicago was to be awakened. "We must work for ourselves for the first few days," said the evangelist. "There's such a thing as praying for others when we ourselves are not yet ready. We must prepare ourselves before we can do any good to others." The preparations which Moody expected of Christians became clear in the subsequent meetings. In his first sermon, Moody called on believers to absolve themselves of all "hindrances" to the revival's success. Specifically, he exhorted his listeners to rid themselves of three "stones" standing in the way of revival: "unbelief," "prejudice against revivals," and a "miserable sectarian spirit." Sankey repeated the exhortation to Christian rededication with the words of an appropriate hymn:

> Only an armour-bearer, proudly I stand
> Waiting to follow at the King's command,
> Marching if "onward" shall the order be,
> Standing by my captain, serving faithfully.

At the conclusion of the service more than fifteen hundred Chicagoans pledged themselves and their labor to Moody and Sankey and to the revival.[2]

In the days which followed, Moody and Sankey continued their efforts to gather Chicago's Christians into a single, united front dedicated to the work of revival. On four consecutive nights, Moody addressed believers at the Tabernacle on the themes of "courage," "faith," "charity," and "compassion." Only as Chicago's church people embraced these qualities, Moody declared, could they enter effectively into the spiritual battle at hand. Again and again in these sermons,

he placed responsibility for the coming of revival to Chicago
on the shoulders and in the hearts and minds of believers:
"If God does not do a great and mighty work here it will not
be his fault, but it will be our own." At the same time,
Moody became specific about the roles that Christian laborers
were to play in the work at hand. Faithful prayer support
and right living were requisite, to be sure. But Moody was
also readying his forces for an aggressive confrontation with
sin. "What we want is a hand-to-hand conflict with the billiard saloons and drinking halls," Moody proclaimed. The
city was to be canvassed and a personal invitation to the
meetings extended to every citizen. If the politicians could
visit every Chicago home in search of votes, said Moody confidently, so could Christians in search of souls. Personal
evangelism by workers was crucial for revival.

> If souls weigh on your hearts, let us go and bring
> them to Jesus. Let us write to them beseeching
> letters if our lips cannot reach them. Let us not
> rest day or night. Let us commence with our fam-
> ilies; let us find our brothers. If our brothers
> have yielded, let us go to our friends.

The exhortations to Christians continued daily at the Tabernacle until Moody was satisfied that he had beside him a core
of committed workers and supporters.[3]

The enthusiasm of these early meetings was dampened
only slightly by the absence of Moody for several days during the second week of October due to the death of his
youngest brother. Large crowds continued, however, to fill
the Tabernacle to hear Sankey sing and to listen to Moody's
stand-in and longtime friend, Daniel Whittle. Indeed, the
unabated interest in the revival services despite Moody's absence was proof to some observers that the work was of God.

On Sunday, October 15, Moody returned to Chicago,
"more subdued, somewhat saddened," and addressed a packed
Tabernacle with a sermon entitled appropriately, "He First
Found His Own Brother." The sermon was a masterful example of the revivalist's ability to adapt personal circumstances
to the task of evangelism. For fourteen years, said Moody,
he had prayed for his youngest and dearest brother--the
"Benjamin" of the family. Finally, in the last year the boy
had become a Christian and immediately set to work for Christ.

Now he was gone. A bittersweet joy exuded from Moody and touched many in the crowd. One listener commented, "The great congregation seemed to feel as though it had been their brother, as well as Mr. Moody's, whom he had just been away to bury." Then he issued the challenge:

> If you, my dear Christian friend, have a brother out of Christ, go bring him in. You will by and by have to stand by the open grave of some dear brother, and to be without Christ, how can you bear it? ... Begin at once your mission lest it be too late forever.

At the conclusion of the service, thousands moved into the inquiry rooms to take up the challenge.[4]

This sermon marked the onset of the third stage in the revival program--what one contemporary called the "first wedge" in the quest for converts. Moody's sermons from the day of his return from Northfield assumed a decidedly evangelistic tone. The revival and unification of Christians seemingly accomplished, the evangelist focused his labors now on the conversion of those outside the churches.

From October 15, 1876, to January 15, 1877, Moody, Sankey, and their Chicago workers labored to evangelize the city. Their efforts centered around a rigorous schedule of meetings held at Farwell Hall and the Tabernacle. Evening meetings were conducted daily at the Tabernacle, except Saturdays. At the precise hour scheduled, the services began, unless the building had been packed early; in such cases, the services began even earlier. The first half hour was spent in congregational singing. The hymns were usually the gospel songs popularized by Sankey, Bliss, Phillips, and other contemporary evangelical composers, and the singing was led by a local director or by George Stebbins, the choir director imported from New York by Moody. Exactly half an hour after the music had begun, the two evangelists entered the Tabernacle, Moody going to his pulpit and Sankey to his organ. After a moment of silent prayer, Moody would announce the next hymn and sometimes comment upon its appropriateness to the subject of the evening. A prominent minister then led a prayer, Sankey would sing a hymn or two, and Moody would read the evening's Bible lesson. The service closed with a prayer and an invitation to those desiring further

spiritual guidance to come to the inquiry rooms. As the congregation stood to sing a concluding hymn, the inquirers
moved to the designated areas.

For the first month and a half of meetings, this daily
fare of revival services, similar in format and procedure,
was conducted at the Tabernacle. The more informal noon
prayer meetings at Farwell Hall, spiced with testimonies and
prayer requests, provided some variety in service form.
Still, the danger that the meetings would become overfamiliar
concerned the evangelist. How could a high level of vitality
and enthusiasm be maintained over ninety-three days and
nights of continuous services? Moody anticipated the problem
and planned accordingly.

Beginning in mid-November, Moody introduced into the
revival schedule a series of specialized meetings. Special
services for young men, young women, businessmen, parents,
Germans, and "fallen women" were held in the later weeks of
November and throughout December.[5] Marshall Field and Levi
Leiter released four hundred of their employees from the
afternoon work schedule to attend an exclusive service with
Moody at Farwell Hall. Temperance meetings for converted
alcoholics were held on Fridays and special sessions for new
converts were scheduled for Monday evenings. A week of
all-day personal inquiry meetings held at the Tabernacle in
late December lent an even greater variety to the revival
work. The Advance reported the new schedule:

> From 1 o'clock til 10:00 p.m. on Monday, Tuesday,
> Thursday, and Friday, the Tabernacle will be open
> for inquiry meetings, at which Mr. Moody and others
> [will] give personal instruction. The women's meet-
> ing and the men's meeting from 1 to 1:30 p.m., the
> temperance meeting from 3 to 4 p.m.; a young ladies'
> meeting from 4 to 5 p.m.; and the reformed men's
> meeting, the boy's meeting and the young converts'
> meeting, in different rooms of the Tabernacle from
> 8 to 9 p.m. From 9 to 10 p.m. there would be a
> men's meeting at Farwell Hall, at which Mr. Moody
> would preside.[6]

In short, there was a special meeting for almost anyone in the
city who wished to attend. Instead of diminishing interest
as the revival meetings became familiar, the variety Moody

incorporated into the meetings worked to maintain the desired
level of religious interest and excitement.   In mid-December,
the Northwestern Christian Advocate was able to report larger crowds and more prayer requests than ever before.   "The
Chicago meetings," the writer said, "are like that wedding
in Cana; we are having the best of the wine at the last of
the feast."[7]

Clearly, the revival techniques Moody employed in Chicago enhanced the probability of the success of his meetings.
Equally significant, however, was the incorporation into the
revival structure of what Sandra Sizer has termed the "basic
forms of social religion"--prayer, testimony, and exhortation.
Sizer argues that in the early nineteenth century, revivalists
employed this "new complex of religious practices" in order
to bridge effectively the earlier Puritan distinction between
the private religion of confession and conversion and the
public religion of worship and praise.   Revivalists like Charles
Finney, she argues, intended these worship forms "to create
a community of intense feeling, in which individuals under-
went similar experiences and would thenceforth unite with
others in matters of moral decision and social behavior."
This "community of feeling," they hoped, might provide the
moral undergirding necessary if Christians were to engage
effectually in the building of a godly America.   By the time
of the Moody and Sankey revivals in the 1870s, she contends,
revivalism had removed itself from the public sphere.   Prayer,
testimony, and exhortation continued to be foundational to
their gatherings, but the aim was now "a happy medium of
controlled affection, shared by a community and directed to
God."   The images of home, mother, and family proved especially useful to Moody in keeping uncontrolled passions in
their place.[8]

Sizer's thesis suggests a way to estimate the social
impact of the Moody revivals.   She rightly relates the extensive use of domestic imagery in Moody's sermons to the culti-
vation of certain kinds of feelings and attitudes.   This feature
of the Chicago sermons will be explored in a later chapter.
Here, the concept of "social religion" will be adopted as a
frame of reference from which to examine the roles of prayer,
testimony, song, and story in the Chicago meetings.

Prayer and testimony were part of the regular fare of
the revival services.   Both forms of worship were, of course,

vital and familiar activities in the spiritual life of evangelicals.[9] In evangelical congregations, attendance at and interest in the weekly prayer meetings was understood by some
as a kind of barometer of the level of spiritual vitality in a
church. As a writer for the Baptist Standard phrased it,
the "prayer meeting is both an index to the religious life of
a church and a medium through which that religious life may
be reached and elevated."[10]

Most evangelicals also believed that prayer was requisite
to the experience of conversion. Divine help was sought in
order that unbelievers might comprehend and receive the Gospel. In a related function, prayer was thought to be an indispensable instrument in the periodic showering of revival.
Henry C. Fish, in his 1874 handbook on revivals, argued
that prayer "enters into the plan and structure of the universe." "God would as soon give the rain without the clouds
or the electric fluid," Fish argued, "as revivals without the
prayers of his people."[11] Prayer revitalized and refreshed
individual believers, provided an avenue for divine aid in the
work of evangelism, and was requisite to the occasional revivals that brought fresh life to the churches. It was only
to be expected, then, that Moody would incorporate this
activity into the revival program.

Prayer functioned at yet another level of experience
equally significant to the interests of the revivalist. Prayer
was a social and unitive activity. In a series of articles in
the Interior, the Reverend A. E. Kittridge of Chicago's Third
Presbyterian Church articulated these aspects of the prayer
meeting. It was "a family gathering of the disciples," said
Kittridge, "where each one comes bringing some leaf or bud
of experience to cheer and comfort others." He advised ministers to "work up" the meeting with lively songs and testimonies. They should strive for brevity, informality, and
widespread participation, said Kittridge. People should be
seated close together in order to cultivate a "warm sociable-
ness." The goal of the prayer service, he concluded, was
that "all hearts will melt together and become as one heart."[12]

Prayer sessions were conducted daily at noon in the
YMCA auditorium at Farwell Hall with Moody and Sankey often
in attendance. The room usually was crowded, and late-
comers stood in the aisles or sat on the platform steps. Moody
approved of the closely packed quarters, resisting suggestions

that the services be moved to the more spacious Tabernacle.13
The physical proximity of attendants, he believed, facilitated
"a sense of close contact" which benefited the meetings. The
prayer meeting began with a hymn. A local minister followed
with prayer. After singing a single verse of another hymn,
Moody commented briefly upon a selected Scripture passage.
Prayers, prayer requests, testimonies, and songs filled the
remainder of the hour. Brevity was enforced strictly. Prayers and comments were limited to three minutes. Only single
verses of requested hymns were sung. Participation was
wholly voluntary and as inclusive as possible. The revival
prayer meetings, Moody declared, were to be "free, social
meeting[s]."14

By design, revival prayer meetings united participants
in common sympathy and shared concerns. They were "experience" meetings. In the meetings, participants offered
their individual and corporate expressions of confession and
thanksgiving. Needs, worries, and anxieties were shared in
an atmosphere of common concern and support. The activity
provided an opportunity for personal affirmation and drew
disparate individuals together in spirit and purpose. Furthermore, the prayer meetings reinforced virtuous conduct among
participants by delineating models of sinful behavior.15 Social
pressure to avoid such activities resulted from their castigation by the larger group. Thus the prayer meeting aided in
disciplining individual behavior--an important concern of the
revival. Said a contributor to the Independent about the
beneficial effect of prayer meetings on personal conduct, "You
need the habit of them, the impulses gained at them, the sus-
taining and restraining and sanctifying power of them."16

Like prayer, the sharing of testimonies provided a
means to articulate emotions and share experiences socially.
C. L. Thompson, the pastor of Chicago's Fifth Presbyterian
Church and a participant in the 1876 revival, suggested that
testimony was a useful evangelistic technique because it best
suited the constitution of the human mind and the nature of
the Gospel itself. "Moral influence," he wrote,

> is at its highest when it moves from one heart to
> another.... God has adjusted every moral force in
> the universe for the purpose of accelerating the
> progress of truth. Chief among these moral forces
> are those which lie in the line of the human and

natural affections. The gospel gets an impulse in
passing through a human heart which it could not
have if it were shot through the lip of an archangel.

In generating influence, he concluded, it is useful to put
people of the same class or condition together (men, women,
inebriates, and so on), because "levels of influence are
strongest" among similar persons.[17] Moody agreed. Evangelism, he believed, is "sometimes best done by believers
giving an account of the joy they experience in believing, instead of exhorting."[18]

In both prayer and testimony, then, lines of influence
emerged from the sharing of personal experience--in prayer
when one shared publicly a need or worry, and in testimony
as one related a private religious experience or that of others.
Yet, as in the prayer-meeting revivals of 1857 and 1858 studied by Sizer, the sharing was virtually anonymous. Chicagoans at the Tabernacle probably knew only a small number
of the persons in the audience. But the purpose of the activity was not to create intimate relationships. Rather, the
prayers and accounts of conversion articulated the like-
mindedness, the similar feelings, and the common experiences
of people unknown to one another.[19] They functioned also
to suggest positive and negative sets of images to listeners
and to inculcate models for behavior and "right" feelings. A
letter Moody received from a young woman and read at a noon
prayer meeting was typical in tone and content of the many
testimonies related at the revival services.

Dear Mr. Moody:
    For years my mother (who is now in Heaven) and
myself have been praying for a wandering son and
brother, who had given himself up to the demon Rum.
Since my mother's death I have kept on praying although I was not sure whether he was living or not.
For eighteen years I have not seen his face. This
winter I have prayed that he might be led by the
Providence of God into some of the religious meetings at the West ... and with strong cries I have
asked the Lord to take from him the appetite for
rum. Now, dear brother, hear how the Lord has
heard and blessed my soul and his. On the 27th
or 28th of November last (he visited me on New Years
Day) he found himself (he knows not how he wandered

> there) at Chicago and there went to one of your
> meetings, was impressed with the truths you spoke,
> rose for prayers, went in the inquiry room and the
> Lord then and there took away his appetite for rum
> and since then he has been resting on Jesus' love....
> I write this to beg of other mothers and sisters, to
> keep on praying for their wandering and intemperate
> ones, and the dear Lord will hear their cries and
> take the appetite.[20]

Such tales evoked the sympathy of listeners, identified clearly
the sources of good and evil, and created bonds between
those with similar concerns.

The most dramatic use of testimony occurred in December with the conversion of a young Scotsman named Willie.
Because the testimony elicited a remarkable response, it deserves some recounting and brief analysis. During the first
days of the Chicago meetings, Moody received a letter from a
prayerful and "broken-hearted father and mother" from Scotland begging the evangelist's aid in locating their son, Willie,
who "had been a wanderer for many years." Moody read the
letter publicly at the Tabernacle on the off chance that the
young man might be in Chicago. Receiving no response,
Moody gave the letter to Brother Sawyer, who was leading
the temperance services, "for it was believed that the lost
one would be found among that class, if he was in Chicago."

The expectation proved correct when a week later a
lad named Willie with a Scottish accent came forward for prayer.
Upon further inquiry it was discovered that he was the Willie.
The following evening at the Tabernacle, Moody concluded
his sermon by relating the astounding events and then asked
Willie to add his own personal testimony, which he did.

> Twenty years ago I was a happy boy in Scotland.
> My father wished me to be a doctor; but my mother
> hoped I would be a minister. When I was at school
> I fell in with bad companionship; and, as a result,
> my life has been one long day of debauchery.... My
> wife was one of the sweetest little women that ever
> drew the breath of life. She was a Christian, the
> daughter of a minister. Well, in three years she
> died of a broken heart. I killed her by my profli-
> gate life; and when I saw them shut the black coffin

lid over her white face I felt that I had lost my best
friend and that in her death my last hope was gone....
I took my only little child in my arms to kiss her
goodbye.... My dear mother gave me a hug, as if
her arms were iron; but I broke away from them
all. And since that hour I have roamed the wide
world over--hungry, naked, and miserable--a blot
on the face of the earth. When I first came to Chicago I resolved to live a better life; but I soon
went back to my cups, and lost my situation, lost
my friends, lost all. But a week ago Mr. Sawyer
handed me my father's letter, and I found that my
parents loved me still and were ready and longing
to welcome me back. Then Christian friends prayed
with me.... I bowed at the foot of the cross ... and
He has saved me. And today I would rather live on
crusts of bread, moistened with my tears, than to
go back to my life of sin.

As he sat down, a reporter observed, "thousands in the
Tabernacle were weeping." And in the minutes following,
hundreds of inquirers flooded into the inquiry rooms.[21]

Willie's tale illustrated well the function of testimony in
the revival context. The story was dramatic and attention
getting, roused the sympathies and emotions of listeners,
and evoked familiar images--the rebellious and wandering son,
the evils of liquor, the destruction of a pure and innocent
Christian wife and mother (a minister's daughter), the break-
up of a family, the degradation of the drunkard, and the
ultimate redemption of the young man by the prayers of loving parents reaching even across an ocean. Related again
and again, such stories fostered among those in attendance a
commonality of attitudes, feelings, and expectations.[22]

Testimony, prayer, and the sharing of prayer requests
dominated the daily noon-hour services conducted by Moody
at Farwell Hall. These sessions included pronouncements
against deleterious behavior and toward good conduct. Exhortation clearly was secondary to testimony and prayer at
the noon meetings; in the evening sessions, however, Sankey's
songs and Moody's exhortative preaching highlighted activities.
Still, the goal of the services remained constant--to influence
nonbelievers to enter the community of faith and virtuous living. To this end, the revivalists integrated the forms of
prayer, testimony, and exhortation into both song and sermon.

Moody's "singer of the Gospel" was Ira D. Sankey. A
devout Christian and experienced church musician, Sankey
was an effective complement to Moody. Tall, always gracious,
and physically attractive, Sankey offered a sharp contrast
to the rugged, stocky, brusque Moody. Whereas Sankey was
graceful in bearing and unassuming in manner, Moody was
aggressive and commanding. Both men, however, had the
ability to read an audience correctly and move them emotionally in the direction desired. A perceptive reporter for the
Chicago Inter-Ocean compared the two evangelists and noted
that

> neither ventures to approach a crowd until it is in
> the right mood, and never leaves it until every
> heart is throbbing responsively. In studying Mr.
> Moody we are driven forward to the contemplation
> of the results of his work. In studying Mr. Sankey
> we linger over the sweet voice, the trembling tones,
> the tender words. Mr. Moody startles us and
> arouses us, while Mr. Sankey soothes and comforts.
> Mr. Moody, earnest as he is, succeeds without the
> grace of voice and manner. Mr. Sankey, earnest
> as he is, succeeds because of grace in voice and
> manner. [23]

Sankey was an effective, but not overly impressive,
soloist. His range was limited, and music critics sometimes
commented negatively on his habit of sliding from note to
note. [24] He made his impact largely through the earnestness
and conviction he was able to convey to his listeners. Commentators remarked frequently on the "pathos" of his voice
and on his "exquisitely touching rendering" of the hymns.
Not infrequently, his solos brought tears to the eyes of
listeners and, sometimes, the singer himself wept openly at
the conclusion of a hymn. The music, like the prayers and
testimonies, evoked feelings which effectively prepared listeners for the sermons which followed. A Chicago commenta-
tor, assessing the impact of Sankey's "sweet songs," observed
that "the evangelist without the singer would be lands unbroken to the sower." However, the songs were also musical
statements of the same Gospel which Moody preached and were
understood by the revivalists as evangelistic tools. Sankey
was to "sing the Gospel," Moody was to preach it. [25]

Sankey's understanding of the purpose of his music

affected directly his performing style. Because the message
was all-important, he took special care to enunciate the
words.[26] For similar reasons Sankey varied his singing from
verse to verse. "I never sing the second verse of a tune as
I sang the first verse, nor do I sing the third as I sang the
second," he explained. "Why should I? The words are different, the meaning is different and so the rendering must
be different." Sankey designed the rhythm and tune of his
songs to fit and make more effective the desired impact of
the lyrics. The Nation observed of Sankey's songs, "the
time is now slow, now rapid, constantly changing, the notes
of every variety of length, and the general effect of the
whole designed to give pronounced meaning to the words."
The variety of tempo, length of note, and alterations in volume
gave to Sankey's music a highly dramatic quality, continually
creating moods appropriate to the message.[27]

Sankey's songs also appropriated the basic forms of
social religion. One of his most popular hymns, "I Am Praying for You," combined all of these forms.

> I have a Saviour, He's pleading in glory,
> A dear, loving Saviour tho' earth friends be few;
> And now He is watching in tenderness o'er me,
> But oh, that my Saviour were your Saviour too.
>
> [Verses follow with "I have a Father," "a robe,"
>   "a peace."]
>
> When Jesus has found you, tell others the story
> That my loving Saviour is your Saviour too;
> Then pray that your Saviour may bring them to
>   glory,
> And pray'r will be answered--'twas answered for
>   you!
>
> Chorus:
> For you I am praying, For you I am praying,
> For you I am praying, I'm praying for you.[28]

The hymn offered testimony, prayer, and an exhortation to
listeners.

One of the singer's favorite lyrical conventions was to
adapt a familiar Biblical episode to hymn form. Examples are
Stebbins's song, "The Prodigal Son," Sankey's "Jesus of
Nazareth Passeth By," and his immensely popular "The Ninety
and Nine."

There were ninety and nine that safely lay
In the shelter of the fold,
But one was out on the hills away,
Far off from the gates of gold,
Away on the mountain wild and bare,
Away from the tender Shepherd's care,
Away from the tender Shepherd's care.

But all through the mountains, thunder-riv'n,
and up from the rocky steep,
There arose a glad cry to the gate of heav'n,
"Rejoice! I have found my sheep!"
And the angels echoed around the throne,
"Rejoice! for the Lord brings back his own!"
Rejoice for the Lord brings back his own! [29]

A reporter for the <u>Alliance</u> described Sankey's rendering of
this hymn at the Tabernacle as "highly dramatic.... The
hearer can see the wandering sheep, the mountain 'wild and
bare,' 'the tender shepherd' as he crosses the deserts and
climbs the mountains 'to find his sheep.' " Songs like "The
Ninety and Nine" contemporized and personalized familiar Bible
stories. Like Moody's Biblical anecdotes, they were applauded
by most commentators for their vivid portrayals and their
earnest delivery. [30] And like the evangelist's stories, they
functioned both to join listeners in common emotional experience and to exhort them to a positive response to the Gospel
message.

Sankey's solo singing was supplemented in the revival
meetings by congregational singing. Congregational singing
occurred at various points in the services. As noted above,
it was not uncommon for the audience to spend up to thirty
minutes singing before the evangelists entered the auditorium.
Sankey frequently would invite the congregation to join him
on the choruses of his solos, and often the choir would sing
but one verse of a hymn and then the congregation would
join for the remaining verses.

The songs were most often simple, catchy, lively tunes
which were learned quickly by the congregation. After the
meetings, some participants commented that the tunes recurred
to their minds for days following. The beat of certain of the
gospel songs was such that some Chicagoans were discovered
dancing to them. Varied as the hymns were in subject, tempo,

and mood, they were songs which caught the attention of
the audience and were a joy to sing. As the editor of the
Nation observed about the revival songs, "determine the
pleasure that you get from a circus quick-step, a negro-
minstrel sentimental ballad, a college chorus, and a hymn all
in one, and you have some gauge of the variety and contrast
that may be perceived in one of these songs."[31]

The nightly song service at the Tabernacle produced
numerous desired effects in the context of social religion.
It provided another means of linking together thousands of
individuals as a body; it heightened the emotional level of
the service while at the same time allowing for the release
and expression of those emotions; it reinforced the theme of
that portion of the meetings by restating it in lyrical form;
and it helped to create and maintain the kinds of attitudes
and mood which might facilitate the call to conversion and
consecration.[32] Commentators remarked repeatedly about the
impressive, almost awesome, atmosphere which resulted when
the eight to nine thousand persons at the Tabernacle joined
their voices in singing a gospel song.[33] The Reverend J. T.
Sunderland, the Unitarian minister opposed to the revival,
perhaps expressed best the overwhelming impact which the
congregational singing could have upon participants.

> I insist that the greatest power of the music of the
> great meetings held has not lain in Mr. Sankey's
> singing. It has lain in the sweeping, surging, ir-
> resistible, overwhelming, singing of the congrega-
> tions.... And you, too, though you have only gone
> in as an indifferent and critical spectator, before
> you know it you too are drawn into the enchanted
> current, and are being borne with strange intoxica-
> tion on the bosom of the wild but wondrous song....
> A theology which in sober thought a man would cast
> away with loathing, he would find himself before he
> knew it joining in the singing of, with the multitude;
> and finally, through the singing, he would be drawn
> actually to embrace it. Only he knows that who has
> himself stood in the midst of the great multitude, and
> that day after day and night after night, and felt
> himself thrilled and awed and borne away by the
> strange power of its mighty choruses.[34]

As much as Sankey and his music contributed to the

success of the Chicago meetings, the moving force behind the
revival was Moody. His naturally swarthy complexion was
darkened further by a full dark beard which had thickened
noticeably during the years in Britain. His abrupt mannerisms
combined with deep-set, darting eyes to convey the idea of
a compressed bundle of vitality. Moody's level of energy
seemed always high, and he was able to express a boundless
enthusiasm and intense conviction which attracted people
rather than a nervous tension that might have repelled them.
Dressed in the dark suit he commonly wore, Moody appeared
to some as the very embodiment of the rugged, aggressive,
Yankee businessman--a first-generation-off-the-farm aspiring
merchant or salesman whose honest, efficient, hard work
marked him for certain success.[35]

Moody focused his energies upon revival work with an
intensity and drive that sometimes amazed and awed those
who observed him. In Chicago as elsewhere, Moody spent
long hours every day doing the work of evangelism. His
fervor perhaps stemmed from his oft-expressed conviction
that the world was like a sinking ship, and the task God had
given him was to save as many as possible before the boat
went down.[36] A convinced premillennialist, Moody's zeal in
witness was inspired further by the belief that the time was
short before Christ would return. Henry Ward Beecher once
remarked about Moody's premillennialism, "He thinks that
Christ may come even tomorrow. I should be a burning fire
all the time if I believed like that."[37] Moody did believe "like
that," and the result was a relentless urgency that made every
situation an opportunity for evangelism. Abby Farwell Ferry,
the daughter of Moody's close friend, recalled how, as a child,
she had sat spellbound watching the evangelist in action at
the Chicago meetings "beckoning to us to 'Come to Jesus.' "
"It seemed as if he lifted us up, in spite of ourselves. 'Are
you a Christian?' became an arrow point directed to every
man, woman and child in Chicago, collectively and individu-
ally." Evangelism was his obsession, as she remembered it.
"He shouted [the Gospel message] from the platform, he
whispered it in the narrow passageway, seated at your side
at the dinner table, as he joined you on the sidewalk, in
fact, everywhere."[38]

Moody was confrontational, abrupt, and often blunt in
his evangelism. In some instances, especially early in his
career, people reacted hostilely even violently, to his pigeonhole

style of witnessing. But most were overwhelmed by his apparent utter sincerity, his personalized but never condescend-
ing manner, and his ability to convince others of the magni-
tude of a personal decision about the Christian Gospel.[39]

As a speaker, Moody expressed the depth of his convictions. His abrupt, but certain, actions in the pulpit conveyed to observers the picture of a man of decisiveness,
seemingly in control of every situation. Contemporaries related episodes in which Moody took troublesome or annoying
situations and turned them to his own advantage. One impressed reporter for the Inter-Ocean described such an occasion in Chicago in which a small child began to cry in the
middle of the sermon. As persons in the audience turned to
look, the child's mother reluctantly got up and began to go
out. Moody stopped and said, "My good woman, don't go
out. You are here to hear the gospel. Your dear little baby
does not disturb me and I am sure the people about you who
want to hear the gospel won't be disturbed either." The
woman went back to her seat, and almost immediately the baby
stopped crying. The reporter, Thomas McMillan, noted that
"the effect on the audience of this incident was tremendous."[40]
Obviously, Moody's actions worked to enhance his rapport
with the congregation as well as to diffuse possible tensions
and regain the attention of his listeners. The revivalist's
evident skills in moderating crowd response probably contributed further to the sense of unity and community achieved
by the services.

Moody had his critics, to be sure. Commentators described his Chicago discourses on several occasions as "in-
elegant" and "ungrammatical." Some commented negatively
on his "locomotive" style of delivery. Others thought his
sermons totally unorganized.[41] In a letter to the Tribune,
one unsympathetic listener wrote, "It is Mr. Moody's plan to
start his discourse with a text in the orthodox style, and
then to ramble all around creation for bits of religious wisdom, which may or may not have a connection with the topic."
This listener went on to disparage the emotional quality of
Moody's presentations.

> To the female portion of his audience Mr. Moody ap-
> peals through his anecdotes about the conversion
> and death of children. These are narrated in a very
> pathetic manner. The tears well up to the preacher's

eyes, and the ladies, probably more affected by
the manner than the matter, weep from pure sympathy. [42]

However, the critics were in a clear minority. Even those
who commented negatively on the evangelist's crude, un-
polished style as a speaker were usually captured by the
earnestness and drama of his presentation. As one journalist
present admitted, after criticizing mildly the evangelist as a
speaker, "to a disinterested auditor, Mr. Moody's earnestness atones for everything."[43]

Moody was an effective speaker. Besides his earnest,
convincing manner, he possessed a marvelous ability to tell
a story well. The bulk of Moody's sermons were, in fact,
composed of anecdotes and stories used to illustrate spiritual
points. Most of the stories placed characters in family set-
tings. They related events of daily life similar to those ver-
balized in testimonies at Farwell Hall. For this reason, the
story-sermons functioned much in the manner of a testimony.
They provided models of experience and behavior to listeners
and created lines of influence between preacher and pew sitter.

Biblical tales provided Moody with one important source
of illustrative materials. Job, David, Samuel, and Daniel
were several of the Biblical characters Moody fleshed out into
nineteenth-century form. In Moody's rendition, the prodigal
son was transformed into the rebellious lad down the street
who fled and, in time, returned to the home where he was
truly loved. Moody brought to life for Tabernacle listeners
the traumas, tensions, joys, and sorrows of the familiar Bible
stories. Moody himself was captured by the tales and was
able to convey successfully the intensity of his feelings to
others. D. W. Whittle described the process at work on one
occasion as Moody read aloud to a few friends the familiar
tale of the good Samaritan. "His eyes would fill and his
voice tremble as he read over the description to me of the
wounded man and glisten with joy as he came to the account
of the kind Samaritan.... His power is in [the story's] reality to him."[44] Years after the Chicago meetings were
memories, Henry Sloane Coffin recounted what it was like to
listen to Moody.

I can see him now in the Northfield pulpit, speaking
about "Dan'l." "Dan'l" was down there in the lion's

> den and Mr. Moody, speaking in the name of the
> King, leaned over and said: "Oh, Dan'l, servant
> of the living God, is thy God whom thou servest
> continually able to deliver thee from the lions?"
> Then from this profound pit came the voice: "Oh,
> King, live forever. My God has sent his Angel and
> has stopped the lion's mouths."

"There was nothing bizarre, nothing spectacular, nothing
theatrical, nothing irreverent," recalled Coffin. "This was
the Word of God, but it was so vivid to him that he made
us feel that we were right on the spot."[45]

To audiences composed largely of people who had grown
up listening to these Bible stories, Moody's powerful, vivid,
contemporized renderings likely stirred deep-seated memories.
For they drew effectively upon the "collective thought" of his
audience.[46] The Biblical stories were among the foundational
"myths" of nineteenth-century Protestant American culture.
Such myths, as Mircea Eliade has explained, undergird every
culture functioning to create "exemplary models" of conduct
for that society.[47] A modern student of Bible stories, John
Shea, has explicated further their mythic function. The individual growing up in a Christian culture, argues Shea, is
encouraged and critiqued by the great Bible stories. They
establish for him "the inner meaning and ultimate values of
life situations ... setting boundaries and modeling behavior."[48]
From this perspective, one can see how Moody's rendering of
the classic Bible stories functioned socially to create ultimate
models of behavior. The revivalist's contemporization of
these stories made their lessons even more explicit for listeners. Furthermore, his family stories can be seen as ex-
tensions of the Bible stories. For the domestic tales both
reiterated and further contemporized the behavioral and at-
titudinal models set forth in the Bible stories. The collective
recollection of these stories itself was important in engendering a sense of community among listeners.

Whether a contemporized Bible story or, more commonly,
a personal anecdote, the story-sermon in combination with
prayer, testimony, and song, evoked precisely the kind of
emotional ethos the revivalist deemed necessary for effective
evangelism. The employment of these worship forms in Chicago was extensive and certainly must be considered in assessing the revival's attractiveness to Chicagoans as well as
the ultimate social significance of the meetings.

   While it is difficult, if not impossible, to measure accurately the success of Moody's first month of meetings, there
is little doubt that by November the evangelistic team was
having a significant impact on the city's evangelical churches
and had captured the attention and interest of a large portion of the city. The November issue of the Independent reported that Chicago's "pastors are finding their hands more
than full with cases of peculiar religious interest in their
own fields." "Wherever you go," the writer continued, "you
hear the names of Moody and Sankey, and on the horse-cars,
in counting rooms, and even in saloons and gambling dens
men are discussing the services in the Tabernacle and the good
which these services are accomplishing." The religion pages
of the local newspapers contained frequent reports of the surprising number of conversions both at the Tabernacle and
in the local churches, the large numbers of new members reported by pastors, and the heightened interest in local prayer
meetings and Sunday worship services.[49]

   Numerous Chicago ministers expressed their excitement
about the spiritual awakening they witnessed in their respective
congregations. Arthur Mitchell, the pastor of the First Presbyterian Church, testified that mid-November "had been the
best of all my eight years pastorate.... During last week
there began to be conversions among us, and sinners are in-
quiring what they must do to be saved." The minister of
the Third Presbyterian Church, the Reverend A. E. Kittridge, reported that "at the inquiry meeting after the sermon
last night there were fifty persons present, and throughout
the Church there is an unprecedented desire for and activity
in the work of saving souls." The pastor at First Congregational Church stated "that the work of salvation was going
on gloriously in his Sunday School, where 100 had already
accepted Christ, and fifty more were seeking Him.... They
had organized a Christian Bureau," he added, "and 100 persons, both men and women, were busy every night visiting
from house to house in the name of the Lord." The cleric
of the Second Presbyterian Church perhaps expressed most
poignantly the conviction that revival had, indeed, descended
upon Chicago.

         I have invited people to come to me as inquirers a
         good many times; but seldom anybody came. But
         now there were so many people coming that I can
         hardly find time to speak to them all. I have a long

list of names in my book, so many cases that I can
hardly overtake them. I am not usually tired on
Mondays, but today I am tired.... These are like
the times spoken of in the Acts of the Apostles,
when the Lord added to the Church daily of such
as should be saved.[50]

The enthusiasm of Moody's supporters was buttressed
further by reports of revival successes in other Midwestern
cities where Moody's associates had initiated services.[51] Testimonies of dramatic conversions and answered prayers were
offered daily at the noon prayer meetings. Beginning in November a weekly publication entitled the Tabernacle was issued
from the evangelist's headquarters at Farwell Hall. The paper
repeated portions of Moody's sermons, detailed accounts of
conversions, and related revival news from the local churches
as well as those outside the city.[52] In large part the characteristics of a true revival seemed already in evidence in
Chicago by mid-November.[53] Interest in religion and religious
questions was extraordinarily high among both the churched
and unchurched, the simple Gospel was being proclaimed
regularly, and conversions were occurring in unusually large
numbers both at the Tabernacle and in the local churches.

But the harvest was not yet complete. From November
to mid-January, the revival work continued at the Tabernacle
and in evangelical churches across the city. The long-planned
visitation campaign was undertaken with great success. Every
home, business, bar, and billiard hall received its visit from
the revival workers.[54] A formal Prayer Alliance was enjoined
with ministers and lay leaders outside the city at the conclusion of a Christian Convention held at the Tabernacle in late
November.[55] Thousands of outstate clergy flooded the city
to learn from Moody the secrets of revival. As they returned
home, they took with them the excitement of the awakened
Christians of Chicago. In the latter weeks of December the
normal schedule of events was interrupted, and Moody instead opened the Tabernacle daily from one o'clock in the
afternoon to ten o'clock in the evening for personal sessions
with inquirers. The temporary change in evangelistic strategy
proved eminently successful. Moody told a reporter from the
Christian Advocate that "he had never led so many souls to
Christ in one day in all his life as during the second day"
of personal inquiry work at the Tabernacle.[56] The evangelist
ended his labors in Chicago on an equally high note, addressing

more than six thousand "new converts" at a special farewell
meeting and collecting more than $60,000 for the YMCA build-
ing fund at the final Tabernacle meeting. More than twenty-
five hundred new members had been added to the rolls of
the churches of Chicago during the period of Moody's activities in the city, and numerous more had professed similar
interests.57

In surveying Moody's Chicago meetings in 1876, several
observations are warranted. First, the revival program was
a masterpiece of planning and organization. This involved
nothing sinister. It meant simply the effective use of advertising, the careful financial arrangements for a building that
would be most advantageous to his labors, the employment of
professional associates to do tasks for which he lacked the
necessary skills or time, the recruitment of large numbers of
workers to infiltrate the city on his behalf, and an overall
strategy designed ultimately to bring a maximum number of
Chicagoans into contact with Moody and his message. Second,
the Chicago meetings point up the crucial role of Moody in
the success of virtually every phase of the enterprise. Moody's
skill as an organizer and recruiter, his power as a speaker,
and his ability to inspire others with a zeal for the same Gospel he loved was at the heart of whatever success the services
achieved. Finally, the revival structure incorporated effectively the forms of social religion--prayer, testimony, and exhortation. These procedures were intended, of course, to
prepare listeners for evangelistic appeal. But they were also
intensely social strategies aimed at engendering among Moody's
hearers a sense of community grounded in shared feelings
and similar attitudes.

At this point, it is appropriate to examine the social
dynamics that underlay the Chicago revival. Numerous important questions remain to be answered. Who were the people who responded positively to Moody's message? Did the
social stress which Chicagoans experienced in the 1870s cause
certain of them to ally behind Moody and revival religion?
What was there about the evangelist's message and the man
that particularly soothed the hurts and comforted the anxieties
which these Chicagoans felt? Out of the hundreds of thousands of people in Chicago in 1876, why did certain individuals
find comfort and relief at the Moody meetings while others remained unresponsive? Only when such questions are answered

can one begin to understand the social function of the Chicago revival in 1876. The remaining chapters are devoted largely to this task.

Chapter VI

THE RESPONSE

There is an impressive scholarly consensus that the Moody
and Sankey revivals of the 1870s were a nostalgic response
on the part of thousands of recently come-to-the-city folk to
the complexities of metropolitan living. William G. McLoughlin,
the premier historian of American revivalism, argues that
Moody attracted the "country-bred, evangelically oriented,
intellectually unsophisticated, and sentimentally insecure individuals who made up the bulk of the nation's churchgoers"
and were troubled by the social, economic, and political
changes which occurred in urban America during the last
quarter of the nineteenth century. Bernard Weisberger agrees
that "the millions who heard Moody gladly did so because
they yearned for an echo of that simplicity which was disappearing with agrarian America." And Marion Bell, who has
studied Moody's Philadelphia meetings of 1876, explains his
warm reception there as "a nostalgic backward glance at a
simpler America of the past."[1]

These scholars assume further that the revivals were
responses to social unrest, but they fail to describe adequately its specific content. Weisberger finds social sources
of stress in the "urban and scientific upheavals which were
proving so unsettling to the churches of the seventies."
Bell attributes the religious excitement Moody generated in
Philadelphia to the anxieties of rural-oriented evangelicals
about "the new technical advancements, heavy immigration,
and social displacements that were inherent in America's industrialization process." McLoughlin offers a more instruc-
tive, but still highly generalized, interpretation of the social
origins of the Moody revivals. He describes the revivals as
the product of important changes in the structure of the nation's life: from an agrarian to an industrial economy, from

a rural to an urban-centered population, from an anticolonial
to an imperialistic nation, from a relatively homogeneous to a
heterogeneous people, and from a system of relative laissez
faire to the first stages of governmental social control.[2]

The present study aims to understand more specifically
the social roots of that unrest which disposed certain persons in Chicago in 1876 to respond positively to revival religion. It was shown in a preceding chapter that the possible
sources for social unrest in Chicago during the 1870s were
many--chronic unemployment, decreasing wages, labor violence,
and ethnic and religious distrust being only the more prominent. Indeed, socioeconomic and political conditions in the
city were such that in 1876 many, perhaps most, Chicagoans
experienced serious social stress of some sort. But only a
portion of the city's population found comfort in revival religion. Who were these people? What drew them to the revival meetings? What needs were met by conversion or by
affiliation with a revival church? What motives led individuals, under the revival influence, to profess membership in
a church? If these and other related questions can be answered with some specificity, a fuller understanding of the
social functions of the Chicago revival will be obtained.

Historians most often have assessed the social impact
of revivals by reviewing the recorded observations of con-
temporaries--the comments of journalists or the impressions
recorded in letters and diaries by ministers or interested lay
persons in attendance. However, the value of these sources
as a guide to the social composition of the revival congregations is limited. Frequently the observations of eyewitnesses
are vague and unsatisfactory. Nor is attendance at the
services necessarily indicative of a positive response by those
who heard Moody's message. Certainly, thousands of Chicagoans entered the Tabernacle out of curiosity alone. Some
more definitive response is needed to identify with greater
certainty those who embraced revival religion. It is, therefore, both helpful and necessary to study carefully not only
the extant literary evidence but also church membership lists,
census materials, city directories, and other sources which
taken together suggest at least partial answers to the critical
questions of who listened and who responded affirmatively to
the evangelist's words.

The most modern studies of Moody's revivals argue that

the revivalist addressed a predominantly middle-class audience.[3] A perusal of the literary sources describing the Chicago meetings tends to confirm this opinion, but with some
significant qualifications. A reporter for the Inter-Ocean
described the listeners at Moody's first meeting in October
as "composed almost entirely of representatives of the middle
and upper strata of society." A second journalist for the
same paper agreed, observing that the "bulk of the people"
who attended the early meetings "seemed to be of the more
respectable portion of the community, or to consist of drafts
from city chapels and churches." Assessments of this sort
appear to have been based on the clothing worn or the man-
ners evidenced by listeners. The most common word employed by those describing the Tabernacle crowds was "respectable."[4]

    The middle-class caste of Moody's congregations is sug-
gested also by certain criticisms leveled against the revival
meetings. The most common lament commentators voiced about
the services was the absence of the working class and the
poor. "One would suppose that the lowest orders would be
attracted to these meetings, if it were possible to attract them
to any place of devotion," one observer remarked, "but one
looks in vain for many representatives of that class of men
and women, whom one would like, above all others, to see
among the crowds at the Tabernacle." The Chicago-based
Methodist weekly, the Northwestern Christian Advocate, also
reported on the failure of the meetings to reach "the foundations of society," but defended Moody against the city's own
clergy in this regard. "There are about ten flights of stairs
which you preachers never get down; Moody and Sankey get
down one or two lower than the rest of you, but there are
at least eight lower layers that they do not reach."[5]

    Criticism of this sort troubled both Moody and the
evangelical clergymen who supported the revival effort in
Chicago. Many of the city's ministers likely shared the concern voiced by Protestant leaders in the 1870s about the
presence of increasingly large numbers of unchurched people
in the city, especially among the lower classes.[6] Most often
these commentators attributed the difficulty in attracting the
unchurched working classes to pew rents, which the poor
could ill afford, or to the ostentation and formality of many
Protestant churches, which made the poor feel out of place.
Moody and Sankey, as was suggested earlier, appeared to

some as a possible solution to the problem. Since the revival
meetings were free (not even an offering being taken) and
held in a large public hall rather than a church building, it
was expected by some Protestants that the poor would flock
in, be won to Christ through the ministrations of the evangelist, and be ushered subsequently into the evangelical fold.[7]

Moody himself was disturbed by his relative lack of
success in reaching the masses. He had come to Chicago with
a very carefully conceived strategy for evangelizing the entire city. First, the local ministers and lay Christians would
be revived; second, with the aid of these enlivened Christians, the revival message would be conveyed to the poor,
the destitute, the unchurched, and the unsaved. Moody expected that the largest numbers of such people would be
found among Chicago's working classes. While the first stage
of the strategy appears to have met with astounding success,
the second stage achieved only limited results.

The problem was obvious. The working classes and
the poor were not finding their way to the Tabernacle in the
large numbers that Moody expected. The reasons for the
problem are not difficult to surmise. The Catholic allegiance
of a significant portion of the lower classes obviously restricted their receptivity to the revival meetings.[8] Cultural
antipathies and language difficulties dissuaded numerous immigrants among the poor from attendance at the Tabernacle.
The issuing of tickets of admission probably hindered others.
Moody had initiated the ticket system in Philadelphia earlier
in the year, intending thereby to ensure that people of every
class might gain entrance to the services.[9] Tickets were
given out on a first-come-first-served basis with no priority
to class or church affiliation. However, the ticket system
probably worked to discourage lower-class attendance. Working families apparently did not have either the time or the
energy to walk to Farwell Hall and stand in line for tickets.
Indeed, the Tabernacle was often full at 7:00 p.m. when some
factory workers were probably just being dismissed from their
jobs.[10] Those with the time and the determination to gain
access to the meetings were most often middle- and upper-
class church members eager to see the Moody and Sankey
team in action. Complaints about the predominance of the
churched at the Moody services ranked second only to complaints about too few of the working class and the poor in
attendance.[11]

This is not to suggest, however, that Moody's audiences were a homogeneous group or that he failed totally in his efforts to reach the unchurched and the poor. Numerous bits of evidence combine to suggest the opposite. Newsmen described a number of services at which the common people were especially well-represented and the assemblage "made up chiefly of non-church people." The report of the Chicago Times about the October 1 afternoon service depicted a socially diverse crowd. The congregation consisted, the Times said, of "men and women of all ages and every condition, the devout and the undevout, the church-goers and the Sabbath-breakers, Sunday-school children and hoodlums, without regard to age, sex or previous condition of service." Several weeks later, the Independent reported that "all classes are represented.... The majority every evening are men, and very many of these are evidently from the laboring classes, most of whom we never see inside the walls of our churches."[12] At about the midpoint of the campaign, Francis Hemenway, a professor of theology at the Garrett Bible Institute, wrote in his journal that "the movement has taken hold of the low, the ignorant, the degraded, the dissipated, and that too with most extraordinary power." Charles Sawyer, who accompanied Moody as a temperance specialist and conducted large meetings each Friday, remarked that "90% of his work had been with the poor." And, in a most telling statistic, it was discovered that only one in ten of the more than six thousand persons who attended a farewell meeting for new converts had any previous connection with a church.[13]

The difficulty in generalizing accurately about the kinds of people to whom Moody spoke at the Tabernacle is obvious. It seems likely that on-the-scene reporters themselves had great difficulty in assessing the true makeup of any congregation at the Tabernacle. The sheer size of the crowds would tend to make generalizations about an audience relative to the eye of the beholder. How reporters distinguished the "churched" persons from the "unchurched" in the large throngs is even more problematic. Clothing was, at best, an unsure gauge of either social or spiritual condition. Yet, most assumed apparently that well-dressed, respectable-appearing individuals must be middle-class churchgoers.[14] That the "unchurched" could slip quite unnoticed into the Tabernacle was indicated in an interview with an admitted prostitute following a special service held in December for "fallen women." A reporter asked her, "Have you been interested in the services?" "Yes," she replied,

> but I have been here before when I felt much better
> satisfied, and when it was not so easy to tell who
> were the fallen and who were the saved. Now that
> we are crowded together like criminals in a sort of
> public exhibition, I do not like it. [15]

In sum, the impressions of observers regarding the social
composition of audiences at the Tabernacle are imprecise at
best, and in numerous instances contradictory. If any general statement is suggested by this data it is perhaps that
while the average attendant at a Moody meeting in Chicago
was more likely to be a middle-class churchgoer than not, the
congregations were of a miscellaneous nature and varied
greatly from meeting to meeting.

While a precise counting of the social characteristics
of Tabernacle audiences would provide interesting material
for the student of revivalism, it should be recognized that
in a very real sense, far more Chicagoans "heard" Moody, or
at least had ready opportunity to do so, than attended the
Tabernacle meetings. The leading city newspapers all carried
running accounts of Moody's words and activities from the
opening meeting in October to the farewell session in mid-
January. At the same time, Moody's workers were canvass-
ing the city in a house-to-house visitation program to distribute an abbreviated form of the Moody message. The popularity of the meetings and the fame of the revivalists made
them and their beliefs the focus of discussion for some curious
Chicagoans who perhaps never attended a Tabernacle meeting. In short, Moody's audience was not restricted to the
congregations gathered in the revival auditorium.

Certain Chicagoans did engage in positive and public
forms of response to the revival message. Most often these
took the form of conversion[16] or formal affiliation with a revival church--that is, a church which shared the attitudes,
values, and feelings expressed at the Tabernacle. It was
these latter persons who were, perhaps, influenced most
significantly by the Chicago revival. In some fashion, Moody's
words, Sankey's songs, and the activities and atmosphere of
the Tabernacle, in part or as a whole, took on a vivid rele-
vance for them and generated a personal reorientation. But
if this reorientation was personal, it was also social. For
"conversion," as defined within the revival, included the acceptance a particular world view and its accompanying moral

values. The further step of church membership occasioned
the public affiliation of the convert with a community which
shared those values and that world view. The act was a profound social statement.

        In mid-January 1877, a farewell meeting was held for
new converts. At the service the names and addresses of
these persons were recorded carefully by inquiry-room workers
for the purpose of follow-up by local ministers and church
workers. Moody was adamant in his concern that new believers
quickly be ushered into the fellowship of the local evangelical
churches.[17] More than six thousand tickets were issued for
the farewell service. This figure is the only available guide
to the actual number of conversions garnered at the Chicago
meetings. Several commentators did suggest, probably correctly, that the total number actually approximated eight
thousand, since not all converts could be present at any one
meeting.[18]

        Unfortunately, a diligent search has failed to uncover
any trace of the list of converts. Again, one is forced to
rely on the impressions of contemporary observers to ascertain who these people were. And, in this instance, the evidence is sketchy and inconclusive. At least one feature of
this group is, however, certain and noteworthy. Converts
present at the farewell service were asked to indicate their
church membership or, if none, their church preference.
Ninety percent of those present declared no church membership, and several of these, citing ignorance of such matters,
listed no religious preference at all. The obvious unchurched
character of the converts suggested in this report is significant.[19]

        The social composition of the converts is also impossible
to determine specifically but commentators did make frequent
mention of the large numbers of "inebriates" at the inquiry
rooms. The Chicago Weekly Journal estimated that "as many
as a thousand drinking men ... [had] been first 'converted,'
and thereby saved, from their enslavement to affliction and
vice." A careful reading of other press reports from the daily
meetings reveals further that the foreign-born, the unemployed,
the poor, and prostitutes were among the converted, though
in small numbers. It is possible that many of the converts
came from the ranks of unemployed workers and transients
in the city rather than from the working poor.[20] Transients

and the unemployed had time to attend the meetings (especially
Friday afternoon temperance meetings), whereas workingmen
probably did not. While it would be helpful to have more
exact information on which to base conclusions, the distinct
impression gained from contemporary literature is that conversion at the Tabernacle was not an exclusively middle-class
phenomenon and that most converts came from outside the
evangelical churches. [21]

    A second group of persons who responded in public
fashion to the revival effort was those who joined evangelical
churches engaged actively in the Moody meetings. Contemporary estimates of the total number of additions to these
churches during the months of Moody's presence in the city
varied, but a consensus figure is about twenty-five hundred
persons. [22] The Appendix reproduces a list of additions to
thirty-seven Chicago Protestant churches for the two months
preceding Moody's departure from the city in mid-January.
It is significant that almost three times as many new members
joined these churches by profession of faith than by transfer
of letter. These persons evidently were not newly arrived
Chicagoans who were simply transferring their membership
from one church to another. It is also noteworthy that twenty
of the churches listed had received more than fifty new members by mid-January. The unusual surge in membership was
not reserved to a few churches but was spread broadly among
churches supportive of the revivalist. [23]

    It is, of course, impossible to determine how many of
these new church members were converted at the Moody meetings. Ministers themselves recognized the difficulty, although
many attributed the large increase in membership in their
churches directly to the influence of the revival. [24] However,
since only one-tenth of the converts at the farewell meeting
in mid-January 1877 had as yet joined any church at all, it
seems obvious that the additions to the Chicago churches, at
least to that time, did not involve predominantly those persons who professed faith in the inquiry rooms of the Tabernacle. It is impossible to determine exactly how many Tabernacle converts did finally join churches. When local clergymen checked the addresses reported in cards filled out by
converts, they discovered a number to be fictitious or, reflecting the sense of humor of some converts, the sites of
breweries, saloons, or houses of ill-repute. Apparently,
not all of those who signed cards were sincere, and some upon

further reflection decided they wanted nothing more to do
with the matter.[25] The evidence at hand is inconclusive but
does raise questions about the effective transition of Tabernacle convert to church member.

Numerous churches in Chicago did, however, experience
large increases in membership, and these they attributed un-
hesitatingly to Moody and the revival meetings. In all like-
lihood, most of the new members had attended the Tabernacle
sessions and been directed to seek fellowship in revival
churches. In some cases, their words of testimony indicate
that they experienced conversion outside the Tabernacle--in
church services, Sunday school meetings, or in private counsel with a pastor or church worker.[26]

Revival churches were easily identified by any halfway
discerning Chicagoan. They were active and vocal in their
support of Moody and Sankey. They frequently held special
Bible studies and prayer sessions in conjunction with the revival meetings. Their ministers were conspicuous by their
regular presence at the Tabernacle and their vigorous support of the meetings. Their lay people filled the ranks of
ushers, choir members, inquiry-room workers, and other positions of responsibility in the services. And the wealthy
and prominent among them staffed the committees which
financed and managed the campaign. The endorsement by
such churches of the basic theology, values, and attitudes
expressed by Moody at the Tabernacle could not have escaped
the attention of many candidates for membership, which was
perceived as a logical extension of the revival experience.
Joining such a church, therefore, was a deliberate act to
affiliate oneself socially with the revival community and to
signal adoption of its values and attitudes. By their request
for membership, these persons sought entrance into a community which shared in many ways common moral, economic,
and even political points of view.

The remainder of this chapter is devoted to an examination of the social characteristics of persons who responded
to the revival excitement by voluntarily joining evangelical
churches in Chicago. To facilitate the inquiry, a microstudy
of five selected revival churches was undertaken. Such a
study, like the examination of contemporary observations, has
its limitations, since it is not inclusive of all Chicago evangelical churches. Yet it does shed further light upon the social

composition of a representative group of new church members
and, thereby, makes possible a level of understanding about
these persons which the history of revivalism has not often
achieved.

The five churches selected for examination in this chapter shared several characteristics. They were thoroughly
evangelical in theology; they supported Moody and Sankey
with enthusiasm and urged their members to involve themselves in the revival work; they garnered large numbers of
new members relative to the size of their respective congregations; and they attributed the increases to the revival.[27]
Two of the churches were Congregationalist, two were Presbyterian, and one was Methodist. The choices are appropriate
since these three denominations far outdistanced all others
in the numbers of new members added during the revival
months.[28] The churches were scattered across the city--
Fifth Presbyterian in the southern section, New England Congregational in the north, Centenary Methodist and Third
Presbyterian in the west-central, and Tabernacle Congregational lying northwest of the city's business hub. All of these
churches, except Tabernacle Congregational, were also situated in middle-class residential areas, although all were within easy walking distance of working-class and ethnic concentrations.[29] New England Congregational Church bordered
the largest German and Swedish communities in Chicago.
Fifth Presbyterian was bounded on the west by large concentrations of Irish, Swedish, and German people. Tabernacle
Congregational was located in a working-class area and bordered a large Swedish population. Centenary Methodist and
Third Presbyterian were also located near Scandinavian communities. The size of the churches ranged from the 304 members at Tabernacle Congregational to the 1,093 members of
the Third Presbyterian Church.[30]

Obviously, the composition of the surrounding community
affected directly the kinds of persons who might be expected
to join particular churches. It might be anticipated, then,
that the churches examined here would attract middle-class
Anglo-Americans. While this consideration is recognized, the
data remain useful. Since these churches were near ethnic
and working-class populations, and because evangelical leaders
in the city desired to evangelize and attract to membership
the unchurched working and ethnic people by means of the revival, the degree to which they were successful assumes

significance even if the actual numbers are small. Moveover,
it is my contention that the five churches analyzed here are
representative of the revival churches in the city which profited most, in terms of new members, from the Moody meetings. The Appendix reveals that twenty of Chicago's Protestant churches added at least fifty new members to their
church rolls in the final two months of the campaign. An
examination of the locations of those twenty churches shows
that none was located in a working-class area, only two were
situated in areas of high ethnic or racial concentration (both
in black neighborhoods), and three more bordered ethnic
areas.[31] In short, it was the evangelical churches located
in middle-class residential districts that reaped the largest
portion of the harvest of new members. The five churches
examined in this study were at least as accessible to working
people and the foreign-born as were most other identifiably
revival churches.

The perimeters of this study are drawn to include only
those new church members who were added by "profession
of faith" from November 1, 1876, to March 31, 1877.[32] The
115 persons who joined these churches by letter of transfer
are excluded since their affiliation to evangelicalism probably
was established quite apart from the revival experience.

The further delimitation of the study to new members
added in the five-month period following November 1, 1876,
is determined by several considerations. It is assumed that
the process of affiliation with a revival church required
several weeks at least. Evangelical churches usually conducted intensive examinations of persons interested in church
membership. Individuals had first to discuss their case with
the minister. A meeting before the church board or session
normally followed at a later date. Finally, those candidates
satisfying their examiners were received into membership,
usually on a Sunday morning during the worship hour.[33]
Because the meetings at the Tabernacle began on October 1,
it is reasonable to begin with an examination of members
joining in the subsequent month. Determining the terminus
ad quem was somewhat more difficult. I selected the date of
March 31, 1877, for two reasons. First, the revival meetings at the Tabernacle continued for some time after the revivalists had gone to Boston under the leadership of Moody's
associate, Daniel Whittle. While Whittle's successes did not
rival Moody's, according to press reports he did keep the

flickering flames of revival burning in Chicago.[34] Second,
an examination of the records of the churches reveals that
unusually large numbers of new members continued to join
the churches through the month of March, at which time there
followed a marked and constant diminution in the number of
new admissions. The final profits of the Moody meetings for
church membership were apparently being cashed in during
the last weeks of March.

From November 1, 1876, to March 31, 1877, 533 persons
joined by profession of faith the five churches selected for
study.[35] Social data for many of these individuals was collected from the Federal Census for 1880 and the city directories for 1876 and 1877.[36] Fifty-five percent of the new
membership was female. This figure suggests that although
the number of new women communicants outnumbered that of
men in every church examined, their presence was not so
large as to permit characterization of the Chicago revival as
a female phenomenon. Nor was a disproportionate number of
new members drawn from the ranks of adolescence. Nineteen
percent were under the age of 18 years, and the average age
of those joining the churches was a mature 28.8 years. These
figures do not, of course, indicate adequately the possible
inpact of the Moody meetings in precipitating youthful conversions. While there is no evidence that a large percentage
of the Tabernacle converts were adolescents, the local Sunday
schools did report sizable numbers of conversions at their
weekly sessions during the revival months.[37] For many
churches, the reception of young people to membership was
a protracted process, requiring not only profession of faith
but also completion of "cathechism" or "communicants" classes
and the attainment of an age considered appropriate for church
membership by the congregation's leaders. Hence, most new
members were adults. Their numbers were such as to ne-
gate any thesis that the Moody revival in Chicago served
primarily as a rite of passage for evangelical youth.[38]

Table 1 reveals that the overwhelming majority of the
new church members were of Anglo-American nativity, most
having been born in the United States, Great Britain, or
Canada. Significant, though perhaps not surprising, was
the small number of Irish, German, and Scandinavian-born
who sought formal fellowship in the churches. These three
ethnic groupings accounted for 28 percent of the city's population in 1880, just three years after the revival. Yet, they

comprised only 8.7 percent of the new church members in
the five churches.[39]

TABLE 1

Distribution of All New Admittants to
Selected Chicago Revival Churches from
November 1, 1876, to March 31, 1877, by
Place of Birth

	Abs. Freq.	Adj. Freq. (%)
Northeastern United States	98	31.7
Illinois	70	22.7
Other Midwestern States	45	14.6
Southern United States	11	3.4
England/Scotland	39	12.7
Canada	17	5.5
Ireland	16	5.2
Germany	5	1.6
Scandinavia	6	1.9
Other	1	0.3
All	308	100.0

Several observations help to explain the apparent lack
of interest on the part of these groups in the revival churches.
First, non-English-speaking Germans and Scandinavians would
have been unlikely candidates for membership in English-
speaking churches even had they been influenced seriously
by the revival meetings. At the same time, the Catholic
loyalties of many Irish and German immigrants would have
reduced their receptivity to the Tabernacle activities. Certainly, the style of revival religion was unfamiliar to these
persons. And although Catholic leaders in Chicago did not
condemn Moody and Sankey, there is no evidence of sympathy
with the revival effort.[40] Catholic leaders, moreover, were
doubtless aware that the conversions Moody aimed for would
entail for Catholics a conversion to evangelical Protestantism.

Only a careful statistical analysis of all the Chicago
churches and a precise understanding of the posture of these
churches toward the revival could tell with certainty what

impact Moody had upon the foreign-born and Roman Catholic
populations of Chicago. At least one piece of evidence indicates that there was some interest. The Reverend A. Miller,
a city missionary to the German population of Chicago, issued
regular reports of the revival's progress among those peoples.
In November 1876, Miller wrote,

> The Moody and Sankey meetings are still the absorb-
> ing topic of conversation. They continue to grow
> in interest and are the means of saving multitudes....
> It may be supposed that the foreign element is not
> reached by this English service, but I am glad to
> say that many have been attracted to it and have
> embraced the Gospel. Among the inquirers may be
> seen Roman Catholics and infidels. Some come to
> gratify their curiosity, but are convicted and sub-
> mit themselves to Christ.

Miller's January report noted that "union meetings continue
with unabated interest. The various churches are still receiving large accessions.... Not only the pastors, but also the
missionaries are reaping a rich harvest." The missionary's
last report about the impact of the revival on the German
churches was scarcely less enthusiastic than his earlier comments. "Scores are coming into the various churches," he
wrote, "and a deep religious feeling pervades the entire community."[41] Moody and Sankey conducted special German
meetings in the first six weeks of services.[42] After a November 13 meeting attended by fifteen hundred German-speak-
ing Chicagoans, however, the effort apparently was discon-
tinued--at least no similar service was reported again. Perhaps the language problem caused interested German ministers to localize their revival efforts in the ethnic churches
and, thereby, away from the Tabernacle setting.

The evidence is too meager to justify more than qualified
observations about the revival's impact upon the foreign-born
population of Chicago. While Miller's report indicates some
interest among Germans, there appear no grounds for sug-
gesting that revival excitement was widespread among Chicago's foreign-born or that the city's ethnic churches benefited significantly because of the revival. Reports in newspapers and magazines rarely mentioned conversions of Catholics or foreign-born persons. Those foreign language newspapers published in Chicago which were examined for this

study also had little to say about the Moody and Sankey
services. Their absence of comment perhaps suggests that
the meetings had little interest for the majority of their
readers.[43]

Records of Chicago's ethnic churches admittedly are
scarce, but those extant suggest that the revival did little
to increase membership among the foreigh-born congregations.
Chicago's four largest German Methodist Episcopal churches
gained only thirty-nine members cumulatively in 1876. The
following year, aggregate membership for the four churches
actually decreased by six persons.[44] The Swedish Methodist
Episcopal churches of Chicago reported no unusually large
numbers of either probationers or new members.[45] Evidence
of a similar nature is offered by examining again the list of
thirty-seven churches which the Times described in mid-
January as "directly interested" in the Moody and Sankey
meetings (see Appendix). Of these churches only three were
ethnic congregations. The Holland Presbyterian Church added
twenty-four members, the Zion German Methodist Episcopal
Church received eighteen additions, and the black Olivet
Baptist Church added one new communicant. In short, Chicago's ethnic population appears to have been little inclined
to take any overt step of evangelical affiliation because of
the Moody services.

The new church members examined in this microstudy,
then, were overwhelmingly Anglo-American, almost as likely
to be male as female, and most often young adults in their
twenties or thirties.[46] Only one person was black and every
individual reported in the census was able both to read and
write.[47] Eighty-eight percent of the communicants resided
with at least one other family member in a city which received
daily large numbers of single adventurers and transient
workers. Only 58.2 percent of those over the age of eighteen were married, but 53 percent of the adults who remained
single continued to maintain residence with their immediate
families. While the data in this instance are merely suggestive, the marked tendency on the part of these new church
members to locate themselves at home or with members of
their immediate families is perhaps reflective of the importance
they attached to family. If other factors, such as literacy
rates and occupational status, identify these individuals with
Chicago's middling classes,[48] then their location in family set-
tings may shed light on their warm reception to revival rhetoric.

Moody glorified home and hearth in his sermons, reflecting
the prevailing middle-class elevation of domesticity.[49] The
home, as shall be observed in a later chapter, he depicted
as a locus of salvation, and the family (especially mothers)
as a redemptive influence. Such preaching was perhaps
more attuned to the sensibilities of persons living at home
(even as single adults) than to boarders.

In certain instances, church membership itself was a
family act. A counting of the new church members in this
study revealed that 24 percent joined one of the five selected
churches simultaneously with a spouse or other family member.[50] In yet other cases, new members affiliated with
churches in which another relative was already an active
church member. A prominent example was E. W. Blatchford,
a wealthy manufacturer and leading figure in the revival
work. Blatchford received the rewards of his labors for
Moody when in the course of the revival three of his children,
aged fifteen to twenty-one, professed faith publicly and were
received into the membership of the New England Congregational Church.[51] The case was the exception not the rule,
yet family connections among those who joined the churches
were not unusual.[52]

The most accurate gauge of the social standings of those
persons who affiliated with the selected revival churches is
provided by an examination of occupations.[53] Sixty-eight
percent of the individuals included in this study were identified by occupation in the city directories for 1876 and 1877
or in the 1880 federal census.[54] The new church communicants represented seventy different stated occupations.

Table 2 indicates the large number of clerks and bookkeepers who affiliated with these churches and, in marked
contrast, the relatively few laborers who became members.[55]
Clerks and bookkeepers occupied the lower end of the white-
collar labor force in nineteenth-century cities.[56] Some of
these folk were unemployed because of the depression; a
large portion of the employed probably had suffered decreases
in wages.[57] Clerks and bookkeepers were not commonly union-
ized in the nineteenth century and were unlikely candidates
for labor violence. Instead, they were more often individuals
still confident that their present situations would be better
in the future. In this study, they were most often young
men near the bottom of the commercial ladder but probably

men with high hopes. They were, perhaps, not unlike the
young Moody, who had himself clerked in a Chicago shoe
store, carefully saving his earnings and intending to accumulate a good living. These young men had a stake in the continuance of the economic status quo. They held jobs. They
shared the middle-class faith in the free enterprise system.
They admired the Marshall Fields, Cyrus McCormicks, and
Philip Armours rather than resenting the successes achieved
by such men. They believed that hard work would, in time,
bring to them personal social and economic success.58

TABLE 2

Occupations of New Male Admittants to Selected
Chicago Revival Churches from November 1, 1876,
to March 31, 1877

	Abs. Freq.	Adj. Freq. (%)
Clerk	47	24.5
Bookkeeper	17	8.9
Salesman	10	5.2
Nonworking Child	10	5.2
Merchant	9	4.7
Printer	8	4.2
Carpenter	6	3.1
Machinist	5	2.6
Lawyer/Doctor	5	2.6
Laborer	5	2.6
All	192	100.0

The large number of clerks and bookkeepers exemplifies
the middling-class character of most persons attracted to membership in the five selected churches. This characterization
is evidenced further by examining the occupational status of
"heads of households" of the new church members. "Heads
of households" offers the best indicator of the kinds of families from which the revival churches drew their new church
members. Table 3 shows again the predominantly middling-
class character of these families. Fewer than 12 percent had
lower-class origins.59

TABLE 3

Occupational Status Ranking of "Heads of
Households" of All New Admittants to Selected
Chicago Revival Churches from November 1,
1876, to March 31, 1877

	Abs. Freq.	Adj. Freq. (%)
High White Collar	57	16.0
Low White Collar	158	44.3
Skilled Artisans	101	28.3
Unskilled Laborers (specified occupations)	23	6.4
Unskilled Laborers (unspecified occupations)	18	5.0
All	357	100.0

Status rankings are based upon Theodore Hershberg et al.,
"Occupation and Ethnicity in Five Nineteenth-Century Cities:
A Collaborative Inquiry," Historical Methods Newsletter (June
1974):   174-216.

Clearly, then, the five selected revival churches examined here garnered their new members primarily from the
middling classes of the city and from those Chicagoans of
Anglo-American parentage.   Nonworking children under the
age of eighteen who joined the churches came much more frequently from upper-class families than did the average new
communicant (see Table 4).   By far the most commonly listed
occupation of the heads of these households was "merchant,"
followed by "manufacturer" and "lawyer."   It is almost certain that nonworking children in their early teens would have
joined churches in which their parents were already members.
If true, this bit of evidence suggests again the solidly middle-
and upper-class character of the membership of the revival
churches.   The new members who were added to their rolls
as a result of the Moody meetings, then, were not unlike the
old or, perhaps, were aspiring to similar social and economic
positions.

TABLE 4

Occupational Status Ranking of "Heads of
Households" for Single Young Persons of Ages
Nine to Eighteen

	Abs. Freq.	Adj. Freq. (%)
High White Collar	20	32.8
Low White Collar	26	42.6
Skilled Artisans	13	21.3
Unskilled Laborers (specified occupations)	2	3.3
Unskilled Laborers (unspecified occupations)	0	0.0
All	61	100.0

Status rankings are from Hershberg et al., "Five Cities Study."

This, then, is the composite social portrait of these
persons who voluntarily affiliated themselves with churches
supportive of the revival effort and the Moody Gospel. They
were most often young adults, almost equally male and female, equally married and single, and usually from the families
of skilled artisans or white-collar workers. The great majority were native-born Americans--most of these born in
either Illinois or in the Northeastern states. The greatest
percentage of the foreign-born originated in Great Britain or
Canada and were, on the average, eight years older than
the typical native-born new church member. The group as a
whole (but of particular interest, the single adults) tended
to live with their families at home. Nine of every ten lived
with other family members. Most of the adult women were married or widowed and listed as their vocation "housewife" (see
Table 5). The few women who labored outside their homes
held jobs in fields traditionally acceptable, for women in the
nineteenth century, such as teacher, seamstress, or servant.
But these women were in the minority and most who worked
outside the home still resided with their immediate families.

TABLE 5

Occupations of New Female Admittants to Selected
Chicago Revival Churches from November 1, 1876,
to March 31, 1877

	Abs. Freq.	Adj. Freq. (%)
Housewife	93	50.8
Nonworking Child	46	25.1
Seamstress	8	4.4
Teacher	8	4.4
Servant	5	2.7
Other	23	12.6
All	183	100.0

TABLE 6

Family Status of All New Admittants to Chicago
Revival Churches from November 1, 1876, to
March 31, 1877

	Abs. Freq.	Adj. Freq. (%)
Head of Household	97	27.5
Children	109	30.9
Wife of Head of Household	94	26.6
Relative or In-Law of Head	7	2.0
Servant	6	1.7
Boarder at Hotel or Rooming House	28	7.9
Boarder with Nonrelated Family	12	3.4
All	353	100.0

The new members were drawn almost equally from the several segments of the family structure. Table 6 shows that husbands who headed the family were as likely to join the churches as were their wives or children. A shared characteristic of the communicants was location within a family setting. The new church members were drawn most often from the middling classes. They were likely to be "respectable," neither exorbitantly rich nor poverty-stricken, espousing middle-class values, and attached to family and home.

The results of a microstudy of this kind are, of course, fragmentary and only suggestive. Yet this examination of five revival churches does suggest strongly that Moody and Sankey did not succeed in bringing the masses into the fold of evangelicalism in large numbers. There is no evidence here that the religious excitement generated at the Tabernacle resulted in large increases in the membership of ethnic evangelical churches, nor did it apparently transcend the class and ethnic bias of the several mainline evangelical congregations examined intensively. Chicago's Methodist, Presbyterian, Congregational, and Baptist churches tended to be composed of middle-class Anglo-Americans in 1876, and the revival did not alter significantly those characteristics.[60] This is not to say that Chicago's unchurched foreign-born and poor were untouched by the Moody meetings.[61] Some certainly were touched, whether by direct visitation, media reports, or attendance at the Tabernacle. But the revivalist's desire to usher large numbers of these folk into the nurture and care of the city's evangelical churches was not achieved.[62]

The reasons for the relative absence of the poor and non-Anglo-Americans among the new church members are apparent. Simply put, these individuals would have felt out of place in most of Chicago's evangelical churches. By the 1870s in Chicago, class and ethnic lines had come to be more and more distinct. Rather than transcending this increasing fragmentation of the population, the evangelical churches often reflected it. Well-to-do evangelical Protestants flocked in large numbers to the Reformed Episcopal, Congregational, and Presbyterian churches, often located on the fashionable avenues of the city. While Methodist and Baptist churches had historical roots in the lower classes, their urban congregations were composed predominantly of middle-class Chicagoans. A study of fourteen Methodist churches in Chicago in 1870 shows that only three were located in working-class

districts, and the combined membership of these congregations was a meager 11 percent of the total Methodist enroll-
ment in the city.[63] The Baptists were represented by eleven
churches, of which one was black, three were German or
Scandinavian, and one a mission church to the poor.[64] While
all the evangelical denominations reported significant growth
in the early 1870s, their gains lagged consistently in proportion to Chicago's population increases.[65]

Location of the churches, pew rents, language, the
dissimilarity of other members, and the unfamiliar styles of
worship associated with evangelicalism probably disinclined
most of the unchurched foreign-born and poor from membership in the city's revival churches. Perhaps equally important, however, were the attitudes and values they associated
with these churches. When workingmen joined in strikes to
gain what they understood to be their fair share, they sensed
only token sympathy from the evangelical churches of the
city. Moreover, they sometimes found the evangelical clergy
voicing opinions similar to those held by the men who employed and underpaid them--that wage reductions stemmed
not from the greed of employers but came as a result of
economic laws "as inexorable as the laws of gravitation." In
a statement of mainline Protestant doctrine, S. J. McPherson
of the Second Presbyterian Church of Chicago declared that
labor was merely a commodity and, therefore, any attempt to
evade the laws which controlled it, particularly through collective action, connoted "abysmal ignorance."[66] Confidence
in the Protestant ethic continued to influence much of the
social and economic thinking of Protestants in the 1870s. The
Congregationalist voiced the familiar line of reasoning when
it declared confidently, "In this country, every industrious,
prudent, skillful, healthful laborer can acquire a handsome
competence by the time he is fifty years old, if that is what
he desires."[67] Chicago's working poor were left to ponder
the causes of their continued struggle with poverty.

Cultural attitudes regarding Sabbath observance and
alcohol also separated evangelicals from many of the foreign-
born and the poor. A. C. Hesing, the outspoken editor of
a leading Chicago German-language newspaper, voiced the
antagonism some foreign-born workers doubtless felt about
middle-class evangelical moralizing.

They give you no cheap concerts and lectures to

educate you. They will not even let you go to the
Exposition on the day when you can dress up and
appear like them, but they go whenever they please
and make you and their clerks do their work. They
go there and look at the machinery and furniture
and fabrics you have made at wages of a dollar and
a half a day. I ask Dr. Kittridge and Dr. Fowler
[both active in the revival], who preach morality
and try to crowd their words down your throats,
to lay their hands on their hearts and answer if it
is right for them to rob the poor of their privileges.
I ask them what harm there is, after you have been
working hard in a dirty, dusty shop all week, for
you to go to Lincoln Park on Sunday with your
wives and babies to breathe a little fresh air the
Lord they pray to made? I ask them what harm it
would be for you to hear a little music there as
they hear it in their churches? I ask them what
harm there is if, when you return, you take a glass
of lager or wine to refresh you? You are a pack of
slaves if you suffer laws that prohibit this.68

Not surprisingly, then, the largest portion of immigrant
workingmen and their families who sought church fellowship
found it in the burgeoning Roman Catholic and Lutheran congregations of Chicago.69 For many the action reflected church
loyalties established in the old country. But others probably
felt more warmly received and better understood in the Roman
Catholic and Lutheran congregations. They predominated in
numbers in these churches and were able to worship on a
common social plane. Significantly, the leadership of the
Catholic churches especially approached the problems of the
workers with greater sympathy and more tolerance than did
most Protestant clergymen. Certainly, the Catholic church
was also more understanding and accepting of ethnic and cultural traditions and mores, and the forms of worship there
were more familiar to the immigrant. Still, the majority of
Chicago's poor and foreign-born were not Roman Catholics
but were unchurched. It was perhaps not so much a distaste
for the revival style of religion or the competition of Catholicism which disinclined these persons from the evangelical
churches as it was those churches' obvious lack of understanding and sympathy for the plight of the poor.70

Even the best efforts of Moody and Sankey failed to win

many of the foreign-born and poor to evangelicalism. What this chapter has demonstrated is that the new membership of the revival churches was very much like the old. Indeed, Moody and Sankey probably served as catalysts who enlivened and reinforced the existing middle-class orientation of these revival congregations. Certainly, the cultural heritage of middle-class, Anglo-American listeners better prepared them to respond sympathetically to the images and feelings evoked by worship at a Moody and Sankey meeting. Furthermore, as will be shown in the following chapters, the terms of salvation offered at the Tabernacle were set squarely in the context of middle-class social values and expectations. It is inadequate, however, to explain Moody's revival successes in Chicago primarily in terms of middle-class nostalgia. The revivalist's words offered listeners more than an attractive "backward glance" at a simpler America. They also provided receptive Chicagoans with specific and satisfying explanations of the social turmoil in the city and strategies for corrective action. Moody's sermons thus provide a crucial source of insight into the nature of the revival's social appeal. His words help to explain further the large ingathering to the revival churches of young, middle-class Anglo-Americans and, in contrast, the disinterest of the poor and foreign-born in these communities of fellowship.

Chapter VII

THE RHETORIC OF REVIVAL: THE
GOSPEL, EVANGELICAL AND SOCIAL

Several students of revivalism have attributed Moody's evangelistic successes primarily to his innovative revival techniques and the sentimental appeal of his sermonizing.[1] In
their preoccupation with what Moody did and how he preached,
these scholars seldom have taken seriously what he said. The
nature of Moody's sermons perhaps explains this gap in
scholarship. As one of his hearers claimed, they were "extremely diffuse ... unconnected, rambling and given to re-
petition."[2] In this chapter it will be shown, however, that
the doctrinal and social content of the Chicago sermons was
important in attracting certain kinds of urban dwellers toward evangelicalism while perhaps alienating others in the
city. Further it will be demonstrated that Moody's preaching
functioned to ease in several ways specific sources of social
distress experienced by native-born Chicagoans of the middling classes--that group which was most supportive of the revival and from whose ranks came the bulk of the new church
members.[3]

In preface to this examination of Moody's preaching,
several comments are in order. First, Moody's sermons were
pragmatic discourses designed primarily to effect conversions.
Nearly all were lacking woefully in careful exegesis and were
often theologically inconsistent. In part, this was probably
the result of Moody's total lack of formal theological training.
Unlike most seminary students, Moody was never taught a
theological "system." Instead, he accumulated an understanding of Christian doctrine through years of question-and-
answer sessions with other Christians, intense personal Bible
study, and common sense. Furthermore, Moody was always
less concerned with the logic of his sermons than with their

110

Biblical integrity and commonsense application. In an exposition, "How to Study the Bible," Moody declared that "truth"
is best found in an "unbiased" study of Scripture. "A great
many people believe certain things," he observed.

> They believe in certain creeds and doctrines, and
> they run through the book to get Scripture in ac-
> cordance with them.... But if we go to seek truth
> the Spirit of God will come. Don't seek it in the
> blue light of Presbyterianism, in the red light of
> Methodism, or in the light of Episcopalianism, but
> study it in the light of Calvary.[4]

The sufficient and essential Gospel truth was to be found in
the Bible. No other external source of instruction was necessary.

The pragmatic intent of Moody's sermonizing did much
to shape the simple Gospel he preached. He summarized this
Gospel in a sermon at the Tabernacle as "the ruin of man by
nature, redemption by the blood, and regeneration by the
Holy Spirit."[5] W. H. Daniels, discussing Moody's theology
in his 1877 narrative of the Moody revivals, cited the three
phrases and observed that "outside of them, in the region
of speculative, historic, or inferential theology, [Moody]
does not go; not even into the realm of the Church or its
institutions, orders and sacraments." This core of doctrines,
it should be recognized, was amenable to every stripe of
evangelicalism and, probably, to many outside the evangelical
fold. More important to Moody, these truths formed the
heart of the salvation story. Daniels quoted Moody as saying, "I have in all about seven hundred sermons, but there
are only about three hundred of them that are fit to convert
sinners with." By this rule of fitness, said Daniels, Moody
"tests the ideas which present themselves to his mind. If
there be salvation in them he adopts and uses them; if not,
he casts them aside."[6]

A further important characteristic of the sermons is
the constant emphasis placed upon the love of God and the
person of Jesus Christ.[7] Here again, Moody's choice of subjects was a pragmatic one. Proclaiming God's love of sinners,
Moody reasoned correctly, was a more effective means of making converts in 1876 than was, for instance, preaching about
the terrors of hell. "If I wanted to scare men into heaven

I would just hold the terror of hell over their heads and say,
'go right in.' But that's not the way to win men.... Terror
never brought a man in yet," said Moody. And, in a subsequent sermon, he observed, "Mark you, my friends, I believe
in eternal damnation; I believe in the pit that burns, in the
fire that's never quenched, in the worm that never dies, but
I believe that the magnet that goes down to the bottom of the
pit is the love of Jesus."[8]

Similarly, the emphasis upon Jesus in Moody's preaching reflected the importance contemporary evangelicalism placed
generally upon a personal religious or conversion experience
in which the figure of the Redeemer was central. Ministers
of an evangelical persuasion often stressed the need to "preach
Christ first," for it was through Christ that individuals were
brought to know God and transformed into persons of faith.[9]
But Christ was more than a Savior; he was a Friend. The
dealing of God with men, argued a contemporary of Moody,

> compels them to turn ... to the man Christ Jesus,
> for sympathy; to the Saviour, Christ Jesus, for
> atonement and pardon; to the Intercessor, Christ
> Jesus, for an answer to prayer; and to the glorified
> Christ for a heavenly inheritance.[10]

Increasingly, the person of Jesus dominated virtually every
aspect of spiritual life for evangelicals.[11] Moody shared this
supposition and gave frequent expression to it in his sermons.[12]

Analyses of Moody's theology are readily available. It
is sufficient here to note that the revivalist stood in the
mainstream of nineteenth-century evangelical thought. Moody
preached an old-time Gospel, both familiar and appealing to
many Protestant, middle-class listeners.[13] There were differences between Moody's thought and that of earlier evangelical spokesman, to be sure. Most significantly, Moody's premillennialism with its inherent pessimism toward broad social
reform was largely new to nineteenth-century evangelicals.[14]
But Moody minimized this potentially divisive doctrine in his
Chicago sermons and in his emphasis upon the mercy of God
and the love of Christ, the redemptive quality of Jesus'
death, the absolute necessity of a conversion experience, and
the essential ability of men and women to respond to the offer
of salvation by a conscious decision of faith the revivalist was
in tune with the thinking and the theology of most of his

evangelical contemporaries. Furthermore, Moody's expectation that personal moral reform should follow upon conversion coincided with contemporary Protestant convictions.

It is appropriate to wonder what ingredients in this
old-time Gospel particularly appealed to the many middle-class
Anglo-Americans who responded positively to the 1876 revival.
First, these persons were most likely attracted by Moody's
emphasis on the freedom of individuals to choose or reject
salvation.   There existed in Moody's preaching an inherent
democratic impulse. When preaching to a congregation at the
Tabernacle, Moody declared, "They don't have any slaves in
heaven. They are all sons, and they must accept salvation
voluntarily." In a later sermon about the conversion of Naa-
man, the evangelist observed that "many people expect to get
salvation by some sudden shock, some great event happening
to them, or some sudden flash of light to break upon them."
But, he continued, "the battle is fought on this fact, if you
will--not because you can't." Essentially, salvation was for
Moody an act of the individual's will. In reply to a statement
that sin is what stands between man and Christ, Moody replied, "It isn't, it's your own will! That's what stands between the sinner and forgiveness."[15] Moody had no doubt
but that every person had sufficient ability to make a choice
about salvation. The question was what that choice would
be.[16]

Moody's preaching, then, was in tune with the Arminian
tendencies in nineteenth-century evangelical thought.[17] It
was also in harmony with the democratic, self-determinative
impulses in middle-class thinking. God through Christ, taught
Moody, and brought circumstances to the place where an individual determined his or her own destiny. Moody rejected
outright the fatalism which some attached to the doctrine of
election. "How many men fold their arms and say, 'If I am
one of the elect I will be saved, and if I ain't I won't. No
use of your bothering about it.' " Salvation, Moody contra-
dicted, was no more predetermined than was success in business. "Why don't some of those merchants say, 'If God is
going to make me a successful merchant in Chicago I will be
one whether I like it or not, and if he hasn't I won't."[18]
In either case a man was finally responsible for his future
well-being. His destiny was self-made. Both notions made
sense to the many Anglo-American, middle-class persons who
joined revival churches in Chicago or supported the revivalist's

efforts there. These folk had been reared to believe that
hard work, frugality, and honesty were prerequisites for
economic and social success. It was entirely logical, therefore, that a man by his actions and response to God should
determine his own eternal destiny.

Perhaps even more appealing to such persons were the
expected results of conversion implied in Moody's preaching.
New believers, Moody made obvious, were not only converted
"to" Jesus Christ but were also converted "from" the world.
In Moody's understanding of salvation, acceptance of God's
grace in Christ was always and necessarily paralleled by repentance from sin. Moody defined repentance in one Chicago
sermon as "a turning right about and forsaking sin." Repentance involved a change in actions and living resulting
from an inner change of heart. The regenerate man, said
Moody, "loves his enemies and tries to repair all wrong he
has done.... If this sign is not apparent his conversion has
never got from his head to his heart." And again, "If a man
don't turn from his sin he won't be accepted of God, and if
righteousness don't produce a turning about--a turning from
bad to good--it isn't true righteousness."[19] In short, the
convert was literally a new creation of God in Jesus Christ.
His attitudes were altered by the experience. His living and
activities would subsequently reflect the righteousness of
God himself.

Moody never stated explicitly all that might be involved
in "turning from bad to good." But the evangelist's remarks
left little doubt but that authentic Christian living involved
the rejection of or abstinence from certain practices frowned
upon by many contemporary evangelicals. Swearing, lying,
dancing, card playing, gambling, business speculation, laziness, drinking, and Sabbath breaking Moody condemned from
the Tabernacle pulpit.[20] By and large, Moody urged believers
to adopt an evangelical and middle-class ethic. Disciplined
outward behavior was the necessary evidence of inward regeneration.

The "sins" Moody condemned most frequently in his
Chicago sermons were Sabbath breaking and drinking. Both
practices worried many evangelicals. From the days of Puritan New England, evangelical Protestants had been devoted
to Sabbath observance. Moody, like many other native-born,
middle-class Protestants, had been reared in this Sabbatarian
heritage. Not surprisingly, he found the laxity of Sunday

observance in Chicago particularly distressing. In letters written to his family during his first years in the city, Moody complained about the "wickedness" of a city where the Germans spent the Sabbath frolicking in beer gardens and the stores were open for business.[21]

Moody's preaching about Sabbath breaking affirmed traditional evangelical conceptions. He had no time for Sunday "amusements," deplored the reading of newspapers on the Sabbath, and condemned persons who patronized the rail and horsecar companies on Sundays. In one sermon in Chicago he stated bluntly that "no man can work seven days a week and save his soul."[22] He thus condemned outright scores of Chicago's common laborers and factory employees. Moody also held the belief that persistent Sabbath breaking would cost a city or a nation its prosperity and peace. In a prayer-meeting talk, he implied that the fire of 1871 and the panic of 1873 were God's judgments upon Chicago for its lax observance of the Sabbath. "Ten years ago you had your theatres shut on Sundays. There was a law against this thing then. Ten years ago the people used to go to Church, but now they have their Sunday newspapers and their printed sermons and keep out of Church." Ten years ago "we had great advantages." But, "you know how after that, people--Sunday school teachers and all--got a few straws and dollars together, and then they became careless, went out riding on Sunday, and enjoyed the world after their fashion, and forgot God." It was no coincidence, he concluded, that a few years later came the fire and then the depression.[23] Similar judgment faced the nation that turned from God by desecrating the Sabbath. "If this country falls into neglect of the observance of the Sabbath, it will go the way of France, Mexico, and Spain. Every nation that gives up the Sabbath must go down."[24]

Moody's statements clearly condemned those Chicagoans who failed "to keep the Sabbath holy" and implied further that such behavior was not only immoral and un-Christian but also un-American and unpatriotic. It is not difficult to ascertain the appeal of such pronouncements to native-born Chicagoans of the middling classes. Moody's comments could easily be construed as an indictment of immigrant behavior in the city. Although Moody carefully avoided any such outright criticism of ethnic groups per se, some evangelicals in Chicago already had connected Sabbath breaking with the foreign-born. The revivalist's strident castigation of Sabbath

breakers, therefore, may have sanctioned existing fears about
the danger of the foreign-born population and thereby reinforced nativistic attitudes.

But Sabbatarianism not only functioned as a release
for ethnic hostilities. It also was thought to be integral to
the maintenance of a rightly ordered society. The Interior
in 1872 observed that "to break down the idea of a Sabbath
in a community, is to remove a chief support of thrift, social
order, and religion, and to invoke instability, dissoluteness
and crime."[25] It was shown earlier that many Chicagoans in
the 1870s were concerned intensely about social disorder.
Unemployment, labor violence, poverty, political corruption,
and personal immorality gave evangelical observers abundant
evidence of increasing social chaos. They deemed immigrants
and Catholics especially disruptive of the traditional order,
but life in the city generally seemed out of control. The
need of the day, they reasoned, was for a revival of discipline. Sabbatarianism provided a way of inculcating such behavior. As a writer for the Advance told Chicago readers,
Sabbath observance "tended to form the valuable habit of
self-control."[26] Moody's own Sabbath practices, related in
Tabernacle sermons, provided appropriate models of disciplined behavior. In one sermon he related how on one Sunday
he had walked sixteen miles rather than ride in a horse car in
order not "to break the Sabbath of any man." He further criti-
cized those who even owned stock in companies which conducted
business on the Sabbath. Strict self-discipline, even self-
negation, characterized the revivalist's Sabbath ethic.[27]

Disciplined behavior further was integral to the Protestant work ethic. Disciplined persons were frugal, hard working, and industrious. They caused few social problems and
lived circumspectly. Such persons were suited admirably to
the industrial, capitalistic economy of 1876 Chicago. Sabbatarianism, as Christopher Hill has argued, rationalized "a
regular day of rest and meditation suited to the regular and
continuous rhythm of modern industrial society."[28] Obviously,
Chicago businessmen who supported Moody were cognizant of
the economic benefits of the Sabbath doctrine. Disciplined
workers following planned work schedules promised optimum
efficiency and production. As the Interior noted, "One day
of physical rest in seven is surely needful, if ever, in these
days of hot haste to obtain the largest possible amount of
material good."[29] The Reverend C. L. Thompson best summed

up the social benefits of Sabbath observance from an evangelical perspective in a sermon preached in Chicago in 1872.   The
pastor of the Fifth Presbyterian Church emphasized first the
economic advantages for both workers and employer.   Regular
periods of rest are necessary, said Thompson, "or the physical
machinery would ... soon wear out."   But the Sabbath, he
continued, must of necessity be "properly kept."   It should
be a day for "religious instruction" and "sober reflection,"
not for "revelry," said Thompson.   For the Sabbath rightly
observed promoted personal discipline and moral behavior.
The worker who so disciplined himself by strict adherence to
the Sabbath proscriptions, Thompson concluded, would "stand
straighter, look steadier, work harder and live longer."[30]

   Moody's Sabbath preaching, then, reaffirmed existing
Sabbatarian attitudes among Chicago's Protestants.   It further
promoted the Protestant ethic and provided a means to extend
control over personal behavior in the city.   The regular
periods of work and rest it encouraged also fitted well the
laissez faire urban economy.   Not surprisingly, aspiring clerks
and bookkeepers and the city's prominent business leaders
found the Sabbath ethic attractive.

   Regenerate living also meant for Moody abstinence from
alcohol.   Moody attacked liquor and the liquor industry repeatedly from the Tabernacle pulpit.   "These grog shops here
are the works of the devil--they are ruining men's souls
every hour," he declared in his second sermon in Chicago.
"Let us fight against them, and let our prayers go up in our
battle....   It may seem a very difficult thing for us, but it
is a very easy thing for God to convert rumsellers."   He
urged Christian men especially to enter into a "hand-to-hand
conflict with the billiard saloons and drinking halls."   The
revivalist's condemnation of alcohol and the liquor trade could
hardly have been more fervent.   He warned his Chicago listeners in no uncertain terms:

>   Woe be to the man that put the bottle to his neigh-
>   bor's lips.   My friends, I would rather have that
>   right hand cut off before I would give the bottle
>   to a man.   I would rather have my right arm cut off
>   than deal out death and damnation to my fellow-men....
>   No drunkard shall inherit the kingdom of heaven.[31]

   Moody's sermons also made clear his opinion that religious conversion was the sole effective remedy for the

drunkard. Indeed, regeneration meant, in part, that the evil
influence of the bottle had been conquered by the omnipotent
influence of the Spirit in the life of a believer. Moody himself was openly pessimistic about the prospects of rehabilitat-
ing the alcoholic without first converting him. In a "Temperance Talk," Moody remarked, "Now as I understand it,
there is no hope for any drunkard till he has been born of
God. A resolution can't save him. Signing the pledge can't
save him." Only Christ "can give you the power to resist
the cup of temptation."[32] The logic of Moody's thinking regarding the reformation of drunkards explains in part his
pessimism about broad social reform apart from the simultaneous conversion of large numbers of individuals. If alcoholism
was a root cause of many social ills and regeneration was the
only true cure for alcoholism, then regeneration must necessarily be the only viable means of effective social reform.[33]

It is not difficult to understand the popularity with
the middling classes of Moody's statements about drink. First,
his preaching made clear that alcohol threatened the well-
being of family life. Chapter Five showed that the new members of the revival churches generally lived with other family
members. Furthermore, their class and cultural backgrounds
predisposed them toward middle-class sentiments elevating
family life. Family relationships probably were important to
such persons. It is significant, then, that Moody emphasized
the malevolent effects of alcohol on family life.

Moody treated liquor as an evil influence which seemingly overpowered a man, broke him down, and destroyed
his family relationships. This scenario was typical:

> Why, there was a man whom I knew who was an in-
> veterate drinker. He had a wife and children. He
> thought he could stop whenever he felt inclined,
> but he went the ways of most moderate drinkers.
> I had not been gone more than three years and,
> when I returned I found that that mother had gone
> down to her grave with a broken heart, and that
> man was the murderer of the wife of his bosom.
> Those children have all been taken away from him
> and he is now walking up and down those streets
> homeless.[34]

A similar experience befell a young New Yorker who, Moody
related, "learned the habit of drinking" as a boy until liquor

became to him "like water." He soon was drawn into gambling, lost all of his money, stole from his employer to repay
his debts, and was forced to flee as a fugitive from justice.
His marriage fell into shambles and his children had no idea
of the whereabouts of their father.[35] In both stories the
bottle not only debilitated the individual drinker morally and
spiritually but also destroyed the family. Such tales were
effective particularly with those listeners whose cultural heritage elevated the home and family.

Drink also interfered with the orderly work patterns
important to aspiring middle-class urbanites. Native-born,
middle-class Chicagoans anticipated and idealized upward
social and economic mobility.[36] Drink inhibited mobility by
diminishing self-discipline and industriousness in workers.
Drink "universally encourages idleness," argued a contributor
to the Advance. The Presbyterian Interior listed as the ill
fruits of the drink habit, it "beggars mothers and children,
multiplies and peoples jails ... [and] destroys the products
of industry."[37] Similarly, in Moody's sermons drinkers
abandoned their families, became lazy, lost their jobs, and
sometimes turned to thievery to further indulge their drink
habit.[38] Embracing religion, however, meant the convert
was now subject to the strict moral codes of evangelical Protestantism. Indulgence and idleness were among the major
vices which the religious man swore to avoid. In this sense,
as Joseph Gusfield has argued, temperance marked "the man
bent on improving his conditions of income and his status in
the community."[39] One way of preventing such social problems
as urban unemployment and poverty was, evangelicals believed,
to inculcate middle-class habits of industry throughout society. Chief among these habits was the discipline of so-
briety.[40]

Temperance and Sabbatarianism thus functioned in similar
fashion. Both were concerned with extending disciplined, industrious behavior throughout society. Both focused on con-
crete evils which could be attacked and hopefully conquered.
And both could be associated readily with the foreign-born
population. In the context of this conflict of cultures, temperance and Sabbatarianism provided ways to release tensions
in the native-born, middling-class population and simultaneously
to exert control and discipline over those segments of the
city's population whose behavior was deemed dangerous to the
general social welfare.

In his study of the temperance movement in America,
Gusfield has argued that temperance and Sabbatarianism were
means by which native-born, middle-class Americans attempted
"to preserve, defend, [and] enhance the dominance and prestige of [their] own style of living within the total society."
By the end of the nineteenth century, he argues, the conflict of cultures which had produced the temperance issue
had come to characterize the opponents.

> Dry men were native Americans; they were Protes-
> tants who took their religion with seriousness; they
> were the farmers, the small-town professionals; and
> their sons and daughters, while they had migrated
> to the big city, kept alive the validity of their
> agrarian morals. Wet men were the newcomers to
> the United States; the populations that supported
> the political machines of Boston, New York, and
> Chicago; the infidels and heathen who didn't keep
> the Sabbatarian laws of Protestantism; and the so-
> phisticated Eastern "society people."[41]

Gusfield's analysis depicts accurately the class and ethnic
alignment of temperance and Sabbatarian advocates in Chicago. Their efforts aimed broadly toward the continuance of
middle-class cultural hegemony in the city. Moody's preaching coincided with and affirmed their beliefs. It might have
been anticipated correctly, then, that the revivalist's supporters and the new membership of the revival churches
would be drawn primarily from such persons.

Moody taught that the initial work which every truly
regenerate man or woman should evidence was a "peculiar"
life-style. "Peculiar" people, in the "Biblical sense," said
Moody, are those who "give up sinful, worldly pleasures,
and separate themselves to live and work for God."[42] Sabbath observance and abstinence from drink were two important ways by which "God's people" might be distinguished
from the "world." But more generally the call was to disciplined and moral living. In his "Address to Parents," Moody
urged fathers and mothers to enter into "fasting" from "amusements, and from theatres," as testimony to their children of
the authenticity of their Christian faith.[43] To do less, he
suggested, was to desecrate Christ's act of love on Calvary.
For, "when Christ died it was to separate His church from
the world, and how can a man who has consecrated himself

as a child of God, go back to the world without trampling
that blood under his feet." The first and preeminent work
of the new believer, then, was to demonstrate in his day-to-
day living his new allegiance to Jesus Christ. The inner
transformation of heart was to be evidenced by an outward
conversion to an evangelical and middle-class life-style.

In his sermon, "Work," Moody spelled out certain of
the activities which especially constituted authentic Christian
service. His opinions reflected again the individualistic and
pietistic attitudes which characterized much of evangelical
thinking in the 1870s. "Doers of the Word," he said, involve
themselves in Wednesday night prayer meetings and Sunday
evening worship services. They hold "cottage prayer meetings" at their homes and engage themselves in Sunday-school
work and in the labors of the Bible, mission, and tract societies. True believers, Moody declared, would support the
local evangelical churches with their time and money. Such
activities were "good works" and evidenced genuine conversion. The foremost "good work," however, was the labor of
evangelism. To work was to witness, to attempt to win souls,
and every Christian was responsible to be engaged in this
activity. Said Moody, "If a man be a true Christian he wins
souls." And, in a subsequent sermon, "If it is not a good
work to talk to a soul burdened with sin, what is a good
work?"[44] Humankind's primary need was for personal spiritual
renewal, Moody believed. The Christian's foremost priority,
therefore, was to respond to that need by a witness of word
and deed.

Moody's sermons also affirmed the social attitudes voiced
most often by evangelical Americans in the 1870s--attitudes
called into serious question in Chicago by the social and economic problems of the poor. Moody did not dismiss the importance of other forms of social aid, but he did subsume all
efforts at social reform under the more important task of
evangelism. Thus Moody supported actively the social programs of an organization like the YMCA, but only because
that institution had as its ultimate aim the conversion of lost
souls to Christ. "Opportunities have been afforded for reaching a large number of people with the gospel of peace, other-
wise almost unapproachable, simply because its forerunners
were bread, coal and clothing," Moody said of the YMCA.
"The heart as naturally opens to such kindness as flowers to
the sunshine; and when Christianity thus opens human hearts,

its power with God and men is recognized and felt."45 Social welfare was a means to an end. But ultimately reform,
to be effective, must be aimed at a change in the individual's
sinful nature. "Whitewashing the pump won't make the water
pure," Moody was fond of saying. "A heart that is right
with God and man seldom constitutes a social problem....
Nine-tenths of social betterment is effected by the convert
himself and the other tenth by Christian sympathy."46

If witnessing was the highest form of Christian work,
Moody informed a Tabernacle audience, it was not the only
work in which believers should be engaged. All hard work
was good and virtuous in Moody's judgment. Indeed, the
more physical the labor the better. "Don't try to get your
living by your brains and wits," he advised a group of reformed alcoholics in Chicago. "Work like a man.... We are
commanded to earn our bread by the sweat of our brows.
Get something to do. If it is for fifteen hours a day, all
the better, for while you are at work Satan does not have so
much chance to tempt you." Laziness, on the other hand,
was a blight upon society for which the revivalist evidenced
no compassion. "If a man will not work, let him starve,"
Moody told one group of listeners. In this sermon he went
on to express his doubts that a lazy man could become a
Christian at all. He had more hope for the salvation of a
drunkard, thief, or harlot, he said, than for that of a lazy
man. "Any honest work is better than idleness," declared
the evangelist.47

Much of the abject poverty that evidenced itself in
America's cities in the 1870s Moody attributed to laziness and
sin. He told listeners at the Tabernacle that "one reason
why people are poor, is because they refuse the gospel. If
they would only seek the Kingdom of God and His righteousness, God has promised to add all other things." In a November sermon, he cited his personal experience as proof that
God uses poverty to bring the sinner to his knees but will
finally bring prosperity to the believer. "My friends," he
said,

> I know just what [poverty] means. I have walked
> the streets of Boston out of work, out of money,
> and not knowing what I was going to do for a liv-
> ing. The whole of my early life was one long struggle
> with poverty, but I have no doubt it was God's way

of bringing me to Himself. And since I began to
seek first the Kingdom of God, I have never wanted
for anything.[48]

If sin was the root cause of much poverty, as Moody thought
it was, then regeneration by conversion was the necessary
remedy for the ills of the poor.

Moody did not lack compassion or sympathy for society's
downtrodden. He recognized that some Christian folk, honest
and hard-working individuals, were poor. Moody himself had
known want and hardship. His labors for the YMCA and the
Christian Commission evidenced a genuine concern to aid the
needy. Consequently, Moody distinguished in his preaching
between "the Lord's poor and the devil's poor."[49] The Lord's
people were sometimes poor so that they might bring glory
to God by their faith and perseverance in their peculiar, although temporary, circumstances. The devil's poor, however,
were poor because of sin; laziness, Moody believed, was the
chief of their sins. Charity, therefore, was to be meted out
with care. Gifts to idle and lazy persons would "only en-
courage them to live on in idleness, and to bring up their
children for the penitentiary."[50] In one Chicago sermon,
Moody expressed concern lest acts of charity might actually
interfere with the more important work of evangelism. When
engaged in work for the City Relief Society, Moody recalled
to his Tabernacle listeners,

> I supposed that I could open a poor man's heart by
> giving him a load of wood or a ton of coal when the
> winter was coming on, but I soon found out that he
> was not any more interested in the Gospel on that
> account. Instead of thinking how he could come to
> Christ, he was thinking how long it might be be-
> fore he got another load of wood. If I had the
> Bible in one hand and a loaf in the other, they al-
> ways look first at the loaf; and that was just con-
> trary to the order laid down in the Gospel.

When it was suggested at a Thanksgiving service that a collection be taken for distribution among the poor, Moody responded, "If it were known that we had some money to give
away, there are plenty of people who would be very anxious
inquirers at our meetings in order to get some of it."[51] There
was in Moody's preaching at times a thinly disguised suspicion

of the poor. His own experience had been a kind of Horatio Alger success story, and he was genuinely convinced that God would take care of true believers. "It may be a hard chance to get the first footing, but if you hold on, God will open a way for you."[52] These convictions, placed alongside his seemingly natural tendency to empathize with the down-trodden, may help to explain the contradictions which characterized Moody's preachments on social aid to the poor.

Henry F. May has described correctly the basically conservative outlook of the evangelical denominations toward the pressing social and economic issues of the 1870s. "In 1876," asserts May, "Protestantism presented a massive, almost unbroken front in its defense of the social status quo."[53] As has been shown, Moody's expressions on social and economic questions during the Chicago meetings suggest that he fitted May's perspective well. Moody had been reared in rural New England and imbibed in his youth the principles of rugged individualism and the Protestant ethic. His own experience as a penniless but hard-working shoe salesman who achieved quick success in the commercial world probably reaffirmed for him the validity of his convictions and instilled in him a boundless confidence in the American economic system. His strong religious convictions acquired by his conversion to evangelical Christianity in the 1850s did nothing to unsettle these basic beliefs.

Moody shared the prevailing middle-class faith in the Protestant ethic. Hard work, frugality, honesty, and Christian living would result ultimately in prosperity.[54] James F. Findlay has observed correctly that Moody "never questioned in any ultimate sense the values of the ruthlessly acquisitive society that characterized America in his adult years, nor the men who governed that society."[55] In part this explains his great popularity with the middle classes. They shared his confidence in the competitive, free-enterprise society in which they had been reared. They shared his individualistic assumptions about social ethics. It was the native-born middle classes who, like Moody, saw in the Sabbatarian and temperance movements righteous crusades to preserve the moral order of so-called Christian America--their world. They understood his values and attitudes and were comfortable with revival religion. Even the revivalist's occasional condemnation of selfish materialism, fraud, corruption, and lack of charity among the well-to-do had a therapeutic value to middle-

class Americans troubled somewhat by the ruthless competitive-
ness of the system.   If Moody condemned Chicagoans who
worshiped "silver and gold ... more than any other god,"
he also applauded the Marshall Fields and John Farwells who
used their wealth for the Lord's work.   The quest for success and prosperity was not sinful provided the wealth acquired was used in part for charitable and religious ends.
Moody questioned the morals of individual capitalists, but he
did not question seriously the adequacy of the system or suggest a restructuring of society in light of changing realities.[56]

Considering Moody's preachment on work and his acceptance of the social and economic status quo, it is not surprising that so many of the leading captains of Chicago's
business and industrial community supported his efforts.
Commercial leaders could hardly dislike an evangelist who told
his converts, as Moody did, that "there is many a man that
will help you if you will show a disposition to help yourself."
"If you want to get these employers always under obligation
to you," he added,

> you must be such true men and be so helpful to
> your employers that they cannot get along without
> you, and then you will work up, and your employers
> will increase your wages.   If a man works in the
> interest of his employer, he will be sure to keep
> him, and treat him well, but if he only works for
> money and don't take any interest in his employer's
> business, he will let him go at any time.

And, considering the multitude of strikes in Chicago in the
summer of 1876, businessmen probably felt like applauding
when Moody advised Chicago workers, "If you can get only
twenty-five cents a day go to work for that."[57]

In this chapter it has been shown that Moody's sermons
possessed a natural appeal to native-born, middling-class,
Anglo-American listeners--precisely the kinds of persons who
most often joined revival churches and filled the ranks of
Moody's workers.   In theology, the sermons proclaimed the
"old-time Gospel"--a strong emphasis upon personal sin, an
even stronger focus on God's willingness to forgive the sinner, and an appeal to embrace the godly life.   The egalitarian
spirit in which Moody couched God's offer of salvation to all
who would believe augmented the attractiveness of this familiar

Gospel to middle-class ears. When Moody chose to emphasize the love of God and minimize preachments about the terrors of hell, he made an astute decision of rhetorical strategy in light of the sensibilities of middle-class hearers. Other elements in his preaching also coincided with the attitudes and values of these folk. Moody's advocacy of Sabbatarian and temperance goals affirmed the rightness of evangelical and middle-class moral conceptions. And the revivalist's belief in the nobility of hard work, his commitment to an individualistic social ethic, and his confidence that diligent work, honesty, and Christian faith would breed success for any and every man confirmed middle-class confidence in the economic and social status quo.

This cluster of attitudes and opinions which Moody shared with native-born, middle-class Chicagoans shed light on the extraordinary number of such persons who responded positively to the revival meetings by seeking fellowship in revival churches. But the revival functioned for the new church members at deeper levels than the mere coincidence of opinions. By offering almost prophetic sanction of the correctness of their social and moral attitudes, the revival served to quell doubts about the adequacy of the present social system or the absolute rightness of their cultural mores. The social ills of the city, Moody assured them, were rooted in immoral behavior and ungodly living. And his definitions of such behavior allowed blame easily to be placed upon the foreign-born population. The revival also offered to middle-class and native-born Chicagoans a means to ensure the retention of cultural hegemony precisely at a time when it appeared threatened by a massive influx of immigrant and Catholic peoples. Conversions at the meetings or through the efforts of the revival churches meant, Moody taught them, the adoption of a life-style and social ethic much like their own. In short, revival religion offered reassurance to troubled middle-class Chicagoans as well as a possible means of maintaining social order by effective evangelism.

At this point it is possible to understand the sources of social stress which found comfort and answer in revival religion, and also to survey the manner in which the Chicago revival functioned socially. First, however, the sermons must be examined from the viewpoint of sentiment and feeling, for the emotional context of the sermons perhaps proved as comforting to some distressed listeners as did their social content.

Chapter VIII

THE RHETORIC OF REVIVAL:
SENTIMENT AND FEELING

In the first half of the nineteenth century, American culture
experienced a broad and profound transformation described
variously by historians as "romanticization," "sentimentaliza-
tion," or "feminization."[1] Reflecting the broader cultural
changes, evangelical religion itself became more emotional,
more soft and accommodating, more sentimental. Such harsh
doctrines as the idea of infant damnation died quietly about
the middle of the century. God was more commonly likened
to a loving father and Christ to a suffering, sacrificial wife
or mother. Clergymen praised the home as a kind of heavenly
haven from the hellish world around. The family joined the
church as a locus of grace, purity, and salvation. Domesticity was glorified, and women were placed upon a pedestal.
Immense power, in the form of "influence," was attributed
to mothers and housewives who maintained a purity and piety
lost to men (and wayward women) who ventured out into the
aggressive, masculine world of business and politics. The
salvation of America itself was placed by some in the virtue
of "True Women." "Yours it is to determine," one minister
solemnly informed his female parishioners, "whether the beautiful order of society ... shall continue as it has been" or
whether "society shall break up and become a chaos of dis-
jointed and unsightly elements."[2] The maintenance of the
traditional domestic virtues was deemed crucial to the survival
of the social order.

It is significant that Moody, Sankey, and most other
native-born, middle-class Americans had been reared in a
cultural and religious milieu which glorified domesticity and
was imbued with sentimentality. As shown in earlier chapters, it was this middle-class and family-located population

which both swelled the rolls of Chicago's revival churches in
1876 and 1877 and supplied the revivalist with hosts of volunteer workers. These persons probably shared Moody's
social views and his interest in disciplining individual behavior. This chapter analyzes how the revivalist's anecdotes
and stories suggested ways to exert that discipline upon society through passive forms of influence. It also examines how
the stories, by asserting sets of positive and negative images,
imparted to revival supporters a sense of shared attitudes,
which in effect contributed to the growing fragmentation of the
city's population along religious and ethnic lines. Finally, the
analysis clarifies how Moody's illustrative materials were attuned
to middle-class sentimentality, which explains in part his popularity among the native-born, middling classes.

   Many religious spokesmen at midcentury assumed that
men, women, and children were susceptible to "influence"--
both positive and negative--in nature. The term appeared
with astounding regularity in contemporary religious periodicals, particularly in discussions addressing questions of social and personal morality. Moody also employed the word
frequently in his Chicago sermons. Influence was a passive
means of exerting power. It was attributed most often to
women and religion, both of which in the nineteenth century
were deprived of direct access to the active centers of power--
the worlds of business and politics. Perhaps troubled by the
increasing secularization taking place in the American processes
of decision making and the pervasive corruption in business
and politics, many religious and secular leaders joined in eu-
logizing the saving influence of the home and church.[3] And
because both spheres of influence aimed at a salvation that
included religious renewal and moral reform, both were truly
evangelical in nature.[4]

   Moody's illustrations most often revolved around the
relationship of mother and child or wife and husband. Almost invariably, the godly woman was the heroine of the
tale. She was depicted in the stories as noble and pure, a
wholly redemptive though passive influence upon those closest
to her.

> I remember being in the camp and a man came to me
> and said, "Mr. Moody, when the Mexican war began
> I wanted to enlist. My mother, seeing I was resolved,
> said if I became a Christian I might go. She pleaded

and prayed that I might become a Christian, but I
wouldn't. I said when the war was over I would
become a Christian, but not till then. All her pleading was in vain, and at last, when I was going away,
she took out a watch and said: 'My son, your
father left this to me when he died. Take it, and
I want you to remember that every day at twelve
o'clock your mother will be praying for you.' Then
she gave me her Bible, and marked out passages,
and put a few different references in the fly-leaf.
I took the watch, and it was twelve o'clock. I had
been gone four months, but I remembered that my
mother at that hour was praying for me. Something
prompted me to ask the officer to relieve me for a
little, and I stepped behind a tree away out on those
plains of Mexico, and cried to the God of my mother
to save me."[5]

Little wonder that Moody could say at one point, "There's
no influence like a mother's." Or, in another sermon: "Bless
God, boy, for that mother. Do not treat that mother con-
temptuously; do not deny her prayer tonight; do not make
light of your mother's cries to God this night. God's best
gift on earth to you is that praying mother."[6]

In Moody's imagery the godly mother often assumed
Christ-like qualities. In numerous instances the forgiving
character of Jesus was exemplified in the patient, always
forgiving, always praying mother. One such story related
the experience of an estranged, rebellious daughter, a hardened runaway, who became convinced that her mother would
never forgive her for her wayward behavior. Unknown to
the girl, her mother began a lengthy, determined search for
her daughter, visiting all the locations in which "fallen women"
were known to reside in this city. Failing to find her daughter, she asked permission to pin her picture on the wall at
one such residence.

Weeks and months rolled on, until at length one
night a poor fallen girl came into the room ... her
eye caught the picture, and gazing at it for a moment, she burst into a flood of tears. "Where did
you get it?" she sobbed. They told her how her
mother came there, heart-broken, and asked to have
her picture hung up on that room, in the hope of

> finding her daughter. The girl's memory went back
> to her days of peace and purity, recalling the acts
> of kindness of that beloved mother, and she then
> and there resolved to return. See how that mother
> sought for her and forgave her. Oh, poor fallen
> ones, the Son of God is seeking for you tonight.
> If you haven't got a mother to pray for you, the
> Son of God wants to be everything to you.[7]

The godly mother, in this instance, was strikingly reminiscent
of Christ, the Good Shepherd, seeking the lost sheep.

In Moody's stories, the Christian mother was identified
most often as the source of redemption. In some instances,
however, it was an innocent, saintly child who proved to be
the saving influence within the family setting. Moody told
of one young convert who prayed faithfully for his drinking
father. The boy was ordered by his irreligious parent to
cease the practice or be flogged. But, said Moody, the lad
"was filled with God and couldn't stop praying." One day
his father arrived home drunk, found the boy at prayer,
beat him, and sent him out of the home.

> The mother knew it wouldn't do to try to keep the
> boy when her husband had ordered him away, so
> she drew him to her bosom and kissed him, and bid
> him good-bye. When he came to the door his father
> was there, and the little fellow reached out his hand
> --"Good-bye, father; as long as I live I will pray
> for you," and left the house. He hadn't been gone
> many minutes when that father rushed after him.
> "My boy, if that is religion ... I want it."[8]

The story asserted, in much the same fashion as did Moody's
tales about godly mothers, the power of passive moral influence.

Occasionally, fathers assumed such redemptive qualities,
as when Moody compared the love of God for sinners to a
contemporary father's loving search for his wandering son.[9]
More commonly in the sermons, however, fathers were themselves in need of redemption rather than a redemptive source.
Consider the sad tale Moody related about a wealthy father
whose dying boy asked him, "Won't you pray for my lost soul,
father? You have never prayed for me." At this, said Moody,

the old man only wept. "During the seventeen years that
God had given him his boy he had never spent an hour in
prayer for his soul, but the object of his life had been to
accumulate wealth for that first-born."[10] The world of business, the story implied, had corrupted this father's spiritual
perceptions. It was the godly mother, maintaining her virtue
and spirituality by restricting her activities to domestic and
religious affairs, that was the missing ingredient in this tra-
gic tale.

　　Not all mothers in Moody's stories were pure and pious.
This did not lessen their influence. Moody told of one German mother whose son was "impressed" at Sunday-school
meetings he conducted in Chicago in the 1860s. But this
mother thought her son was a "good enough" boy, and did
not need to be converted. On Sundays, he recalled, she
took the lad to the beer gardens rather than allowing him to
attend Sunday school. "I pleaded with that mother, but all
my pleading was of no account. I tried my influence with
the boy; but while I was pulling one way she was pulling the
other. Her influence prevailed. Naturally it would." The
sad end of the story pointed up the destructive influence of
the ungodly mother, for the boy ended up in the county jail.[11]
A similar fate befell the son of a mother and father who let
their boy "do as he would." They had no time for God or
religion. That boy, said Moody, ended up in prison for ten
years and when he returned home discovered that his father
was dead and his mother had gone insane.[12] Yet another
episode told of a father who "brought his children up to treat
all religion with contempt." As a result of his influence,
said Moody, "his sons have gone down to their graves drunkards, and his daughter has died of a broken heart."[13] Stories of this sort were less frequent in the Chicago sermons
than were those which testified to the effectual and redemptive influence of a godly mother or a faithful father, but
they did provide for Moody's hearers an important set of negative symbols. Drunkenness, insanity, broken hearts, prison,
families in disarray--these were the fate of persons outside
the influence of a godly home.[14]

　　If the evangelist's anecdotes are an accurate barometer
of his thinking, Moody believed that a mother's influence was
most effectual through prayer. Prayer was a means of exerting influence upon God in the direction of that for which one
earnestly and sincerely prayed. It was, moreover, a passive

vehicle of social influence and thus appropriate to women.
In his second sermon in Chicago, Moody acknowledged to
the mothers in the audience that "we depend a good deal
upon you." He related how in Philadelphia he had called a
"meeting of mothers" which was attended by somewhere between five thousand and eight thousand women. "They
prayed for aid from the Lord, and that grace might be shown
to these sons, and daughters, and husbands, and the result
was that our inquiry-rooms were soon filled with anxious and
earnest inquirers."[15]

The extent of a mother's influence with God through
prayer was such that episodes sometimes described wayward
sons and husbands being reached across oceans and even
from beyond the grave.

> A wayward boy in London, whose mother was very
> anxious for his salvation, said to her: "I am not
> going to be bothered with your prayers any longer;
> I will go to America and be rid of them." "But, my
> boy," she said, "God is on the sea and in America,
> and He hears my prayers for you." Well, he came
> to this country, and as they sailed into the port of
> New York, some of the sailors told him that Moody
> and Sankey were holding meetings in the Hippo-
> drome. The moment he landed he started for our
> place of meeting, and there he found Christ. He
> became a most earnest worker, and he wrote to his
> mother and told her that her prayers had been an-
> swered, that he had been saved, and that he had
> found his mother's God.[16]

"If we had a thousand such mothers in Chicago," said Moody,
"we would lift it."[17] Even from heaven the lingering influence
of a mother's prayers was such that Moody could attribute
to it the reclamation of a family member. Said Moody to one
Tabernacle audience, "How many men have been saved by
their mothers after they have gone up to heaven; and perhaps
her influence made him think sometimes."[18]

At one point in the Chicago meetings, Moody seemed to
become sensitive to the possible ill effects of his overemphasiz-
ing the power of maternal prayer. In a prayer-meeting talk
at Farwell Hall he made a pointed effort to dispel "the impression abroad now ... that it has always been women and a

few weak men who have prayed." In this brief address he
held up Daniel, the Bible's lion tamer, as a man of strength
and courage who was also fervent in prayer. Because of
his faithfulness in prayer, Moody suggested, Daniel was a
more effective politician--he "was a wise ruler and had more
influence than any other man living on earth."[19] Apparently
Moody had become conscious that for some in his audiences
prayer was assumed to be a feminine activity--a passive form
of influence and, therefore, "womanly." When confronted
with difficulty a man acted, a woman prayed. While Moody
would certainly have objected, his stories themselves contributed to exactly this stereotype.[20] Redemptive influence
could be generated in many ways, but the domestic lines of
influence always emerged in the sermons as strongest. Women
and children, the symbols of domesticity, knew best how to
wield the passive power that could be generated through
prayer.

The domestic circle--mother, child, and home--provided,
then, an important model for the kind of controlled behavior
approved of by evangelicals like Moody. It offered further
a means to combat strategically the problems of order and
discipline. By prayer and through personal influence, the
family purified the feelings and behavior of its members. The
home offered a haven of safety from the ill influences of a
surrounding hostile and undisciplined world. Thus Moody
urged his listeners to erect "family altars," to engage in
regular prayer for their children and unsaved family members,
and live circumspectly, for "children are very good imitators."
Such families, his stories suggested, would produce the kind
of men needed to lead the nation back to moral righteousness.

Moody's illustrations themselves were intended to gene-
rate influence with sympathetic and sensitive listeners. The
stories evoked like feelings among listeners creating, thereby,
bonds of shared emotions and experience. An important set
of positive images was provided by godly mothers, saintly
children, and occasionally by a faithful father; an equally
significant set of negative images was provided by alcohol
and the city.

There is no doubt about Moody's outright condemnation
of drink. Here it is necessary only to observe how the revivalist used stories to flesh out his conceptions about liquor
and the drinker. The dominating theme of the revivalist's

stories involving drink was its destructive impact upon family
and home. One such tale described a "rumseller" who "didn't
worship God, but he worshipped [his] boy." "Time rolled on
and his life became such a burden to him that he put a re-
volver to his head and blew his brains out."21 Drink had
destroyed both the family and the individual drinker. Another typical story described a young fugitive from justice
who fell prey to the drink habit, gambled his employer's
money away, and was forced to abandon his wife and family
in an effort to avoid imprisonment.22 Here alcohol was the
root cause of immoral behavior (gambling) and also cost the
young man his job and family. In an "Address to Parents,"
offered late in December, Moody implored the parents in attendance not to offer wine at the New Year's celebrations.
For some young man will feel compelled to take a little who
"hasn't got back-bone enough to resist the temptation.... He
goes to another house, and the same thing is repeated, and
so on, until at night the poor fellow goes home intoxicated
and breaks the heart of some mother."23 Drink was the anti-
thesis of the family--the former a source of destruction and
degradation, the latter a source of grace and purity.

Moody's illustrations commonly placed the drinking man
in the city. The city, in Moody's imagery, was a place of
deception and allurements. His stories sometimes followed a
conventional nineteenth-century romantic story line in which
the innocent young female or the naive, adventuresome young
man lost his or her virtue shortly after arriving in the city.24
"No young man ever comes to the city," said Moody, "but
has great temptation cross his path as he enters it."25

The temptation to which city dwellers most often succumbed in the stories was crass materialism. Moody told of
a country minister who came to visit his son living in Chicago
and found the boy "mad about real estate." He tried to talk
to his son about spiritual things, "but it was no use.... His
only heaven was real estate." In one sermon Moody likened
many Chicagoans to the ancient Babylonians who cried out,
"Give me gold, give me money, and I will do anything." The
city blinded its inhabitants to the more important spiritual
realities. Politics, business, fashion, "worldly" amusements--
all abounded in the city, and all, said Moody, took a man's
heart away from both God and family.26

Bernard Weisberger has suggested that the millions who

heard Moody gladly "did so because they yearned for an echo
of that simplicity which was disappearing with agrarian
America."[27] Although Weisberger's explanation is overly
simplistic, there is an element of truth in his remarks. Urbanization, massive immigration, and industrial growth did bring
new strains to the lives of city residents, many of whom were
recently arrived from the countryside or the rural towns of
the East. In the brief span of twenty years, Chicago itself
had been transformed from a quiet, if aspiring, Western town
into the second greatest city of America and the industrial
capital of the West. Troubled by the complexities of metropolitan living, some Chicagoans doubtless longed for a more
simple life which they associated with their rural past. Moody's
characterizations of the purity of country and family life and
the immorality of city life probably evoked in them a nostalgic
response. For the city, in Moody's stories, was not depicted
in neutral terms with potential for good and evil, but was itself a destructive force. A multitude of ills besetting middle-
class Chicagoans could be rationalized by the influence of the
city.

The degrading and immoral effect of the city upon a
young, recently come-to-the-city woman is illustrative of the
negative symbols Moody's stories related to metropolitan life.

> Just look at her as she comes up to the city from
> the home where she has left sisters and a mother
> as pure as the morning air. She came down to the
> city and is now in a low brothel. Sometimes her
> mind goes back to the pure home where her mother
> prayed for her.... [But] now she is an exile. She
> is full of shame.... In a few short years she dies
> the death of a harlot, and she is laid away in an
> unknown grave.[28]

In the story the city is the site of a fall from innocence into
a life of shame, a place apart from redemptive, purifying
domestic influence, a cause of degraded and damning living,
and ultimately of death. A related set of images appears in
another story where the influence of the city is suggested
by explicit analogy.

> Look at that man in a boat on Niagara River. He
> is only about a mile from the rapids. A man on the
> bank shouts to him, "Young man, young man, the

rapids are not far away, you'd better pull for the
shore." "You attend to your own business; I will
take care of myself," he replies. On he goes, sit-
ting cooly in his boat.... By and by he says: "I
think I hear the rapids--yes, I hear them roar";
and he seizes the oars and pulls with all his strength,
but the current is too great, and nearer and
nearer he is drawn on to that abyss, until he
gives one unearthly scream, and over he goes. Ah,
my friends, this is the case with hundreds in this
city. They are in the current of riches, of pleasure, of drink, that will take them to the whirlpool.[29]

The city is powerful, deceptive, and dangerous, its influence
utterly overwhelming for the foolish and reckless young person. Lot was the Biblical epitome of the young man who
succumbed to the allurements of the city. Just as Lot went
to Sodom to make money, said Moody, so thousands of young
men and women had come to Chicago seeking material prosperity. "No man ever goes into Sodom by God's advice....
It [is] business that takes him there." But the cost is high.
Sodom, as Moody described it, was a "whirlpool" taking its
inhabitants to "sure ruin." As for Lot, his family was destroyed, his character became reproachable, and his children
were reduced to unbelieving gamblers and drunkards. "If
you are in the city of Sodom," he warned his Tabernacle
listeners, "flee from it at once--escape with your lives, for
destruction will come."[30]

The city and drink, often the one in association with
the other, provided sets of negative imagery in the stories.
Moody's hearers were exhorted to "flee" the city, or its
whirlpool-like influence would suck them to destruction. Obviously, Moody's listeners were not expected literally to de-
part Chicago for the more safe confines of country life.
Rather, the sermons implied that the damning influence of the
city could be escaped by a retreat into the safety of home
and family. In a story which combined several of these themes
and images, Moody described an Indiana mother.

Some years ago her boy came up to this city....
He hadn't been here long before he was led astray.
A neighbor happened to come up here and found
him one night in the streets drunk.... [The parents
were then told about this.] Neither of them slept

that night, but they took their burden to Christ.
About daylight the mother said: "I don't know how,
I don't know when or where, but God has given me
faith to believe that our son will be saved and will
never come to a drunkard's grave." One week after,
that boy left Chicago. He couldn't tell why--an un-
seen power seemed to lead him to his mother's home,
and the first thing he said on coming over the threshold was, "Mother, I have come home to ask you to
pray for me"; and soon after he came back to Chicago a bright and shining light.[31]

The city and drink had led the lad to the brink of disaster,
but maternal prayer and domestic influence saved him. His
return to the family in conjunction with divine intervention
brought peace to the out-of-control passions of the wandering
boy.

Stories of this sort are to be found in virtually all of
Moody's Chicago sermons. They drew again and again from
the deep reservoir of family sentiment which characterized
middle-class sensibilities in late-Victorian America. While to
modern readers the stories seem overly romanticized and
heavily stereotyped, to many of Moody's hearers they proved
remarkably effective in generating the kinds of emotional responses the evangelist desired. Tears and quiet sobs were
not uncommon at the meetings. Moody himself wept openly
upon occasion. Even "strong men" were said to have been
moved to tears at certain of the evangelist's stories. What
father, after all, could not have empathized with the man
Moody described who fell asleep one day as his child played
nearby and when he awoke discovered that his little girl had
wandered off and fallen over a cliff to her death. What
young, new-to-the-city Chicagoan would not have been impressed by the sad tale of that rebellious lad who had "an
opportunity for religion," but passed it by. Dying now, he
can only say, "Oh, I have missed it at last." What parents
could have withstood the searching question of the saintly
little girl who, in Moody's story, confronted her unbelieving
mother and father with the words, "Why don't you love Jesus?"
What middle-class, Protestant American in the 1870s would
not have been drawn to the God who, said Moody, "will comfort you as a mother comforts her child."[32] The stories were
effective rhetorical tools among middle-class, Protestant hearers,
particularly when wielded by a storyteller of Moody's talents.

The pervasive sentimentality of Moody's anecdotes is
indicated best by the frequent tales of death and dying.
Death and the loss of family and friends are, of course, constant and real concerns. The Biblical promise of heaven for
believers provided genuine comfort for the grieving and the
lonely. [33]

Moody celebrated the joys of heaven in two sermons
and in frequent illustrations and anecdotes about death and
eternity. The promise of family reunions in heaven had an
especially prominent place in the evangelist's stories. Doubtless, the revivalist sensed in this theme a powerful incentive
toward conversion. In the sermon, "Where Art Thou?" Moody
commented:

> It may be, as you look down the stream of time,
> you see a little grave that marks the resting-place
> of your child. It may be that child took you by
> the hand, and asked you, "Will you meet me in that
> land?" And you promised her that you would meet
> her there. As you looked down into that little grave,
> and heard the damp, cold earth falling down, you
> repeated that promise. Five, ten, fifteen years ago
> you promised this: Have you kept it? [34]

Only the converted would be finally reunited with loved ones
in heaven. Moody was no universalist. He was a pragmatist
when it came to salvation. Reminding his audiences of the
realities of death and eternity was a useful means of bringing them to see the ultimate importance of conversion. As
the testimony of one father indicated, the technique sometimes
was remarkably effective.

> On Wednesday when you were speaking on heaven
> you said, "It may be this moment there is a mother
> looking down from heaven expecting the salvation
> of her child who is here." You were apparently
> looking at the very spot where my child was sit-
> ting. My heart said, "That is my child. That is
> her mother." Tears sprang to my eyes. I bowed
> my head and prayed, "Lord, direct that word to my
> darling child's heart; Lord, save my child." I was
> then anxious till the close of the meeting, when I
> went to her. She was bathed in tears. She rose,
> put her arms around me, and kissed me. When

> walking down to you she told me it was that same
> remark (about the mother looking down from heaven)
> that found the way home to her, and asked me,
> "Papa, what can I do for Jesus?"[35]

Such sentimental tales were common in Moody's preaching. They touched the emotions of hearers, bringing tears
to the eyes of many in attendance and evoking an atmosphere
of sympathy between the revivalist and his listeners. Middle-
class, native-born Northern whites who were the regular con-
sumers of popular romantic literature could enjoy the sentimentality of the sermons yet feel quite comfortable in the
orderly and controlled emotionalism of the services. Moody
was an effective communicator largely because he understood
so well the emotional plane at which many of his listeners
lived and could touch effectively and appealingly those emotions.

In this chapter, then, it has been shown that certain
kinds of metaphors and images--city as whirlpool, mother as
a holy influence, and the like--and the sentimentality of the
stories generally, were part of Moody's sermonic strategy to
evangelize Chicago. Moody probably saw these conventions
as universal. In fact, they were not. The imagery and the
sentimentality were culturally oriented. They made good
sense and had therapeutic value for many native-born, middle-
class, white Protestants in Chicago. Furthermore, the images
explained further for these persons the sources of their social
distress--alcohol and the city--and offered in family and prayer
acceptable ways to maintain order within society. Many of
these folk flocked to the Tabernacle and supported Moody and
Sankey enthusiastically in a variety of ways. For some of
the unchurched middle class Moody's words evoked sufficient
sympathy to lead them to seek formal affiliation with others
of like minds and feelings in the revival churches.

It should be recognized here that the evangelist's sincerity and the genuineness of his love and concern for all
people, regardless of class, may be beyond question. Moody
was consciously committed to the evangelization of all persons.
And conversion, he was convinced, provided the only viable
solution to the personal dilemma of sin and the larger social
problems of the city and nation. In seeking conversions,
however, his sermonic strategy, like his social convictions,
could not escape the trappings of the middle-class, Protestant

culture of which he was a member. Furthermore, the cultural
constraints of his preaching probably contributed to his repeated frustrations in attempts to attract the lower classes
and the foreign-born to the Tabernacle, evangelize them, and
usher them into the revival churches.

It is appropriate at this point to summarize the evidence
accumulated in these several chapters and assess the actual
social results of the 1876 Chicago revival. Clearly the meetings did not produce the consensus of values Protestants
hoped might result from the conversion of the unchurched
masses to evangelicalism and to Protestant, middle-class
ideals. There is little evidence that many of the "dangerous
classes" either embraced the revival rhetoric or affiliated
themselves with local evangelical churches. Reflecting upon
the Moody services in Chicago it is, however, possible to
speculate that the event provided comfort of a different sort
for some worried middle-class city dwellers. It offered to
those who embraced its rhetoric a sense of identification and
community.

Sociologists of religion assert that one function of religion is to create and maintain identity and to integrate order
and meaning in the face of perceived chaos, disorder and
fear.[36] Religion legitimates the values and institutional structure which undergirds a society, says Peter Berger, by relating "the humanly defined reality to ultimate, universal and
sacred reality." In a stable society, Berger adds, the members of that society "look upon key meanings of the social
order" as "inevitable, as part and parcel of the universal
'nature of things.' "[37]

Revival Chicagoans saw their moral, social, economic,
and even political conceptions as, to borrow Berger's phrase-
ology, "fundamental meanings inherent in the universe."
City life in general and the immigrant and Catholic populations in particular seemed, however, to endanger evangelical
hegemony over social values and institutions. From this perspective one can understand the frenzied rhetoric of evangelicals in response to Sabbath breaking, intemperance, the
Hanford murder, and the Bible-and-school questions in Chicago as reactions to fears of social dislocation. If the revival did not remove the sources of those fears, it did reas-
sert the absolute "rightness" of evangelical conceptions by
defining opposition to them as sin.

The Chicago revival, then, worked to define and
strengthen the ethos and world view of middle-class Protestantism in Chicago.   In particular, clerks, bookkeepers,
salesmen, and other lower middle-class Chicagoans found in
the revival rhetoric a means of understanding and coping with
fears of loss of status and severe social dislocation.   For
these persons, the maintenance of a stable social order seemed
essential to their social and economic aspirations.   Not surprisingly, then, from this social group came the large numbers
of new church members, professing their faith and commit-
ting themselves fervently to the ideals of evangelicalism.   Their
profession of faith signaled their allegiance to the evangelical
world view, a world view that transcended denominational
distinctions and was embodied in the revival rhetoric.   Converts believed themselves saved from something frightening
and incorporated into something new and clean and good.
Their sense of identity was given clear definition through
the sacralization of certain social, political, and economic
mores.   Revival Chicagoans talked alike, thought alike, sang
the same kinds of songs, held the same values, and shared
the same feelings.   Any doubts about the ultimate goodness
of the moral and social conceptions they shared were removed,
at least temporarily, by the prophet Moody.   Said one astute
observer of the Moody meetings in Chicago, people find comfort in coming in contact "with a man who knows no doubt."[38]

The 1876 revival thus strengthened a sense of community
and identity among evangelical Chicagoans.   In so doing, however, it also sharpened hostilities toward those whose attitudes, values, and behavior were inimical to evangelical conceptions.   This heightening of cultural tensions and antipathies
would have enduring results in postrevival Chicago.   The
concluding chapter examines the impact of the revival in Chicago on church and society.

Chapter IX

AFTERMATH: THE IMPACT OF THE
REVIVAL ON CHURCH AND SOCIETY

Tuesday evening, January 16, 1877, marked the grand finale
of the Moody services in Chicago. The final service testified
to the evangelist's continued popularity in the city. By seven
o'clock, one-half hour before the service's scheduled beginning, nine thousand people had packed the Tabernacle and an
equal number crowded the areas outside. The scene was reminiscent of the excitement generated at the initial service
fifteen weeks earlier. An impressed reporter for the Inter-
Ocean remarked that "a thermometer freezing mercury would
not have diminished the streams of pilgrims who with hymn-
books under arm and shining evening faces, walked briskly
to the Tabernacle." Seated at floor level were some four
thousand "young converts"--the visible fruits of the revivalist's quest to evangelize the city. The evangelical clergy
was there in full force giving the public a final testimony to
their kinship with Moody and the revival effort. Marshall
and Henry Field and John Farwell led an impressive contin-
gent of business leaders also present and seated conspicuously
upon the platform. 1

     The evening service was unlike those held nightly
throughout the campaign in several features. Moody took
the single offering of the meetings to aid the local YMCA in
alleviating its indebtedness. As the collection was received,
Moody read the names of large contributors and the amounts
pledged by each. He also used the occasion to thank publicly
the city's ministers, press and business leaders, the choir,
committees, and ushers for their aid in the revival work. The
remainder of the meeting, however, was patent Moody. The
initial hymn had a familiar other-worldly theme.

> Oh, think of the home over there,
> By the side of the river of light
> Where the saints all immortal and fair
> Are robed in their garments of white.

Sankey followed with a rendition of one of his popular gospel
hymns. And Moody preached on the word "Able." As one
might have expected, the meeting concluded with a sad and
sentimental tale.

> I remember a few years ago a little child died, and
> just before his soul went home, he asked his father
> to lift him up, and the father put his hand under
> the head of his child and raised it up. But the
> child only said, "That is not enough ... lift me
> right up.... Higher, father, higher!" Till at last
> his head fell back, and his spirit passed up to the
> eternal King--high at last.

"So my dear friends," Moody concluded, "let your constant
cry be higher, higher, more near the cross of the Son of
God." And with a tear in his eye, he bid them goodnight.[2]

Moody and Sankey departed the following morning to
initiate a series of meetings in Boston. Daniel W. Whittle
and George Stebbins remained in Chicago holding regular
evening meetings at the Tabernacle in an effort to maintain
a high level of revival excitement.[3] Moody kept no record
of converts. The only record that mattered, he said, was
that which was kept in heaven.[4] Nor did he pause long
enough at the conclusion of the Chicago meetings to express
his satisfaction or dissatisfaction with the results of the three
and a half months of labor or attempt a careful assessment
of exactly what had happened in Chicago. Instead, he acknowledged simply that by God's grace "we have done what
we have done in this city."[5] Others were left to carry on
the Chicago work and, perhaps, to consider more critically
the actual consequences and results of the Moody services.

Contemporary observers were almost unanimous in their
praise of the Chicago meetings. Not surprisingly, most
emphasized the immediate benefits to the city's churches and
clergy. The Alliance commented:

> The city has enjoyed a religious feast such as was

> never spread in its sight before.... Half-dead mer-
> chants and half-dead preachers, idle ladies of wealth,
> and others, many who have stood around the market
> places without spiritual employment, have gone into
> the vineyard to work. The revival of religious in-
> dustry among Christians must be ranked as next in
> importance to the conversion of sinners.[6]

The Tribune remarked positively on the pervasive interest in
religion which, it believed, had resulted from the Moody services. "Probably never before in the history of the city has
there been a time when public attention and private conversation and introspection have been so largely devoted to religious subjects." The Inter-Ocean thought that the meetings
"gave strength to all religious societies and ... widened the
influence of all religious thought and sentiment." "There
have been about as many conversions in the church as out,"
noted the Chicago Weekly Journal enthusiastically, and "a
good many ministers have evidently experienced a change of
heart and given their church a new minister without a change
in name." Even W. H. Ryder, a popular Universalist clergyman, in a letter highly critical of Moody's Chicago work, acknowledged that "many have been converted; more have been
convicted; more still encouraged to lead a better life" because
of the revival.[7]

The secular and religious press of Chicago was admittedly sympathetic toward Moody and revivalism. One might
suspect correctly that some of those reports at least were
biased or exaggerated in the evangelist's favor. However,
there is a large body of evidence supporting certain of their
claims for the Moody revival. It appears certain that the
city's evangelical churches and ministers did receive a sub-
stantial boost of enthusiasm and vigor because of the revival
campaign. And several of these churches, though not all,
also profited by large increases in membership.

The enlivened spirits of the clergy were celebrated repeatedly by the ministers themselves. The Reverend Samuel
Wyckoff attributed to the revival meetings his own personal
experience of repentance and rededication. God, he assured
a gathering at Farwell Hall, "had heard his prayer and delivered him out of his suffering and sorrow." This morning,
he concluded, "seemed to him like a morning without a cloud,
and he was living in the twelfth chapter of the prophecy of

Isaiah." Other Chicago clergymen testified to similar experiences. C. L. Thompson, the prominent cleric at Fifth
Presbyterian Church, reported that

> he had received great courage and strength from
> his attendance at the Tabernacle and Farwell Hall
> meetings, and from the influence of them he had
> almost forgotten the feelings of desolation, the re-
> membrance of broken vows, which possessed him
> during the early services.

For Thompson and Wyckoff the revival lifted them from feelings of spiritual and emotional despair to renewed fervor and
zeal for God. Their experiences probably paralleled that of
many evangelical ministers. For when L. T. Chamberlain,
pastor of the New England Congregational Church, testified
in December that he had "received a power and a joy altogether beyond what he had ever felt in the past, and, as
a result, more persons had been converted in his church the
last six weeks than in the previous three years," the Christian
Advocate reported that the whole audience, composed primarily of ministers attending the Christian Convention, "fell
upon its knees" to ask for a further blessing of the Spirit.[8]

The revived clergy sometimes conveyed their excitement
to the churches they served. The Advance reported the
story of an outstate minister who visited the Chicago meetings, "received a new baptism of the Holy Spirit, went home
and began an earnest, vigorous work amongst his people,
resulting in one hundred additions to his church."[9] Within
the city, revitalized clergymen enjoyed a similar surge in
religious interest among their parishioners generated apparently by the revival meetings. From mid-October to Mid-
January the city's newspapers reported almost daily on the
revival and the unusual religious happenings in many of
Chicago's churches. Bishop Cheny, a Chicago Methodist,
related a pleasant dilemma not unlike that experienced by
other city ministers.

> I gave up yesterday at the Sunday-school to a pre-
> sentation of the way to be saved, setting aside the
> usual lesson, and trying to make the way of salva-
> tion as plain as possible. I noticed that there was
> a good deal of interest, so I invited any who wished
> to meet me for prayer, to come into one of the little

> rooms, after school, in which I had the sexton place
> ten or twelve chairs for them. But, to our surprise,
> there were so many inquirers that we were obliged
> to take them into the large lecture-room. Not only
> scholars, but teachers, were present, some of them
> seeking Christ themselves, and others bringing mem-
> bers of their classes.[10]

Chamberlain, the Congregationalist, related that "at the close
of my sermon on Sunday morning I was kept for an hour
right in the main audience-room of my church talking to people who wanted to be saved." Bishop Fallows of St. Paul's
Reformed Episcopal Church of Chicago testified in late November that most of the forty new members received into his
church a week previous "had been converted during the
present revival services." One leading Methodist clergyman
protested mildly that "we have inquiry-meetings all the while.
I can't go down town without having an inquiry-meeting at
the corner; can't make a pastoral call but there is an inquiry-
meeting."[11] The Moody revival did boost, at least temporarily,
the morale of the city's evangelical clergy and breathed new
life into many of their congregations.

The long-term impact of the Moody revival on the Chicago churches is more difficult to assess. To be sure, the
spirit of religious interest did not cease immediately upon the
departure of Moody and Sankey to Boston. In February, the
Advance reported that "the religious activity of the Chicago
churches, though less concentrated than when Moody and
Sankey were here, is believed to be greater than ever." Attendance at the noonday prayer meetings at Farwell Hall,
the paper said, regularly numbered more than a thousand
persons. The WCTU reported continued successes in its
temperance efforts. And Sunday afternoon Bible classes at
First Congregational Church and Third Presbyterian Church,
begun as a result of revival interest, still flourished in mid-
February. [12]

Despite the optimism of some reporters, however, signs
of an ebb in revival excitement in Chicago were quickly evident. After mid-January the secular press turned its attention to other items of interest to readers and scarcely mentioned revival except in brief reports of Moody's activities in
Boston. Even the Inter-Ocean, a newspaper always sympathetic to religious work, commented shortly after Moody and

Sankey's departure on the steady decline in interest in the
evening services conducted by Whittle and Stebbins. Initially
held at the Tabernacle, the special services soon were moved
to Plymouth Congregational Church due to the increasingly
sparse crowds. Near the end of February these meetings
ceased altogether, and the revival in Chicago was for all
purpose ended. [13]

One helpful means of gauging the enduring results of
the revival for Chicago's churches is to examine carefully
the numbers of new members or probationers added to the
church rolls during and after the revival. Each of the major
denominations published annual compendiums on church membership which included statistics for the individual churches
as well as for regions. Several intensive studies of this data
have been published which include quantitative estimates of
Moody's impact on particular cities. In at least three cases,
analysts have concluded that the positive effects of the revival meetings on church membership were short-lived. Church
rolls increased significantly during the evangelist's stay and
for a brief period thereafter, but as the revival excitement
wore off, the number of new accessions to the churches declined so as to offset completely the initial gains. [14] A slightly
more favorable assessment of Moody's impact on church growth
is offered by James F. Findlay. Findlay examined Moody revivals in several large cities and concluded that "in terms of
church membership the revivals had a negative effect on the
Congregational and Presbyterian denominations, and a mixed,
or perhaps slightly positive, effect on the Methodists." [15]

This examination of the Chicago revival meetings con-
firms generally the conclusions reached in previous local
studies of Moody revivals. Between 1871 and 1880 the Methodist churches of Chicago averaged a yearly net increase in
membership of 282 persons. In the year following Moody's
Chicago labors the Methodist churches of the Chicago district
enjoyed a cumulative net increase of 428 members, a sizable
increase over the preceding year. The blessing of these
churches was, however, brief. In 1878 cumulative membership for the churches actually declined by 439 persons, and
Methodist "population density" (the number of Methodists
relative to the total city population) fell by three-tenths of
a percent. [16] The gains of the revival year in membership
were lost entirely.

Table 7 indicates that the immediate effect of the Moody

revival on the Methodist churches of Chicago probably is evidenced best by the large number of probationers whom the churches reported that year: 891 individuals began the process leading to formal membership in Methodist churches in the Chicago area in 1877.   The disastrous decline in net membership for these churches in 1878 and the simultaneous return of the number of probationers to prerevival levels suggests that the revival promoted only a temporary surge of interest in church membership for the Methodists.   Indeed, as revival excitement ebbed, the Methodists of Chicago as a whole apparently found it more difficult to attract and retain members than had been their experience in the prerevival years.

TABLE 7

Membership of the Rock River Conference
of the Methodist Episcopal Church,
1871-1880

Year	Membership	Probationers	Density (%)
1871	5237	495	1.6
1872	5495	546	1.5
1873	5988	594	1.6
1874	6463	477	1.6
1875	6997	531	1.8
1876	7017	600	1.7
1877	7310	891	1.7
1878	7738	613	1.8
1879	7299	490	1.5
1880	7779	533	1.5

Source: Methodist Episcopal Church, Rock River Conference, minutes, 1871-1880.

The Presbyterian churches of Chicago seem to have fared somewhat better numerically from the 1876 revival, yet Presbyterian growth in Chicago was almost at a standstill over the final three years of the decade.   During the 1870s, the churches of the Chicago Presbytery received yearly an average net cumulative increase of 559 members.   In 1877,

however, cumulative membership for these churches rose by
1,268 persons. The positive short-term effect of the Moody
revival upon the city's Presbyterian churches is perhaps
even more dramatically illustrated by the surge of new admissions to the churches. Table 8 shows that the number of
new admittants to the several Presbyterian churches in 1877
was almost double that of any other year in the decade. When
the new accessions are further distinguished as received by
"examination," rather than by letter, the increase is almost
triple the average number received in like manner over the

TABLE 8

Membership of the Chicago Presbytery
of the United Presbyterian Church,
1870-1880

Year	Membership	New Accessions	Density (%)
1870	3516	902	1.2
1871	4700	763	1.4
1872	4970	736	1.4
1873	5327	1036	1.4
1874	6071	1122	1.5
1875	6926	1254	1.7
1876	7235	1038	1.8
1877	8503	2093	2.0
1878	8835	1118	2.0
1879	8902	957	1.8
1880	8825	914	1.7

Source: Presbyterian Church, U.S.A., minutes, 1870-1880.

decade.[17] Like the experience of the Methodist churches of
Chicago, the Presbyterian growth was short-lived. The yearly
number of new accessions returned to prerevival levels. And,
most significantly, like the Methodists, the Presbyterian
churches of Chicago found it difficult even to sustain those
membership levels in the latter years of the 1870s. Not only
did the churches cease to grow in numbers, but in the period
from 1878 to 1880, the Presbytery suffered a net cumulative
decrease of 10 members, and the number of Presbyterians relative to the city population declined sharply.

The experience of the Congregational churches of Chicago paralleled closely that of the Presbyterians and Methodists (see Table 9). Like the revival-oriented denominations
examined above, Congregational membership rose significantly
in the immediate aftermath of the revival. Thereafter, church
growth among the Congregationalists returned to normal, if
respectable, rates. But in the final years of the decade,
Congregational membership decreased cumulatively in size by
78 persons.

TABLE 9

Membership of the Seven Largest
Congregational Churches of Chicago,
1870-1880

Year	Membership	New Accessions	Density (%)
1870	1698	464	.6
1871	2041	422	.6
1872	2234	482	.6
1873	2442	317	.6
1874	2427	313	.6
1875	2619	467	.7
1876	2871	376	.7
1877	3037	351	.7
1878	3543	728	.8
1879	3850	383	.8
1880	3772	300	.7

Statistics are inclusive as of September 30 of the preceding
year.

Source: Congregational Quarterly, 1870-1878; and the Year-
book, Congregational Association of Illinois, 1879-1880.

This brief examination of Methodist, Presbyterian, and
Congregationalist membership in Chicago in the 1870s supports
most previous assessments of Moody's effect upon local church
growth. These three denominations, along with certain Baptist and Reformed Episcopal congregations, were the most
supportive of the revival effort. They anticipated positive

benefits as a result of the coming of Moody and Sankey to
Chicago. What happened, in fact, was a sizable, but temporary, increase in membership and religious interest.   In
1877 the experience of several Chicago churches warranted
the enthusiastic reviews which most clergymen gave of the
Moody meetings. The numerical gains, however, were fleet-
ing and reserved completely for the years of the revival.
Perhaps the labor violence of 1877 diminished the spiritual
vitality of evangelicals who had seen in the revival a hoped-
for solution to impending labor/capital conflict.   Perhaps the
city's ministers generally lacked Moody's unique abilities to
organize workers and instill in them a sense of the urgency
of evangelism. Perhaps such extraordinary religious excitement as was stimulated by the revival normally is followed
by a temporary decline, or even depression, of religious life.
Such high levels of emotion and energy must, in time, ex-
haust the most devoted of persons. Yet, one wonders if,
in terms of membership, these churches would have been perhaps as strong or stronger in 1880 had the evangelists not
come to Chicago.

It is, however, probably inappropriate to judge the
merits of the revival for the churches primarily upon postrevival membership rates. It is also perhaps inappropriate
to treat the nonmaintenance of revival energy as a mystery.
For revival itself is the abnormal condition of church life.
And the Moody services certainly did revive interest in the
churches. Christian laypersons and many clergymen did enjoy a season of spiritual renewal and refreshment. The community myths associated with Protestantism in America were
reinforced, hymnody was revitalized, and the Protestant
emphases on preaching and evangelism were reaffirmed. To
ask revival to do more than this is unjust.

In assessing the results of the Moody campaign for the
Chicago churches it is also relevant to inquire into the per-
manence of the new church members in their several congregations. This question addresses the enduring significance
of the revival historically and sociologically. Surprisingly,
historians of revival rarely have addressed it, perhaps because the exercise is fraught with difficulties.

The immediate problem confronting the researcher is
a lack of church records sufficiently complete and extensive
to allow one to follow the church experience of members over

a lifetime. Nineteenth-century clerks of churches were no-
toriously poor record keepers. Data is sketchy and incomplete
with few explanations offered for actions taken with regard
to individual church members. Even more serious is the
loss of records by fire or carelessness.[18] Even if complete
records did exist, the research is tedious and time-consuming
and the results at best, tentative. After all, the sincerity
of religious commitment is finally a subjective matter and the
reason for dropping membership is not necessarily a loss of
personal religious faith.

Recognizing these limitations, I offer the results of a
study of the more than five hundred Chicagoans who joined
five selected revival churches in the course of the revival.[19]
Of this population 20.8 percent remained lifelong active members of the church they joined in 1876-1877 and another 32.2
percent transferred church membership at some point in later
years.[20] Often transfers occurred within a few years of the
revival and were to another evangelical congregation in the
city. What happened to these persons subsequently cannot
be determined. The evidence suggests, however, that more
than half of the church members remained sufficiently committed to their new-found faith to maintain the status of active members or to concern themselves with presenting requests for letters of transfer in order to maintain credible
membership in another church of their preference. At the
same time, a significantly large portion of the persons examined in this study either dropped membership, were "lost,"
or, in the case of Methodist probationers, never followed
through on their professed intention to join the church. How
one interprets this evidence is largely a matter of emphasis.
Since almost half of the new church members or probationers
were lost to the churches, the firmness of their original com-
mitments appears problematic. Were these persons simply
swept up by the emotionalism and excitement of the revival?
On the other hand, more than half of the new admittants
demonstrated a continued interest in their churches, some
holding important church offices. For certain of these persons the revival seems to have marked the beginning of an
enduring spiritual commitment.

In several instances the life stories of individual converts can be followed with some detail. One professed convert, Benjamin Patrick, had inherited a considerable fortune
from his father's business and enjoyed some prestige in Chicago

before lapsing into alcoholism and losing much of his wealth and social prominence. Patrick was converted at a temperance meeting in Farwell Hall. The "Almighty," he said, had beat the plans of his friends to bring him to the Moody meetings that he might be "saved." After his conversion and public testimony, he was received into membership at the Third Presbyterian Church. Patrick remained a member of the church for thirty years. However, his appetite for liquor returned at some point, for Patrick was dropped from membership some years later due to "chronic drunkenness."[21]

For other converts, the transformation of spirit and character which began in 1876 appears to have continued throughout a lifetime. Merton Smith, an avowed atheist, was converted at the Tabernacle, gave up his business, and ultimately entered into full-time personal mission and social work among Chicago's poor. Tony Delight, who was "saved" at a Tabernacle service, "dismissed his mistress, stopped drinking and gambling" and became himself an evangelist. W. O. Lattimore, an army officer who allegedly suffered from alcoholism, was converted upon hearing one of Sankey's gospel hymns. Lattimore took up clerical studies and became a prominent minister. Another of Moody's Chicago converts, Eric Janson, returned to his homeland of Finland and spent the remaining years of his life establishing numerous Baptist churches there.[22] The evidence is too meager to do more than relate examples of this sort. They do make clear, however, the error in either too readily dismissing the significance of the revival for individual persons or of accepting reported numbers of converts or new church members as an accurate gauge of the spiritual impact of the meetings.[23]

The results of the Moody and Sankey meetings in Chicago for the city's Protestant churches can best be appraised as a mixed blessing. There is little reason to doubt that the swell of religious interest during the revival months was real and extraordinary. For certain of the local clergymen and churches, the meetings seem to have revitalized spiritual life and provided fresh enthusiasm for evangelistic outreach and ministry. For some individuals the revival was nothing less than a watershed in the course of their life's experience. Yet, the religious services failed to bridge the chasm between the city's Protestant churches and the laboring poor. And the gains in membership by many of the churches were transient.

The enduring results of the Chicago revival, however, are not to be measured solely in terms of numbers of converts or increases in church membership. Of equal importance was the revival's social impact in the city. Chapter Two demonstrated that Chicago in 1876 was beset by social turmoil. In particular, middle-class, native-born Protestants in the city were troubled by the swelling foreign-born and Catholic populations. To these alien elements in the city, Protestants frequently attributed a multitude of social and economic ills. Revivalism seemed to some Protestants a panacea for their problems--a means to restrain social disorder and promote individual discipline. Moody and Sankey, it was hoped, would lessen the sources of their stress and strain by evangelizing large numbers of the unchurched foreign-born and poor. These converts then would embrace Protestant modes of behavior and ways of thinking. This did not, in fact, occur.

In the months following the revival, relations between labor and capital and between the working poor and the middle and upper classes deteriorated. Nowhere was this evidenced more clearly than in the Protestant reaction to the labor violence which erupted in the summer of 1877.

The strikes began in July when financially troubled railroads in the East cut wages for already underpaid employees. Rail workers reacted by walking off their jobs. Widespread rumors that the railroad companies were managed wastefully combined with bitterness over the arbitrary decreases of pay to fan the flames of worker resentment. The issue seemed clear. That employees had a right to demand higher pay the Tribune conceded, but that a company had the right to lower a man's pay to a cent a day, if it desired, appeared to the paper the prerogative of the company's owners. The Tribune's opinion expressed concisely the understanding of political economy held by most middle- and upper-class Chicago Protestants.[24]

As sensational reports of violence and destruction in the East reached the city, Chicagoans geared for similar unrest. Field, Leiter & Company armed the employees of its wholesale store, and double guards were placed about the reaper plant owned by Cyrus McCormick. When the city's railroad workers formally announced a strike on July 23, thousands of Chicagoans gathered, perhaps significantly, in

the Moody and Sankey Tabernacle, to hear leading citizens
and clergymen discuss the preservation of order and the
restoration of business life. The Chicago veterans equipped
two companies of members with breech-loading rifles and offered their services to the city. Members of the Board of
Trade pledged to arm themselves and assemble at the board's
rooms "subject to the call of the mayor for the defense of
the city."[25]

On July 25 mobs composed of a few workers and large
numbers of the idle and curious smashed in the windows of
the Chicago, Burlington & Quincy roundhouse and set off
three days of violence. Frightened policemen, hearing reports of "civil war" in other cities, showed little reticence in
resorting to clubs and guns in suppressing the mobs. By
the time the city was again tranquil at least thirteen men
were dead and scores more had been injured.[26]

Numerous evangelical spokesmen joined employers and
the secular press in condemning the strikes. W. W. Patton,
minister of the First Congregational Church, spoke for many
Chicago evangelicals when he acknowledged the right of
workers "to accept or to refuse a certain rate of wages" but
not "to prevent another man from accepting that rate and
performing the work." Moreover, Patton argued, "in a time
of universal depression ... laborers even in their poverty
must not expect to be made exceptions to the general rule
of loss, but must submit cheerfully to necessary reductions
in wages." One Baptist minister of Chicago argued that the
pay cuts were not the fault of employers at all but rather
"the result of laws as inexorable as the laws of gravitation."
Labor, another Chicago minister asserted, was "indebted to
the capitalists for their living, and when they warred on them
they warred upon themselves."[27]

If employers were not at fault, who was? Evangelical
spokesmen saw behind the trouble the specter of a Catholic
or communistic plot in which "Romish" and atheist leaders
vied to use the large numbers of recent immigrant workers,
now unemployed, for their own schemes to undermine democracy. In a lengthy editorial, the Northwestern Christian
Advocate termed the violence

> communistic ... [and] principally the importation and
> child of the trades-unions. These are foreign to

> our institutions. They are chiefly composed of
> foreigners. They have brought with them their
> infidelity and disregard for the sanctity of the Sab-
> bath, and for the rights of others.[28]

The Reverend Dr. McChesney, pastor of the Park Avenue
Methodist Church, echoed this opinion. "One great cause"
of the turmoil, McChesney believed, "was the flocking to this
country of the criminal classes of the Old World,--brought
here, naturalized, and marched up to the polls to reform the
country!" A Baptist minister, the Reverend N. F. Ravlin,
was careful to observe to his listeners on the Sunday after
the riots that "the mob was composed entirely of foreigners,
and there was a foreign element in this country which threatened our institutions."[29]

Still other spokesmen stressed the Catholic heritage of
the strikers. The Independent described the mobs as "composed chiefly of those for whose character the Catholic Church
is responsible, whose parents lived and died in the Catholic
Church, and whose religious instruction has been received in
the Catholic Church." Obviously, the magazine expected its
readers readily to associate a Catholic upbringing with poverty
and an innate tendency toward violence. If readers were
hesitant to make the association, the Independent made clear
the connection several issues later when it quoted a "very
prominent citizen" and member of the Catholic church as
being "mortified" to have to admit that, indeed, "Catholics
are the worst class of citizens we have."[30]

Such language makes clear, obviously, that the revival
had not lessened the existing religious and ethnic tensions
in Chicago. More probably, the Moody and Sankey meetings
hardened the response of middle-class evangelicals to the
strikers. For, as shown, Moody's sermons reinforced existing Protestant attitudes about political economy. They condemned as lazy any man who refused available work regardless of the wages offered and asserted the credibility of the
Protestant work ethic. The revivalist encouraged company
loyalty among workers and assured laborers of the true benevolence of their employers. He expressed confidence in the
individualistic, competitive, free-enterprise system. And
those who defied the system, Moody made clear, were sinful,
dangerous, and unpatriotic--a threat to the safety of the city
and nation. Their actions deserved immediate and harsh sup-
pression.

The conflict of cultures persisted in other areas of city
life as well. Ethnic and religious interests continued to align
themselves with particular political parties in the postrevival
years. In 1879, the Republican Albert Wright's close identification with temperance cost him enough foreign-born voters
to give the election to Carter Harrison. Harrison, the Demo-
crat, proceeded to enjoy five consecutive terms in office
largely because he was able to identify himself as a lineal
descendant of the Irish, Swedes, and Germans, and to spend
much time in association with members of each group.[31] In
the election of 1883 not even the generous support of businessmen, the appeals to employees by their employers, and the
castigation of Harrison by the Protestant clergy could over-
come the ethnic support for the Democrats, "the great un-
washed," as the Baptist Standard called them.[32]

Antagonisms related to issues of individual behavior
and social morality also appeared heightened in postrevival
Chicago. Sabbatarian and temperance advocates expanded
their efforts, seeking to impose Protestant morality on all
inhabitants of the city. The Citizen's League, composed of
many Moody supporters and founded in 1877, for example,
sought the enforcement of all laws and ordinances concerning
the sale of liquor to minors.[33] The Chicago WCTU entered
upon a period of sustained growth and social influence.[34]
Evangelical Protestants also filled the ranks of the Relief and
Aid Society and the Charity Organization Society, the latter
founded in 1883. A study of these Chicago organizations
emphasized their Protestant orientation and their role in
disseminating middle-class, Protestant values.[35]

Despite such efforts Chicago Protestants were unable
to achieve the kind of social order they desired. Sabbath
laws were relaxed, and existing statutes frequently went un-
enforced. By the end of the nineteenth century, temperance
efforts had achieved only limited successes in Chicago. And
the laboring poor continued generally to ignore the city's
Prot stant churches. "Have the working classes fallen away
from the churches or have the churches fallen away from the
working classes?" inquired Chicago clergyman Charles F. Goss
in 1892 as he meditated upon the workingman's indifference
and, at times, hostility toward Protestant religious institutions. "There is no place," said Goss, "in the average Chicago church for the poor man ... surrounded by individuals
who not only regard poverty as a disgrace, but by their

vulgar display endeavour to perpetually remind the poor man
of his poverty."36 Only very gradually and in small numbers
were Chicago Protestants able to transcend their cultural
framework and treat more sympathetically the growing res-
tiveness of the urban poor.37

    Clearly the revival did not harmonize the conflict of
attitudes, values, and behavior which so troubled Protestants
in 1876 Chicago. Instead, the Moody services probably exacerbated cultural, ethnic, and religious antipathies and distrust in the city. For the revival, I have argued, strengthened and contributed to a sense of evangelical and middle-
class solidarity based on common sentiments and attitudes.
Certain segments of the city's population increasingly saw
themselves as one. The economic and denominational distinctions among these peoples perhaps seemed to diminish in light
of the broad and generalized population--namely, foreign-
born and Roman Catholic--who did not share their conceptions.
Moody, by his preaching, imparted to these conflicting attitudes a sense of ultimate good and ultimate evil. The salvation of individuals, as well as that of the city and nation, he
connected directly to the maintenance of prevailing Protestant
conceptions of a godly moral and social order. Moody's sermons helped to define for many Chicagoans the kinds of feelings, attitudes, habits, and values which divided the saints
from the sinners, the saved from the lost, the good from the
bad. The revival meetings in Chicago, thereby, probably
worked to fragment the existing social structure into two
loosely defined, generalized camps--the community of the
righteous (middle-class, Anglo-American, and Protestant)
and the community of the unrighteous (foreign-born and
Catholic). While these communities possessed no formal organizational structure and were avowedly apolitical, their
sense of right attitudes and behavior could and did take
political forms. Each saw the other, increasingly, as the
enemy of a just moral and social order.

    The Chicago revival also points up the sometimes inti-
mate relation of religion with ethnic and class identities. This
should be of little surprise since people seem naturally to seek
community with their own kind, with those who share similar
values and interpretations of the ultimate meaning of life.
The revival of 1876 tended to enhance this sense of community
for middle-class, Anglo-American, white city dwellers. Its
rhetoric, in fact, sacralized certain middle-class social and

moral conceptions, bestowing upon them an aura of ultimate and universal validity. While the purpose of this essay has been to examine and assess the significance of Moody and the revival in Chicago and not to make pejorative judgments, it seems appropriate to observe the danger inherent in too readily identifying cultural values with absolute truth. If their violent denunciations of the social habits of immigrants or the labor unrest of 1877 be adequate indication, revival Chicagoans were little able or willing to bridge with sensitivity or understanding the cultural chasm between themselves and the immigrant and laboring poor of the city. They had, perhaps unwittingly, made the New Testament Christ of the poor, hungry, and socially outcast into a sentimental, moralistic, legalistic, and middle-class Savior of the 1870s.

Appendix

MEMBERSHIP INCREASES BY CHURCH
AS OF JANUARY 17, 1877

	By Profession	By Letter	Total
1st Presbyterian	26	8	34
2nd Presbyterian	67	13	80
3rd Presbyterian	126	35	164
4th Presbyterian	15	8	23
5th Presbyterian	68	14	82
6th Presbyterian	50	32	82
Holland Presbyterian	16	8	24
Westminster Presby.	40	8	48
41st St. Presby.	20	6	26
1st Congregational	98	45	143
Union Park Cong.	28	26	54
New England Cong.	48	8	56
Leavitt Cong.	41	16	57
Christ Reformed Epis.	35	25	60
St. Paul's Ref. Epis.	25	25	50
Immanuel Ref. Epis.	10		10
Good Shepherd Ref. Epis.			120
Other Epis.			60
1st Baptist	40	12	52
2nd Baptist	23	29	52
Michigan Ave. Bapt.	22	6	28
4th Baptist	10	16	26
Centennial Baptist	6	12	18
Olivet Baptist	1		1
Free Baptist	12	3	15
1st Methodist Epis.	65	44	109
Wabash Ave. M. E.	65	8	73
Michigan Ave. M.E.	35	43	78
Centenary M.E.	35	35	70

	By Profession	By Letter	Total
Grace M.E.	50		50
Park Ave. M.E.	82	45	127
Ada St. M.E.	35		35
Western Ave. M.E.	25	35	60
Grant Place M.E.	45		45
Zion German M.E.	18		18
Other M.E.			300
Chicago Ave. Church	45		45
TOTAL	1,338	567	2,372

CHAPTER I

1. See, for instance, the October 1876 issues of Chicago Tribune, and Chicago Daily Inter-Ocean.

2. New York Observer, 54 (January 20, 1876): 19.

3. Standard 24 (January 25, 1877): 4.

4. In this study the term "evangelical" refers to those persons who stressed personal religious experience within a theological context in continuity with historic reformed Protestantism. Evangelicals emphasized the theme of God's salvation through faith in Jesus Christ and his efficacious death. They asserted zealously the sole authority of Scripture in matters of faith and worship. Revivals and conversions were sought and accepted by most evangelicals. Evangelicals were convinced that acceptance of the Gospel message would result in immediate personal moral reform and virtuous living. See Winthrop Hudson, Religion in America, 3rd ed. (New York: Charles Scribner's Sons, 1965), p. 80.; William G. McLoughlin, The American Evangelicals 1800-1900 (New York: Harper Torchbooks, 1968), pp. 2-4, 11-13, 14-19; Robert Baird, Religion in America (1856; reprint, New York: Harper Torchbooks, 1970), pp. 173-74.

5. Stanley N. Gundry, Love Them In: The Proclamation Theology of D. L. Moody (Chicago: Moody Press, 1976), p. 10. It is not beyond reason to suppose that Moody did reach such large numbers of people, at least cumulatively. He commonly offered two addresses daily, six days a week. Some services attracted ten to twenty thousand persons. He took few lengthy vacations in his career. When one adds to this the contacts he made through sermons published in the media and in collections for sale, the numbers are even more plausible. While exposure does not equal impact, historians probably have undervalued the significance of Moody's widespread public outreach. For other statistical estimates, see John C. Pollock, Moody: A Biographical Portrait of the Pacesetter in Modern Mass Evangelism (New York: Macmillan Press, 1963), pp. 166, 242, 283-84; and Charles T. Cook and William H. Houghton, Tell Me About Moody (London: Marshall, Morgan & Scott, 1936), p. 117.

6. Martin Marty, in the foreword to James F. Findlay, Dwight L. Moody: American Evangelist, 1837-1899 (Chicago: University of Chicago Press, 1969), p. 1.

7. Findlay's insights into Moody have contributed significantly to the forming of my own judgments about the evangelist. Other biographies of Moody which are sometimes helpful but tend toward hagiography are Richard K. Curtis, They Called Him Mister Moody (New York: Doubleday, 1962); J. Wilbur Chapman, The Life and Work of Dwight L. Moody (Philadelphia: International, 1900); and William R. Moody, The Life of D. L. Moody (New York: Revell, 1900). The last study, by Moody's eldest son, is eulogistic but an indispensable source of information.

8. On the selection and identification of "revival churches," see Chapter Five.

9. In the course of this study I have read a myriad of newspapers and weekly magazines. The Tribune was examined for the five years prior to the revival and the year following it. The Inter-Ocean and Times were read from 1875 to 1877. The several Chicago-based religious magazines--the Presbyterian Interior, the Baptist Standard, the Methodist Northwestern Christian Advocate, and the Congregationalist Advance--were scrutinized closely for the period from 1872 to 1877. Numerous other publications which commented on Moody or expressed popular opinion were also perused.

10. Bessie L. Pierce, A History of Chicago, 3 vols. (New York: Alfred A. Knopf, 1937-57).

11. See, for example, Louise C. Wade, Graham Taylor: Pioneer for Social Justice, 1851-1938 (Chicago: University of Chicago Press, 1964); and the many studies of Hull House. Recent additions of significance to Chicago's religious history are Charles Shanabruck, Chicago's Catholics (South Bend, Ind.: University of Notre Dame Press, 1980); Joseph J. Parot, Polish Catholics in Chicago, 1850-1920 (DeKalb: Northern Illinois University Press, 1981).

12. Pierce, History of Chicago, 3:545.

13. William Tremmel, Religion: What Is It? (New York: Holt, Rinehart & Winston, 1976), p. 17.

CHAPTER II

1. Bessie L. Pierce, As Others See Chicago: Impressions of Visitors, 1673-1933 (Chicago: University of Chicago Press, 1933), p. 171; idem, History of Chicago, 3:64, 2:77.

2. Herman Kogan and Lloyd Wendt, Chicago: A Pictorial History
    (New York: Dutton, 1958), p. 1; Pierce, History of Chicago,
    2:5; Tenth Federal Census, "Report on the Social Statistics of
    Cities," 18:510.

3. Pierce, History of Chicago, 3:469; Harold Mayer and Richard
    C. Wade, Chicago: Growth of a Metropolis (Chicago: Univer-
    sity of Chicago Press, 1969), pp. 97-98; Emmett Dedmond,
    Fabulous Chicago (New York: Random House, 1953), p. 97.

4. Monetary estimates here and elsewhere in this study are in
    contemporary (1876) value amounts.

5. Department of Development and Planning, Historic Chicago:
    The Settlement of Chicago (Chicago, 1976), p. 42; Pierce,
    History of Chicago, 3:3-5; Dedmond, Fabulous Chicago, pp. 97-
    107.   A dramatic pictorial account is in Mayer and Wade, Growth
    of a Metropolis, pp. 107-115.   An equally impressive eyewitness
    account is Alexander Frear, "The Great Fire of 1871," in Pierce,
    As Others See Chicago, pp. 191-206.

6. Tribune, October 11, 1871; Kogan and Wendt, Pictorial History,
    p. 127.

7. Mayer and Wade, Growth of a Metropolis, p. 117; Kogan and
    Wendt, Pictorial History, p. 131; Pierce, As Others See Chicago,
    p. 208; Pierce History of Chicago, 3:19.

8. Quoted in Finis Farr, Chicago: A Personal History of America's
    Most American City (New Rochelle, N.Y.: Arlington House,
    1973), p. 108.

9. Lloyd Lewis and Henry J. Smith, Chicago: The History of Its
    Reputation (New York: Harcourt, Brace & Co., 1929), pp.
    137-38; Pierce, As Others See Chicago, p. 208; Mayer and
    Wade, Growth of a Metropolis, pp. 118-20.

10. A census conducted by the Department of Education in 1876
    listed the population of Chicago at 407,661, reported in Tenth
    Federal Census, 18:   150.

11. Pierce, History of Chicago, 3:21; Farr, Personal History, p.
    118.

12. Pierce, History of Chicago, 3:516.   In 1870 the German popula-
    tion of Chicago formed 36.7% of the foreign-born population, the
    Irish 27.7%, and the Scandinavians 9.5%.

13. Ibid., 3:20-31.

14. Wade and Mayer, Growth of a Metropolis, p. 154; Pierce, History

of Chicago, 3:20-31. See also the excellent map of ethnic concentrations in Historic Chicago, p. 38.

15.   Pierce, History of Chicago, 3:21-31; Historic Chicago, pp. 54-
      55.

16.   Carl Sandburg, Chicago Poems (New York: Henry Holt & Co.,
      1916), p. 3.

17.   Pierce, History of Chicago, 3:108-44; Lewis and Smith, Chicago;
      pp. 143-46; Wayne Andrews, Battle for Chicago (New York:
      Harcourt, Brace & Co., 1946), pp. 79-103.

18.   Pierce, History of Chicago, 3:145-65; Lewis and Smith, Chicago;
      p. 116; Kogan and Wendt, Pictorial History, p. 107.

19.   Pierce, History of Chicago, 3:174-82; Historic Chicago, p. 44.

20.   Pierce, History of Chicago, 3:178.

21.   Ibid., 3:59-66; Farr, Personal History, pp. 120-21; Dedmond,
      Fabulous Chicago, pp. 114-15.

22.   Pierce, History of Chicago, 3:485; Dedmond, Fabulous Chicago,
      p. 117.

23.   There were 39,488 Irish in Chicago in 1870. About three-
      quarters of these persons resided in southwest Chicago. Much
      smaller concentrations of Germans, Czechs, and Swedes also
      lived in this vicinity. See Historic Chicago, "Community Settle-
      ment Map for 1870."

24.   Tribune, June 19, 1873.

25.   Homer Hoyt, One Hundred Years of Land Values in Chicago,
      1830-1933 (Chicago: University of Chicago Press, 1933), pp.
      96-97; Pierce, History of Chicago, 3:52-55; Kogan and Wendt,
      Pictorial History, p. 100.

26.   Chicago Department of Health, Report, 1881, pp. 52, 70-71.
      The inspector, William H. Genung, attributed the high mortality
      rates of children and females directly to housing: "The females
      and children are compelled to remain 'at home' (indoors) day
      and night, and receive such injury as may be caused from
      breathing bad air from defective drains and plumbing, unven-
      tilated rooms, and defective heating apparatus."

27.   Ibid., p. 30. This report shows that the most congested areas
      in the city were the locations of ethnic groups. Wards in which
      native-born Americans predominated were not severely crowded;
      see the table, p. 70. See also Hoyt, Land Values in Chicago,
      p. 104; Mayer and Wade, Growth of a Metropolis, p. 150.

28. Mayer and Wade, Growth of a Metropolis, pp. 150-54.

29. Quoted in Kogan and Wendt, Pictorial History, p. 138; Pierce,
     History of Chicago, 3:398-400, 469, 471, 474-75. Statistics on
     school enrollment are from Tenth Federal Census, 18: 510.

30. Standard 23 (July 27, 1876): 8; Churches of Chicago (Chicago:
     Lakeside Press, 1878). Actual numbers for the major denomina-
     tions were 21 Baptist, 16 Congregational, 17 Episcopal, 7 Re-
     formed Episcopal, 25 Methodist, 23 Presbyterian, and 33 Roman
     Catholic. The largest number of the remaining churches were
     members of small ethnic associations.

31. Pierce, History of Chicago, 3:424-25, 544.

32. See Chapter Five.

33. A brief history and description of the churches of Chicago is
     in A. T. Andreas, History of Chicago from the Earliest Period
     to the Present Time, 3 vols. (Chicago: A. T. Andreas, 1884-
     86), 3:763-833.

34. J. W. Sheahan, "Chicago," Scribner's Monthly 11 (September
     1875): 547.

35. Nation 21 (November 18, 1875): 321. See also Interior 7 (Feb-
     ruary 3, 1876): 4; Northwestern Christian Advocate 14 (Febru-
     ary 8, 1866): 44.

36. Andreas, History of Chicago, 3:793-94; Pierce, History of Chi-
     cago, 3:425. Denominational and interchurch missions in the
     1870s are described in Aaron I. Abell, The Urban Impact on
     American Protestantism, 1865-1900 (London: Archon Press,
     1962), pp. 27-56. A thorough overview of the city mission
     movement among evangelicals in the latter nineteenth century
     is Norris Magnuson, Salvation in the Slums: Evangelical Social
     Work, 1865-1920 (Metuchen, N.J.: Scarecrow Press and the
     ATLA, 1977).

37. These figures are drawn from an examination of the statistical
     records of the denominations for 1876.

38. Pierce, History of Chicago, 3:443. On the YMCA, see C. Howard
     Hopkins, History of the YMCA in North America (New York:
     Association Press, 1951).

39. Pierce, As Others See Chicago, p. 164.

40. Pierce, History of Chicago, 3:543.

41. Interior 7 (August 17, 1876): 4.

42. Kogan and Wendt, Pictorial History, p. 102; Dedmond, Fabulous Chicago, pp. 139ff.

43. Abby Farwell Ferry, Reminiscences of John V. Farwell by His Elder Daughter, 2 vols. (Chicago: R. F. Seymour, 1928), 2:125.

44. See Andreas, History of Chicago, 3:417. In 1877 Moody collected $110,000 in contributions to remove the indebtedness of the Chicago YMCA.

45. Andreas, History of Chicago, 3:709, estimates that the Protestant religious press of Chicago reached at least 300,000 in aggregate circulation. The four papers listed were by far the most significant of the Protestant weeklies.

46. For studies of this nationwide revival, see Timothy Smith, Revivalism and Social Reform in Mid-Nineteenth Century America (New York: Harper & Row, 1957); and Sandra S. Sizer, Gospel Hymns and Social Religion (Philadelphia: Temple University Press, 1978).

47. For a detailed account of these institutions, see Findlay, Dwight L. Moody, pp. 75-80, 100-101, 106-8, 111-12.

CHAPTER III

1. Historical Discourses by the Rev. A. E. Kittridge, Centennial Sabbath, July 2, 1876, Presbyterian Historical Society Library, Philadelphia.

2. In another sermon preached in July 1876, Kittridge urged his listeners to shout a "defiant 'No!' to every demand of the Papacy." He condemned Sabbath breaking and intemperance and urged political activism to combat these evils. "This is God's platform.... Religion and politics! The Savior married them, and what God has joined together, let not man nor party put asunder."

3. Tribune, February 7, 1876.

4. Ibid., October 16, 1876.

5. Western Manufacturer 4 (March 8, 1877): 259; see also Standard 23 (July 27, 1876): 4.

6. There existed in predepression Chicago an extraordinary confidence in the ability of the nation to absorb endless numbers of workers into its economy. In 1874 the Tribune prophesied about the coming era: "Europe will open her gates like a

conquered city. Her people will come forth to us subdued by
admiration of our glory and envy of our perfect peace. On to
the Rocky Mountains and still over to the Pacific our mighty
population will spread.... Our thirty millions will be tripled
in thirty years" (quoted in A Century of Tribune Editorials,
1847-1947 [Chicago, 1947], p. 28). This confidence was shaken
by the depressed economy of the 1870s and the massive unemployment which resulted.

7. Pierce, History of Chicago, 3:240; Andreas, History of Chicago,
    3:714. See Tribune, August 10, 1876, and August 23, 1876,
    for a listing of wage reductions by occupation. During the de-
    pression of the 1870s, average earnings for unskilled labor fell
    from $25 a week in 1873 to $9 a week in 1879.

8. Tribune, December 23, 1873; Pierce, History of Chicago, 3:241-
    42; Chicago Relief and Aid Society, The Sixteenth Annual Re-
    port of the Chicago Relief and Aid Society to the Common Coun-
    cil of the City of Chicago, 1873 (Chicago, 1874), pp. 7-10;
    The Seventeenth Annual Report, 1874, p. 8. An interesting
    study which focuses on the Relief and Aid Society is John Mayer,
    "Private Charities in Chicago from 1871 to 1915" (Ph.D. diss.,
    University of Minnesota, 1978).

9. Quoted in Pierce, History of Chicago, 3:243.

10. Chicago Evening Journal, May 9, 1876; Tribune, May 5, 1876,
    June 4, 1875.

11. Tribune, May 24, 1874.

12. Standard 24 (August 9, 1877): 6; Northwestern Christian Advo-
    cate 25 (August 1, 1877):5. For similar assessments in the
    secular press, see Tribune, May 10, 1876.

13. See the sermons of N. F. Ravlin, Galusha Anderson, and W. W.
    Patton printed in Tribune, July 30, 1877. For similar comments,
    see also the sermons printed in Inter-Ocean, July 30, 1877.

14. Tribune, May 9, 1876. See also Standard 23 (May 18, 1876):8;
    24 (November 11, 1875):3. On the political orientation of Chi-
    cago's newspapers, see Pierce, History of Chicago, 3:408-18.

15. Northwestern Christian Advocate 25 (August 1, 1877):5; Standard
    24 (August 9, 1877):6; Tribune, July 30, 1877. On the roots
    of anti-Catholic nativism, see Ray Allen Billington, The Protes-
    tant Crusade, 1800-1860: A Study of the Origins of the Ameri-
    can Nativism (Chicago: Quadrangle Books, 1938); and John
    Higham, Strangers in the Land: Patterns of American Nativism
    1860-1925 (New Brunswick, N.J.: Rutgers University Press,
    1955).

16. Tribune, February 19, 1876; Harper's Weekly 16 (December 1872):474. Charles Brace, The Dangerous Classes of New York (New York: Wynkoop & Hallenbeck, 1872), pp. 35, 70. See also comments in Tribune, March 12, 1876.

17. Western Catholic, February 26, 1881.

18. Tribune, August 17, October 10, 1873.

19. Advance 9 (August 3, 1876):913. See also Interior 6 (August 26, 1875):1; Northwestern Christian Advocate 22 (April 8, 1874):2; Advance 9 (March 12, 1876):491.

20. This story is drawn from reports in the Chicago Times and the Tribune for March 17 and 18, 1874. An excellent description of the sit-ins in Chicago is in Frances Willard, Glimpses of Fifty Years: The Autobiography of an American Woman (Chicago: Women's Temperance Publication Association, 1889), pp. 335ff.

21. Pierce, History of Chicago, 3:457-58; Sydney E. Ahlstrom, A Religious History of the American People (New Haven: Yale University Press, 1972), p. 867.

22. Willard, Glimpses of Fifty Years, pp. 335-60. The relationship between temperance and evangelicalism was well established by 1876. Willard recalled a temperance meeting several years earlier where "the ministers were on the platform in greater numbers than I have ever seen before or have seen since in that or any other city. They spoke, they sang, they prayed with the fervor of a Methodist camp meeting. Philip Bliss was at the organ and sang one of his sweetest songs."

23. J. F. Richmond, "The Dangerous Classes, and Their Treatment," Methodist Quarterly 55 (July 1873):455-74, suggested that "immigration, Roman Catholicism, alcoholism and overcrowding are the characteristics of our dangerous classes." Similar analyses, if less explicitly phrased, can be found in Standard 22 (October 28, 1875):5; New York Christian Advocate 48 (September 25, 1873):306; Congregational Quarterly 13 (October 1871):537-50.

24. Pierce, History of Chicago, 3:439.

25. John Francis Maguire, The Irish in America (1873; reprint, New York: Arno, 1969), p. 236.

26. Interior 8 (February 15, 1877):4. See also Advance 9 (August 31, 1876):973. Moody typified evangelical reasoning in this matter. His position is stated in James B. Dunn, ed., Moody's Talks on Temperance with Anecdotes and Incidents (New York: National Temperance Society, 1877).

27. An excellent study of the social attitudes and aspirations of
     middle-class supporters of temperance is Joseph Gusfield, Sym-
     bolic Crusade: Status Politics and the American Temperance
     Movement (Urbana: University of Illinois Press, 1963). For a
     discussion of some of the attitudes that gave impetus to the ef-
     forts of evangelicals in temperance work, see Clifford S. Grif-
     fin, Their Brother's Keepers, Moral Stewardship in the United
     States, 1800-1865. (New Brunswick, N.J.: Rutgers University
     Press, 1960), chap. 2.

28. Quoted in Robert T. Handy, A Christian America: Protestant
     Hopes and Historical Realities (New York: Oxford University
     Press, 1971), p. 85.

29. Standard 23 (January 20, 1876):4. Protestant concern with
     Sabbath observance was typified in the reaction of the young
     Moody to Sunday activities in Chicago. In letters written to
     his family during his first years in the city, Moody complained
     about the "wickedness" of a city where the Germans spent the
     Sabbath frolicking in beer gardens and the stores were open
     for business. See Moody to sister, October 6, 1856; Moody to
     brother, October 19, 1856, and December 16, 1856, in the Powell
     Collection, Moody Museum, Northfield, Massachusetts.

30. Findlay, Dwight L. Moody, p. 298; Interior 7 (May 25, 1876):5;
     Standard 22 (December 2, 1875):4. See also Northwestern
     Christian Advocate 15 (January 16, 1867):19; Advance 1 (Oc-
     tober 10, 1867):705; Interior 5 (November 26, 1874):4; 5 (De-
     cember 31, 1874):1; Standard 23 (January 20, 1876):4.

31. For a good discussion of Protestant cultural attitudes and values
     in this period, see the collection of essays in Daniel W. Howe,
     ed., Victorian America (Philadelphia: University of Philadelphia
     Press, 1976).

32. On the controversy over the "school question," see J. S. Kane,
     Catholic-Protestant Conflicts in America (Chicago: Regency
     Press, 1965), chap. 7; Billington Protestant Crusade, chap. 6;
     Robert D. Cross, The Emergence of Liberal Catholicism in
     America (Chicago: Quadrangle Books, 1968), chap. 7.

33. Hudson, Religion in America, p. 245.

34. Bernard McQuaid, The Public School Question (Boston, 1876),
     p. 28; Michael Mueller, Public School Education (New York,
     1873), p. 182.

35. Methodist Quarterly Review 52 (April 1870):206; Interior 7
     (February 17, 1876):1; 7 (September 14, 1876):4. An article
     published in the Baptist Quarterly expressed the Protestant
     argument eloquently: "The Bible ... is the constitution of our

constitution and our sub-fundamental law.... The Bible alone
constitutes us a body politic by the vital principle of authority,
and gives the ethical basis and sanction of our laws. In this
proper, vital, essential sense, is Christianity our national religion.... To know it and enjoy it, then, is a part of the political birthright of every child of our soil" William C. Conant,
"The Bible and the State," Baptist Quarterly 5 [July 1871]:284).

36. Advance 9 (January 20, 1876):353. See also Interior 7 (Febru-
     ary 16, 1876):1; Tribune, January 15, 1876.

37. The reading of the Bible in the Chicago public schools had been
     ended in October 1875.

38. This rendering of the Hanford murder is based upon reports
     for August 7, 8, 9, 1876, in Tribune, Times, and Inter-Ocean.

39. Ibid.

40. Ibid.

41. Northwestern Christian Advocate 24 (August 16, 1876):4; Ad-
     vance 9 (August 24, 1876):963. Virtually the same analysis
     of the events was expressed in Standard 23 (August 17, 1876):4.

42. Tribune, August 13, 1876; Inter-Ocean, August 13, 1876. Five
     sermons printed in these newspapers addressed the Hanford
     murder, and each condemned that Catholic menace which they
     understood to be the root cause.

43. Advance 9 (August 17, 1876):944; Interior 7 (August 17, 1876):4;
     7 (August 31, 1876):4.

44. Pierce, History of Chicago, 3:343-44.

45. Times, September 12, 1875.

46. Pierce, History of Chicago, 3:345.

47. Tribune, January 23, 1876.

48. From several sermons printed in Tribune, March 6, 1876.

49. From sermons printed in Tribune, March 13, 1876.

50. Pierce, History of Chicago, 3:346ff.

51. Ibid., 3:348-49. For contemporary comment on the fraud, see
     Tribune, April 7 through 17, 1876; and Herman Kogan, Lords
     of the Levee (Indianapolis: Bobbs-Merrill Co., 1943), pp.
     102-7.

52. Sermon printed in Tribune, September 11, 1876. For a strikingly similar assessment on the national level, see J. M. Sturdevant, "Church and State," Congregational Quarterly 15 (October 1873):508-35.

53. Tribune, January 1, February 23, 1876.

54. See, for example, Tribune, January 6, March 18, 1876; Times, September 13, 1874, January 26, 1876; Western Catholic, November 6, 1873; Workingman's Advocate, December 9, 1876.

55. Advance 9 (April 27, 1876):631; Tribune, March 6, 1876. The details of the Balknap affair are in Edward McPherson, A Handbook of Politics for 1876: Being a Record of Important Political Action, National and State from July 15, 1874, to July 15, 1876, (Washington: Solomons & Chapman, 1876), pp. 156-70.

56. Advance 9 (March 9, 1876):506; Standard 23 (April 27, 1876):4; Interior 7 (March 23, 1876):4; Tribune, March 3, 19, 1876.

57. Tribune, June 5, 7, 8, 1876. The moral outburst against the Belknap fraud was actually one of many which occurred in the 1870s. A study of popular religious magazines indicates a fear for national morality focused often upon the issue of fraudulent behavior by elected officials. See, for example, the Northwestern Christian Advocate 20 (August 14, 1872):4; 23 (March 3, 1875):4; 24 (January 5, 1876):4; Interior 6 (August 26, 1875):4; 7 (August 24, 1876):4; Standard 23 (July 27, 1876):4.

58. From sermons printed in Tribune, March 6, 13, 1876.

59. The reader interested in the relationship between Protestant moralism and the Republican party in the period is directed to Ronald Formisano, The Birth of Mass Political Parties: Michigan, 1827-1861 (Princeton: Princeton University Press, 1971). The identification of the evangelical churches with sound money and Republicanism in the post-Civil War years is discussed in Henry F. May, Protestant Churches and Industrial America (New York: Harper & Bros., 1849), pp. 43-44. Most denominational papers in the 1870s leaned Republican, although many were critical of the Grant administration. The papers themselves were not unaware of the alliance; for example, the Methodist Northwestern Christian Advocate 23 (September 15, 1875):4, observed that "denominations had often been identified with particular parties and, most recently, the Methodists with the Republicans."

60. Tribune, November 1, 1876; Inter-Ocean, November 5, 1876.

61. Tribune, August 3, September 15, November 1, 6, 1876; Inter-Ocean, November 5, 1876.

62. Northwestern Christian Advocate 24 (August 16, 1876):4; Advance 9 (May 11, 1876):687; 9 (June 22, 1876):801; 9 (July 13, 1876):864; Standard 23 (November 16, 1876):4.

63. On the middle-class character of the evangelical churches, see Abell, Urban Impact, pp. 4, 62-3; May, Churches and Industrial America, pp. 62-63. A recent study by Thomas Lenhart, "Methodist Piety in an Industrializing Society: Chicago, 1864-1914" (Ph.D. diss., Northwestern University, 1981), analyzed the membership of the Methodist Episcopal churches of Chicago in 1878 and found that 65% of the members were from the "non-working" class population, 23% were "skilled" workers, and 12% were factory or unskilled laborers. Lenhart also observed that in 1870, 78% of the Methodist churches were located in "non-working" class districts.

64. I generalize here only about the well-established mainline evangelical Protestant denominations, such as Methodist, Baptist, Congregational, Presbyterian, and Reformed Episcopal. In 1876, these denominations accounted for 105 of the city's 218 churches. Only 15 of this number were directed particularly to ministry among the foreign-born population. In contrast, all 25 of the Lutheran churches listed in the city directory for 1876 were denoted by an ethnic identification. At least one denomination took obvious pride in its Anglo-Saxon heritage. A Methodist wrote about the people in his denomination: "The Anglo-Saxons are muscular, hardy, active and energetic; mentally, clear, cool, shrewd, enterprising and ambitious ... they are the friends of political and religious liberty, and enemies of tyrants, whether spiritual or temporal.... If the race be true to itself ... future races will look back upon its period as the brightest in human history" (Dexter Hawkins, "The Anglo-Saxon Race," Methodist Quarterly 58 [January 1876]:87-111).

65. May, Churches and Industrial America, p. 91, writes that "in 1876 Protestantism presented a massive, almost unbroken front in its defense of the social status quo."

66. Typical was a letter printed in Tribune, January 15, 1876, stating that "all classes of society feel that Rome has taken its position in the struggle for religious supremacy in this country, and it is time for all Protestant denominations to begin marshalling their forces for the fray." Similar comments can be found in Advance 9 (January 13, 1876):353; Tribune, August 13, 1876; Standard 23 (February 7, 1876):4.

67. Standard 23 (April 27, 1876):7; Advance 9 (July 13, 1876):864; See also Interior 7 (May 18, 1876):701. The Northwestern Christian Advocate 24 (January 5, 1876):4, advocated the legislation of Protestant morality throughout the nation. We shall "insist on the morality of Christianity among all classes, even those which refuse its spiritual experience."

68. Tribune, October 16, 1876, November 5, 1876. The fear of
     legislating morality was voiced by the Western Brewer 1 (Au-
     gust 15, 1876):15: "They would prescribe his kind of meat,
     his drink, his style of clothing, the cut of his hair, and fur-
     nish a God ready made to fit each individual taste."

69. Evangelical spokesmen repeatedly voiced both the need to evan-
     gelize the poor and foreign-born and their expectation that re-
     vival was the most effectual method. The Congregationalist
     Advance 9 (January 6, 1876):325, stated typically, "We must
     all recognize that these great convulsions do reach a class of
     sinners, and give them a start that no regular preaching, no
     forces which operate for slow and harmonious growth, ever begin
     to touch." Similar comments occur in Interior 5 (April 2, 1874):1;
     7 (April 27, 1876):4; Standard 23 (February 10, 1876):2; North-
     western Christian Advocate 23 (February 17, 1875):4. For
     statements emphasizing the need to evangelize the poor, see
     Advance 6 (November 20, 1873):9; Northwestern Christian Ad-
     vocate 23 (August 19, 1875);257; Standard 22 (October 28,
     1875):5.

70. On the moral uplift expected from revivals, see Northwestern
     Christian Advocate 23 (September 22, 1875):4; Advance 8 (No-
     vember 23, 1875):211; 8 (October 21, 1875):1002; Standard 23
     (February 10, 1876):2; Tribune, March 13, 1876.

71. See Interior 3 (December 19, 1872):1; Advance 7 (October 22,
     1874):135.

72. Inter-Ocean, September 3, 1876.

CHAPTER IV

1. John V. Farwell, Early Recollections of Dwight L. Moody (Chi-
    cago: Winona Press, 1907), p. 87. Farwell, a longtime friend
    of Moody, noted that some local clergy gave regular reports
    from their pulpits on Moody's work in Britain. A reading of
    Chicago periodicals shows that they, too, followed closely the
    revivalist's labors. See, for example, Advance 7 (February 14,
    1874):11; Northwestern Christian Advocate 22 (June 10, 1874):4.

2. Moody to mother, May 21, 1858, Powell Collection.

3. Moody to mother, October 6, 1856, Powell Collection; W. R.
    Moody, Life of Dwight L. Moody, p. 48; Findlay, Dwight L.
    Moody, p. 61; W. H. Daniels, D. L. Moody and His Work (Hart-
    ford, Conn.: American, 1875), pp. 79-80.

4. Dwight L. Moody, The Great Redemption; or, Gospel Light Under
    the Labors of Moody and Sankey (Chicago: Century Book &

Paper, 1889), pp. 475-76; Robert B. Huber, "Dwight L. Moody: Salesman of Salvation--A Case Study in Audience Psychology" (Ph.D. diss., University of Wisconsin, 1942), p. 228.

5. Moody to mother, January 6, 1857, Powell Collection. On Moody's early relationship to the YMCA, see Findlay, Dwight L. Moody, pp. 69-72; T. R. Alexander, "Dwight L. Moody and His Contribution to the Young Men's Christian Association" (typescript), Moody Museum; F. Roger Dunn, "Formative Years of the Chicago YMCA: A Study in Urban History," Journal of the Illinois State Historical Society 37 (December 1944):342-45. Dunn also points out the strongly evangelical flavor of the YMCA in its early years in Chicago.

6. For comments critical of Moody at this time of life, see Chicago Times, October 28, 1867; Frederick F. Cook, Bygone Days in Chicago: Recollections of the "Garden City" of the Sixties (Chicago: A. C. McClurg, 1910), pp. 307-8. The pony is mentioned in several letters in the Moody Papers at the Moody Bible Institute (Moody to brother, January 13, 1862; Simeon King to A. P. Fitt, November 11, 1908). D. W. McWilliams, in W. R. Moody, Life of Dwight L. Moody, pp. 113-14, relates the following incident: "I called upon Mr. Moody in Chicago, and was conducted through his parish. We went to what would now be called the 'slums.' Soon a crowd of street gamins, boys and girls of all ages, were following us with loud shouts of 'Oh, here's Moody! Come, here's Moody!' Evidently they all knew him as their best friend. He had candy in both side pockets and gave it freely. He was everywhere greeted with affection, and carried real sunshine into these abodes of squalor. He inquired for the absent ones by name."

7. The relationship between Moody and Farwell was one of both financial support and close personal friendship. Farwell's daughter, Abby, remembered Moody always dropping in, and says, "Father had such a love for Mr. Moody as exists only between David and Jonathan.... The least he did for him was to help him financially" (Ferry, Reminiscences, 2; 38, 64).

8. The occasion of this decision and the factors which led to it are discussed in proper detail in Findlay, Dwight L. Moody, pp. 73-81. The reader is also pointed in this matter to comments in Dwight L. Moody, Great Joy: Comprising Sermons and Prayer-Meeting Talks (New York: E. B. Treat, 1877), pp. 154-55; W. R. Moody, Life of Dwight L. Moody, pp. 56-58.

9. The pace of Moody's life in these years was certainly hectic. In a letter to his brother (January 13, 1862 Powell Collection), he described his responsibilities: "So you see I have 3 meetings to attend to every day besides calling on the sick and that is not all that I have to go into the country about every week

to buy wood and provision for the poore also coal, wheat, meal
and corn. Then I have to go to hold meetings.... I do not
get 5 minutes a day to study so I have to talk just as it happens ... it is 11 to 12 every night when I retire and am up in
the morning at light" (grammatical errors are uncorrected).

10. R. B. Huber, "Salesman of Salvation, " p. 230.

11. Findlay, Dwight L. Moody, pp. 112-18. Andreas, History of
Chicago, 2:511-12, relates that in Moody's first year as chair-
man of the visitation committee in Chicago, he called on 554
families and bestowed $2,350 in charity from money raised by
the association for poor relief. Several of Moody's early sermons in connection with his YMCA work are reported in Advance 1 (January 9, 1868): 1 (August 6, 1868); 2 (December
12, 1869).

12. Findlay, Dwight L. Moody, pp. 106-9.

13. Ibid., pp. 112, 119; Ira D. Sankey, My Life and the Story of
the Gospel Hymns (New York: Harper & Bros, 1907), pp. 20-
22.

14. Several factors appear to have led him to this momentous decision. He apparently had a profound religious experience in
which he sensed God's "call" upon him for this larger work.
Also, the Chicago fire of 1871 destroyed most of his posses-
sions and perhaps gave him the immediate impetus to act when
he did. On this matter, see Farwell, Early Recollections, p.
78; and Findlay, Dwight L. Moody, pp. 130-33.

15. An account of Moody's work in England is John Kent, Holding
the Fort (London: Epworth Press, 1978), pp. 132-235. Also
very helpful is Findlay, Dwight L. Moody, pp. 144-91.

16. Findlay uses this fact to argue for the spiritual legitimacy of
the early revivals in Scotland. "In Scotland Moody probably
came closer than at any other time in his career to igniting a
revival in the classic sense in which Christians had viewed that
phenomenon up to the nineteenth century" (Dwight L. Moody,
p. 157; cf. Kent, Holding the Fort, pp. 136-37).

17. Tribune, August 17, 1875; Interior 6 (September 30, 1875):5.

18. New York Tribune, August 16, 1875.

19. New York Times, September 15, 1875; Farwell, Early Recollections, p. 129.

20. Tribune, October 5, 1875; Interior 6 (September 30, 1875):5;
Advance 8 (September 30, 1875):958. Commentators were not

specific about the reasons for Moody's decision not to come to Chicago in the fall of 1875. Certain statements, however, implied that some ministers were dubious as to whether Moody could duplicate his British successes in America and were reluctant to make Chicago the trial horse for the American campaign.

21. Even a partial list of large contributors to the revival fund is impressive: Cyrus McCormick and William Dering, giants in the manufacture of reapers; John Farwell and Henry Field, the owners, respectively, of the second and third largest dry-goods stores in the nation; George and J. F. Armour, leaders in the meatpacking industry; C. P. Kellogg and A. J. Willing, wealthy Chicago merchants; C. M. Henderson, the city's leading manufacturer of shoes and boots; D. K. Pearson, John Crerar, and E. W. Blatchford, Multimillionaire capitalists.

22. The Fields, McCormick, and Crerar all served on the boards of Presbyterian churches in the city. John Farwell spoke frequently at YMCA meetings in the Chicago area and had himself organized a mission Sunday school.

23. Tribune, September 25, 1876. A letter to the editor of the Tribune, December 20, 1876, remarked that there "is a strong undercurrent among businessmen in favor of the revival." The writer then assessed its attraction for the business community as the promotion of the "peace, safety, and good order of the city."

24. Inter-Ocean, June 6, 1876.

25. Ibid., June 3, 1876; Northwestern Christian Advocate 24 (June 14, 1876):4.

26. Inter-Ocean, June 6, 1876.

27. Ibid., June 10, 1876.

28. Ibid., June 12, 1876.

29. Ibid., June 13, 1876; Tribune, June 13, 1876.

30. Inter-Ocean, July 7, 1876.

31. Several local clergy had argued that the meetings would reach the entire city more effectively if held at three different sites.

32. Inter-Ocean, August 12, 1876, September 5, 1876; Northwestern Christian Advocate 24 (September 27, 1876):1. The moving force behind the successful outcome of the committee's work appears to have been Farwell. He resolved the financial haggling by agreeing to pay for the structure himself, sell it to the

YMCA which would own it for the duration of the crusade, and then buy it back at the conclusion of the meetings. The committee, in turn, promised to deduct $6,000 from the repurchase price to cover Farwell's costs in converting the building into a warehouse. The money remaining when the transaction was complete would be given to the YMCA. On this matter, see Farwell, Early Recollections, pp. 40, 159, 161.

33. Descriptions of the Tabernacle are in Inter-Ocean, September 23, 1876; Northwestern Christian Advocate 24 (October 4, 1876): 5; Times, September 28, 1876; Tribune, October 2, 1876. Pictures or drawings of the structure can be found in the Northwestern Christian Advocate 24 (September 27, 1876):1; and E. J. Goodspeed, A Full History of the Wonderful Career of Moody and Sankey in Great Britain and America (Cleveland: C. C. Wick, 1876), p. 624.

34. Inter-Ocean, September 13, 1876.

35. Ibid., September 12, 29, 1876.

36. Chicago Weekly Journal, October 4, 1876; Tribune, September 30, 1876; Chicago Times, September 24, 1876.

37. George C. Stebbins, Reminiscences and Gospel Hymn Stories (1924); reprint, New York: AMS, 1971), p. 99. Stebbins recalled that a total of a thousand singers were recruited for the Chicago meetings and that he began preparations in the city on September 1, 1876.

38. Tribune, September 27, 1876. A copy of an instruction pamphlet used in preparation for the Moody meetings, "Rules for Ushers in Religious Meetings," is at the Moody Museum.

39. Inter-Ocean, August 12, 1876; J. M. Hitchcock, "Reminiscences of the Chicago Revival of 1876," Inter-Ocean, October 27, 1907 (copy at Moody Bible Institute Library); Goodspeed, Career of Moody and Sankey, p. 625.

40. Tribune, January 17, 1876.

41. Inter-Ocean, June 20, 1876; Tribune, September 23, 1876.

42. Among the several trustees of the Chicago YMCA in the 1860s were George Armour, Cyrus McCormick, John Farwell and B. F. Jacobs. See the Ninth Annual Report by the president of the Chicago YMCA (Moody Bible Institute Library).

43. Inter-Ocean, January 17, 1877. The amount collected in this single offering was reportedly $60,000.

44. Moody's policies regarding income were also designed to protect the evangelist from accusations that the revivals brought him and Sankey personal gain. In fact neither of the evangelists was formally paid for his services. In Chicago it seems likely that the two evangelists were given an honorarium for their personal expenses, although I have found no record of it. This practice did occur, however, in other cities in which Moody and Sankey hosted revival meetings. Moreover, close friends (like Farwell) were known to support the evangelist's activities with private financial contributions. Ironically, the private nature of Moody's personal finances sometimes roused public suspicions. Questions about the sources and size of his income were often raised at his meetings. During their careers, both he and Sankey had to state repeatedly that they were not profiting personally from the large sums collected by revival workers. The size of Moody's estate upon his death would seem to verify these disclaimers. He seemingly always had sufficient funds to meet his needs but never accumulated even a modest fortune. On this subject, see Findlay, Dwight L. Moody, p. 203; Tribune, September 14, 1875; Farwell, Early Recollections, pp. 77, 84, 120, 156; Ferry, Reminiscences, 2: 64, 73.

45. Tribune, October 1, 2, 1876; Inter-Ocean, December 17, 1876; Hitchcock, "Chicago Revival of 1876."

46. Tribune, October 8, 1876. See also Tribune, October 1, 2, 1876; and Northwestern Christian Advocate 24 (October 18, 1876):1. Tickets of admission to the Chicago Meetings can be seen at the Moody Museum and at the Presbyterian Historical Society Library in Philadelphia.

47. Moody's understanding of the human and divine element in revival is discussed in Gundry, Love Them In, pp. 77-86; cf. William G. McLoughlin, Modern Revivalism: Charles Gradison Finney to Billy Graham (New York: Ronald Press, 1959), pp. 164-65; and Bernard Weisberger, They Gathered at the River (Boston: Little, Brown & Co., 1958), 176. It should perhaps be noted that Moody himself addressed this matter in his first sermon at the Tabernacle: "God always works in partnership.... There must be honest work of lifting one's self first as far as may be, and then a leaving of the rest to God" (Great Joy, p. 14).

48. The reference here is to the Episcopalian churches of Chicago rather than the Reformed Episcopal churches. In 1873 the Reformed Episcopal Church separated from the larger denomination over the issues of increasing formalism in worship and excessive sacerdotalism. These issues probably explain the Reformed Episcopal support of Moody in Chicago and, in contrast, the nonsupport of the Episcopalian churches. In 1876 Chicago there were seventeen Episcopalian churches and seven Reformed Episcopal churches.

49. Tribune, September 25, November 8, 1876; Advance 9 (December 21, 1876):286; 10 (January 25, 1877):377. For criticism of Moody and Sankey by writers in the Unitarian tradition, see Unitarian Review 7 (May 1877):559-63; and W. H. Ryder, "An Open Letter from W. H. Ryder of Chicago to D. L. Moody, Esq., the Evangelist" (typescript, Boston, 1877), Moody Bible Institute Library.

50. One exception to this generalization is Western Brewer 1 (October 15, 1876):65: "And now the Western Puritans gather at John V. Farwell's Tabernacle and listen to the songs of the divine Sankey--erst an end man of Christy's minstrels--and drink in the swash of the mountebank Moody. And the Chicago preachers of the small-bore order sit on the benches to make out a background of wisdom. Let the business go on. The insane asylums are waiting for the harvest, and will shortly be filled to repletion, as they were by these same hymnbook peddlers over in England."

51. Typical was the expression of Scribner's Monthly 40 (1876): 887: "Revivals seem to have become a part of the established policy of nearly the whole Christian Church. The Catholics have their 'missions,' the Episcopalians have their regular special seasons of religious devotion and effort, while other forms of Protestantism look to revivals occasionally appearing, as the times of general awakening and general ingathering." For similar comments, see Standard 22 (October 7, 1875):4; Congregational Quarterly 13 (October, 1871):551-61; Interior 7 (February 24, 1876):2; Advance 9 (January 6, 1876):325.

52. For example, the Tablet, a national Roman Catholic paper, surveyed Moody's work just before the opening of the Chicago meetings and concluded "this work of Mr. Moody is not sin. It cannot be sin to invite men to love and serve Jesus Christ. It is irregular, unauthorized, but it may be bringing multitudes to a happier frame of mind, in which the Church may find them better prepared to receive her sublime faith" (quoted in W. R. Moody, Life of Dwight L. Moody, p. 284).

53. The traits of "sincerity" and "earnestness" in Moody are mentioned repeatedly by commentators in Chicago and by the revivalist's biographers. See, for instance, Northwestern Christian Advocate 24 (January 19, 1876):4; Inter-Ocean, October 6, 1876; Advance 10 (January 4, 1877):344; Daniels, Words, Work and Workers, pp. 43-45; Chapman Life and Work of Moody, p. 21.

54. Quoted in Findlay, Dwight L. Moody, p. 226.

55. Advance 10 (January 29, 1877):389, took note of this and concluded that it was proof of the relative insignificance of the doctrine of "second Adventism."

56. Moody's response to a question on baptism posed to him during the London meetings is revealing: "Why don't I preach baptism? The Lord has sent me to preach the Gospel. I leave these doctrines to your pastors. I have not come to get up a quarrel in England" (quoted in Gundry, Love Them In, p. 173). In Chicago, Moody took much the same line of response when asked about women praying in public; see Goodspeed, Career of Moody and Sankey, p. 567.

57. R. M. Devins, American Progress; or, The Great Events of the Greatest Century, Also Life Delineations of Our Most Noted Men, 6 vols. (Chicago: Hugh Heron, 1882), 6:455.

58. Inter-Ocean, June 12, 1876.

59. Advance, 9 (March 3, 1876):574.

60. Time, October 2, 1876.

61. David Swing was an extremely popular Chicago Presbyterian minister who was brought before the Chicago Presbytery in 1874 on charges of heresy. Although Swing was acquitted of the charges, he left Fourth Presbyterian Church and formed a nondenominational church which met at McVicker's Theatre downtown. The story of this episode in Chicago religious history is related to broader changes in American religion by William Hutchinson, The Modernist Impulse in American Protestantism (Cambridge: Harvard University Press, 1976), pp. 48-75.

62. Times, September 28, 1876.

63. Farwell, Early Recollections, p. 22.

64. Interior 7 (November 9, 1876):4. Cree's journal is at the YMCA library in Chicago. Its usefulness is somewhat limited, as most entries contain only a listing of places and dates of scheduled activities.

65. Reports of this type can be found in virtually every edition of either the Tribune or Inter-Ocean for November and December 1876.

66. Ahlstrom, Religious History, p. 870.

67. Many of these individuals are described in Daniels, Words, Work and Workers, pp. 489-512. It should be recognized that Moody's ability to gather and hold together these kinds of persons was essential to the mass revivals he sought to engender. The prominence of these persons in evangelical circles and their willing support of Moody certainly must have enhanced the stature of the revivalist in the eyes of Chicago's evangelical Protestants.

68. Chicago Daily News, September 29, 1876; Appeal quoted in the
    opinions column of Advance 9 (October 26, 1876):129; North-
    western Christian Advocate 24 (October 4, 1876):4.

69. Goodspeed, Career of Moody and Sankey, p. 660.

70. Ibid., p. 628.

71. Hitchcock, "Chicago Revival of 1876."

CHAPTER V

1. This account is reconstructed from Goodspeed, Career of Moody
   and Sankey, pp. 626-28; Tribune, October 2, 1876; Inter-Ocean,
   October 2, 1876; Alliance, October 7, 1876.

2. Advance, 9 (October 12, 1876):90; D. L. Moody, Great Joy,
   pp. 13-20; Inter-Ocean, October 2, 1876.

3. D. L. Moody, Great Joy, pp. 13, 26, 58; Inter-Ocean, November 30, 1876.

4. New York Christian Advocate 51 (November 9, 1876):4; D. L.
   Moody, Great Joy, pp. 58-59; Inter-Ocean, October 16, 1876.

5. Inter-Ocean, November 11, December 14, 22, 30, 1876.

6. Inter-Ocean, December 27, 1876; Advance 9 (December 21,
   1876):280. The seriousness with which these specialized meetings were taken is perhaps suggested in a report of the Inter-
   Ocean, December 20, 1876, that "some ladies who were present
   were quite provoked at being requested to leave the meeting,
   and an old lady saying that she had come one hundred miles
   to hear Mr. Moody, and had not heard him; another had never
   been asked out of a meeting before and thought it was not very
   Christian-like to do so."

7. Northwestern Christian Advocate 24 (December 13, 1876):4.

8. Sizer, Gospel Hymns, pp. 50-52, 114. Sizer's interpretation of
   the function of gospel hymnody has aided significantly my own
   conceptions of the social function of Moody's sermons in Chicago.

9. Standard 24 (July 5, 1877):3; Interior 5 (June 8, 1874):1; Advance 8 (March 18, 1875):509.

10. Standard 23 (December 14, 1876):4; 24 (July 15, 1877):3; Ob-
    server 43 (March 23, 1865):89; see also New York Christian
    Advocate 49 (February 26, 1874):70; Interior 4 (May 15, 1873):1.

11. Henry C. Fish, Handbook of Revivals: For the Use of Winners of Souls (Boston: James H. Earle, 1874), p. 299. Fish was not a Chicagoan, but his understanding of prayer as a necessary preparation for revival was common among evangelicals. Similar comments can be observed in Interior 5 (January 7, 1875):4; Advance 8 (February 11, 1875):4; 9 (February 24, 1876):2.

12. Interior 5 (May 15, 1873):1; 5 (May 22, 1873):1; 5 (June 5, 1873):1; 5 (June 12, 1873):1. For similar comments by other contributors to this journal, see Interior 4 (April 11, 1872):1; 5 (January 13, 1873):2. Also Advance 7 (November 5, 1874): 181; 9 (February 4, 1875):411; Northwestern Christian Advocate 21 (May 14, 1873):158; 21 (June 18, 1873):194.

13. Tribune, October 7, 1876.

14. Advance 9 (November 30, 1876):223; Interior 7 (November 30, 1876):5.

15. See the lists of prayer requests in Standard 23 (November 9, 1876):4; Advance 9 (October 12, 1876):91.

16. Independent 3 (July 3, 1851):110. For similar comments, see also Advance 6 (December 4, 1873):2; Interior 5 (October 31, 1874):4.

17. C. L. Thompson, Times of Refreshing (Chicago: L. T. Palmer & Co., 1877), pp. 382-83.

18. Goodspeed, Career of Moody and Sankey, p. 397. Moody said, "If a man is converted I want him to come here and give his experience ... and the result may be that God will use his witnessing to the conversion of many" (D. L. Moody, Glad Tidings: Comprising Sermons and Prayer-Meeting Talks Delivered at the New York Hippodrome [New York: E. B. Treat, 1876], p. 187).

19. Sizer, Gospel Hymns, p. 116.

20. Unsigned letter (dated February 6, 1877) in the files of the Moody Bible Institute Historical Room.

21. D. L. Moody, Great Joy, p. 415; Independent 28 (December 28, 1876):18; Goodspeed, Career of Moody and Sankey, p. 668.

22. Willie, a week after his conversion, "became a member of Mr. Moody's band of evangelists," as the Tribune reported.

23. Inter-Ocean, November 25, 1876.

24. Christian World, April 16, 1875; Inter-Ocean, October 2, 1876.

25. Inter-Ocean, October 6, 1876; Sankey, My Life, p. iii.

26. See, for example, the comments in Independent 28 (March 16, 1876):16; Daniels, Words, Works and Workers, p. 487.

27. Christian World, April 16, 1875; Nation 22 (March 9, 1875): 256.

28. Sizer, Gospel Hymns, p. 589.

29. Ibid., p. 570.

30. Alliance, October 7, 1876.

31. Daniels, Words, Works and Workers, p. 485; Tribune, December 13, 1876; Nation 22 (March 9, 1876):157.

32. Moody emphasized the functionality of music. An acquaintance of Moody, Gamaliel Bradford, D. L. Moody: A Worker in Souls (New York: George H. Doran Co., 1927), p. 168, said of Moody: "He would have nothing whatever to do with a piece of music which only appealed to the sense of beauty. He could form no judgment of its value by hearing it played or sung in private. He must see it tried on a crowd, and could discover in an instant its adaptation to awaken the feelings which he needed to have in action. If it had the right ring, he used it for all it was worth. 'Let the people sing,' he would shout-- 'Let all the people sing. Sing that verse again. There's an old man over there who is not singing at all, let him sing.' No matter how long it took, he would keep the people at work until they were fused and melted."

33. Tribune, December 13, 1876; Advance 9 (December 21, 1876): 286.

34. J. T. Sunderland, Orthodoxy and Revivalism (New York: James Miller, 1876), pp. 111-14.

35. Advance 8 (August 6, 1875):730; Goodspeed, Career of Moody and Sankey, p. 235; Tribune, August 17, 1875.

36. Goodspeed, Career of Moody and Sankey, p. 234; Interior 8 (January 11, 1877):1.

37. Goodspeed, Career of Moody and Sankey, p. 235.

38. Ferry, Reminiscences, 2:65.

39. See the comments in Inter-Ocean, October 6, 1876, and throughout Northwestern Christian Advocate 24 (January 19, 1876).

40. Thomas McMillan, "Twenty Reminiscences" (typescript), Moody Bible Institute Library.

41. See, for example, comments in Inter-Ocean, October 2, 1876; W. R. Moody, Life of Dwight L. Moody, p. 283.

42. Tribune, June 5, 1876.

43. Inter-Ocean, October 2, 1876.

44. Findlay, Dwight L. Moody, p. 223.

45. Henry Sloane Coffin, "Address on the Centenary of Moody's Birth," October 27, 1937, delivered at Carnegie Hall (manuscript copy, Moody Museum).

46. This concept is adapted from Mircea Eliade, Myths, Dreams and Mysteries (New York: Harper & Row, 1960), p. 24.

47. Ibid., p. 32; Mircea Eliade, Myths and Reality (New York: Harper & Row, 1963), p. 8. The term "myth" does not deny or confirm the historicity of a story. Eliade defines myth as a "sacred story" and hence a "true history because it always deals with realities." Most important for my purpose is the function of myth to reveal models, guide behavior, and thus give meaning to the world and to human life.

48. John Shea, Stories of God (Chicago: Thomas More Press, 1978), pp. 51, 57.

49. Independent 28 (November 2, 1876):12; Tribune, November 21, 1876; Inter-Ocean, November 25, 1876.

50. Comments from the Tribune, November 14, 21, 25, 28, 1876; Bishop C. E. Cheney, "Extracts from Tributes," no. 33 (typescript), Moody Bible Institute Library. For similar positive assessments, see Inter-Ocean, January 22, 1877; Tribune, December 31, 1876; Advance 9 (December 21, 1876):286, 292; Northwestern Christian Advocate 25 (January 24, 1877):5; Interior 8 (January 18, 1877):4; Chicago Weekly Journal, December 20, 27, 1876.

51. Tribune, November 21, 1876

52. Inter-Ocean, November 20, 1876.

53. By "true revival," I mean the generally conceived notion of a revival as expressed by Moody's contemporaries. Fish summed up these elements in his Handbook of Revivals, p. 13, as "the renewal of spirituality and vigor among Christians, and the conversion of sinners in considerable numbers to God."

54. Inter-Ocean, November 3, 8, 1876.

55. Detailed accounts of the convention are in Northwestern Christian Advocate 24 (November 29, 1876):6. For criticism of this gathering, see Alliance, December 2, 1876.

56. Advance 9 (December 14, 1876):263; New York Christian Advocate 52 (February 1, 1877):6. The same writer described the scene: "Vast areas dotted all over with people, in groups of two or three, earnestly talking of the things of the Kingdom of God, reading proof-texts from well-worn Bibles, or kneeling in prayer with half a thousand people around them."

57. Northwestern Christian Advocate 25 (January 24, 1877):5; Inter-Ocean, January 17, 1877.

CHAPTER VI

1. McLoughlin, Modern Revivalism, p. 168; Weisberger, They Gathered at the River, p. 213; Marion Bell, Crusade in the City (Philadelphia: Temple University Press, 1978), p. 19. Findlay, Dwight L. Moody, p. 289, offers a generally more positive assessment of Moody, but virtually echoes the prevailing interpretation of his revivals: "The revivals served as a constructive force in the urban centers of the 1870s helping to bridge the cultural chasm that lay for many of the revivalist's hearers between early rural or small-town experiences and the later years of metropolitan living."

2. Weisberger, They Gathered at the River, p. 206; Bell, Crusade in the City, p. 200; McLoughlin, Modern Revivalism, p. 168. Like Weisberger, McLoughlin finds that the new science was productive of religious tensions which, in turn, made the Bible-oriented Moody an attractive religious figure to some. My research suggests that in Chicago in 1876 evolution, Darwinism, and science were being discussed quite congenially by most ministers and scientists. The tone of their conversations indicates that the subjects were of interest to readers but far from threatening or divisive. Advance 19 (February 15, 1877), took a typical attitude, stating "that the Bible and science are but the extreme right and left wing of that movement which embraces the truest thought, the noblest sentiment and the best works of these progressive times." In this regard, see George Marsden, Fundamentalism and American Culture: The Shaping of Twentieth-Century Evangelicalism, 1870-1925 (New York: Oxford University Press, 1980), pp. 17-21.

3. Findlay, Dwight L. Moody, pp. 272-73; William G. McLoughlin, Revivals, Awakenings and Reform (Chicago: University of Chicago Press, 1978), p. 144; Bell, Crusade in the City, pp. 235-36.

4. Inter-Ocean, October 2, 11, November 13, 1876; Northwestern Christian Advocate 24 (November 2, 1876):2; Goodspeed, Career of Moody and Sankey, pp. 670-71.

5. Inter-Ocean, November 13, 1876; Northwestern Christian Advocate 24 (October 18, 1876):1.

6. See Interior 7 (February 3, 1876):4; Advance 6 (November 20, 1873):9; Grant Goodrich, Report of the Conference Committee for the Relief of Methodist Institutions and Churches of Chicago (Chicago: Rand & McNally, 1873), p. 13; "The Ministrations of the Church to the Working Classes," Protestant Episcopal Church, Church Congress, Papers, Addresses and Debates, 1875, pp. 39-73; "Preaching the Gospel to the Poor," Biblical Repository and Princeton Review 43 (1871):83-95; "The Church and the Working Class," Watchman and Reflector 53 (October 31, 1872):6; "Methodism and Our City Masses," New York Christian Advocate 41 (February 8, 1866):44.

7. Expectations of this sort were fostered by reports in the local and national press that Moody had enjoyed tremendous successes with the poor in his New York and Philadelphia crusades. Such reports are probably unfounded. See, for example, comments in Advance 9 (March 3, 1876):494; and National Baptist (February 17, 1876):4.

8. Exact figures for the Roman Catholic population in Chicago in 1876 are unavailable. Interior 7 (August 17, 1876):4, reported a "recent compilation" estimating Chicago's population at 75,000 Protestants, 75,000 Catholics and nonevangelical Christians, and about 250,000 unchurched or "heathen." The paper suggested that the unchurched population was more likely about 216,000 when "interested non-members" were taken into account. Northwestern Christian Advocate 24 (March 8, 1876):2, also estimated the city's unchurched population at 250,000.

9. Inter-Ocean, October 2, 1876. For insight into the problems of this practice, I am indebted to the observations in Findlay, Dwight L. Moody, pp. 273-76.

10. Pierce, History of Chicago, 3:238, 271, notes that in the 1870s most Chicago laborers worked a minimum ten- to sixteen-hour day.

11. Inter-Ocean, October 2, 11, 17, 1876. The overwhelming predominance of church people at one meeting was indicated when Moody challenged all Christians present to "bring one soul to Christ" in the week that followed. Three-quarters of the congregation stood to accept the challenge.

12. Inter-Ocean, October 23, 1876; Chicago Times, October 2, 1876; Independent 28 (October 26, 1876):12. For other reports of a

similar nature, see Inter-Ocean, October 10, 1876; Interior 8
(January 18, 1877):8; Thompson, Times of Refreshing, p. 276.

13. Francis Hemenway, "lessons from the Moody Meetings" (type-
script) Garrett Theological Seminary Archives; Advance 10
(February 15, 1877):483; Standard 23 (November 9, 1876):4;
Times, January 17, 1877; Interior 8 (January 25, 1877):4.

14. This reasoning was common in the late nineteenth century.
Nation 21 (November 18, 1875):321, observed that "one of the
signs of a man's prosperity ... is his appearance in church....
To become a pewholder in all the leading churches ... is to
become a stockholder in a wealthy and flourishing corporation,
and the more powerful the preacher, the more it costs to hear
him." On Moody, the magazine commented, "We have no doubt
that nine-tenths of their hearers, at least, are persons already
connected with religious organizations or the near relatives of
such persons, or members of the well-to-do classes attracted
by curiosity."

15. Inter-Ocean, December 15, 1876.

16. By "conversion" I refer to the religious experience of the new
believer responding to the evangelist's message. Evangelicals
understood the matter to be supernatural in nature--a miracle
of grace--which involved a "new birth," and brought with it a
conviction of salvation and a dedication to warfare against sin.
For Moody's understanding of conversion, see Gundry, Love
Them In, pp. 121-30.

17. D. L. Moody, Great Joy, p. 500.

18. Tribune, January 14, 1877; Northwestern Christian Advocate
25 (January 24, 1877):5; Hemenway, "Lessons from the Moody
Meetings."

19. Chicago Times, January 17, 1877.

20. It is not possible to ascertain the exact number of unemployed
men and women in Chicago in 1876. Certainly, in the midst of
a depression the number was large. Employment for many was
sporadic. Helpful comments in this regard are in Pierce, History of Chicago, 3:240-44.

21. Chicago Weekly Journal, December 20, 1876; Chicago Daily News,
January 15, 1877; Independent 28 (December 21, 1876):15; Tribune, December 2, 1876; Standard 23 (November 9, 1876):4;
Interior 8 (January 25, 1877):4; Thompson, Times of Refreshing, p. 276.

22. Northwestern Christian Advocate 25 (January 24, 1877):5; Chicago

Times, January 17, 1877; Standard 24 (January 25, 1877):4;
Tribune, January 14, 1877.

23. Chicago Times, January 17, 1877. The process of church mem-
    bership varied from denomination to denomination and from
    church to church. However, it is safe to say that an equal
    number of new members were probably received by these churches
    in the months following Moody's departure from Chicago. This
    has been my finding in the cases of individual churches ex-
    amined over an extended period. In every case, the gains in
    membership during the revival months were atypical of normal
    growth rates in previous years.

24. See, for example, comments in Independent 29 (January 18,
    1877):12; Tribune, November 14, 21, 1876; Inter-Ocean, Novem-
    ber 25, 1876.

25. Northwestern Christian Advocate 25 (February 21, 1877):4;
    Times, January 17, 1877.

26. See, for example, the minutes of the Fifth Presbyterian Church
    of Chicago for November 4, 1876, at McCormick Theological
    Seminary Library; Chicago Weekly Journal, December 20, 1876;
    Tribune, November 21, 1876; December 5, 1876.

27. I base these statements upon the remarks of the individual pas-
    tors of the churches in sermons, press reports, and the minutes
    of church meetings. See, for example, Fifth Presbyterian
    Church, minutes; Third Presbyterian Church, minutes and ses-
    sion book; Centenary Methodist Church, minutes; Tabernacle
    Congregational Church, minutes; New England Congregational
    Church, minutes and record book, Chicago Theological Seminary
    Library. For reports on new members added to these churches
    during the revival months and comments by their clergymen
    about the revival, see Tribune, January 1, 9, 16, 1877; Oc-
    tober 9, 1876.

28. See Appendix. It should also be recognized that the selection of
    churches for this study was determined in large part by the avail-
    ability of church records. In the case of the Methodist churches
    of Chicago, for example, I have found records for only two
    churches for these years. Others have apparently been lost.

29. Generalizations about the location of working-class people and
    middle-class residential areas are admittedly imprecise. How-
    ever, it is possible to gain some perspective regarding this
    matter by use of contemporary observations, land value, vice
    areas, and ethnic concentrations. My assertions are based upon
    such factors. Readers are referred to Historic Chicago, "Com-
    munity Settlement Map for 1870"; Hoyt, Land Values in Chicago,
    pp. 96-97, 112-13, 302-3; Mayer & Wade, Growth of a Metropolis,

pp. 54-66. I am also indebted to a discussion of these matters with Thomas Lenhart.

30. Historic Chicago, "Community Settlement Map for 1870." The membership at New England Congregational Church was 337, at Centenary Methodist 981, and at Fifth Presbyterian 350.

31. I have found no evidence to indicate that large numbers of blacks attended the Moody meetings in Chicago. It should be noted however that in 1876, blacks comprised less than 1% of the city's population. In this regard, see The People of Chicago, Chicago Department of Development and Planning, (Chicago, 1976), pp. 16, 20.

32. In the case of Centenary Methodist, I have used the number of probationers.

33. In reading the church minutes of these five congregations, I have discovered that the length of the membership process varied considerably. Methodists welcomed probationers almost immediately upon request. Presbyterians and Congregationalists followed established formats. Nevertheless, because of the rush of new members, special meetings were held frequently for the express purpose of acting on petitions for membership. Two to four weeks seems to have been the common length of wait for a candidate to be received into membership. It should be recognized that this was extraordinarily speedy and reflects the large numbers of petitioners and the eagerness of these churches to receive such persons.

34. Interior 8 (February 8, 1877):4; Advance 10 (February 8, 1877): 417-18; 10 (March 15, 1877):518.

35. The actual number for each church is as follows: Tabernacle Congregational received 25 persons, New England Congregational 89, Third Presbyterian 206, Fifth Presbyterian 111, and Centenary Methodist 102.

36. I was able to identify approximately two-thirds of these persons in either the census or the city directories. Where addresses accompanied names in the church records, I was able to locate with certainty individuals with common names. When more than one family member joined a church simultaneously and the same relationship was indicated in the census or directory, I assumed again that I had identified the correct persons. For about one-third of the cases, I was able to determine only sex and, sometimes, marital status. Missing cases are explained by common names without an accompanying address, transients who tended to be passed over by the city directory, and population movements which took people out of the city by the census of 1880. By chance I discovered that several of these persons

had died by 1880 and that one family had moved to Peoria, Illinois. Problems of this nature are discussed in Stephan Thernstrom, The Other Bostonians (Cambridge: Harvard University
Press, 1973), p. 115.

37. See, for example, reports in Tribune, November 21, 25, 28,
1876.

38. Previous studies of adolescent conversions and revivals do not
provide statistical estimates of the percentage of youthful converts. Joseph Kett calls attention to the "predominance" of
youthful converts during the Second Great Awakening. Nancy
Cott noted that three females to every two males were converted
in this revival. She observed further that most were "youthful." Certainly the percentage of youthful converts in this
study would defy the use of such observations. For examples,
see Joseph F. Kett, "Growing Up in Rural New England, 1800-
1840," in Anonymous Americans: Explorations in Nineteenth-
Century Social History ed. Tamara A. Haraven (Englewood
Cliffs, N.J.: Prentice-Hall, 1971), pp. 1-16; Nancy F. Cott,
"Young Women in the Second Great Awakening," Feminist Studies
3 (Fall 1975), pp. 15-29; Lois Banner, "Religion and Reform in
the Early Republic: The Role of Youth," American Quarterly
23 (December 1971):677-95.

39. Tenth Federal Census, "Population," pp. 538-41.

40. Catholics in Chicago were surprisingly quiet in regard to the
Tabernacle meetings. Certainly they were aware that Moody
opposed the positions they held regarding such matters as
prayer and Bible reading in the public schools. A national
organ of the Catholic church, the Catholic World, did attack
Moody openly in the summer of 1876, satirizing his revivals as
second-rate sideshow entertainment and his preaching as "vulgar
and often unintentionally blasphemous." See Michael Mueller, "A
Revival at Frogtown," Catholic World 22 (February 1876):699-707.

41. Christian World (January 1877):27; (March 1877):88; (April
1877):124.

42. Inter-Ocean, October 18, November 3, 13, 1876.

43. A large number of foreign-language newspapers were published
in Chicago in the 1870s. Unfortunately, few copies remain.
I have examined the Skandinavan, the Norden, and the Kriste-
lege Talsmand--all Scandinavian weeklies published in Chicago
but distributed throughout the Midwest. German language
papers examined included Der Westen, Illinois Staats-Zeitung,
Chicagoer Freie Presse, and Daheim. Only the Skandinavan,
October 10, 1876, and the Staats-Zeitung, October 2, 1876,
make mention of the revival. In both instances the articles were

brief, and the subject did not reappear in subsequent issues.
The Tabernacle meetings were advertised in both publications.

44. Methodist Episcopal Church, Chicago German District, minutes,
    Garrett Theological Seminary Archives. The four churches ex-
    amined were the Van Buren Street Church, the Maxwell Street
    Church, the Clybourn Avenue Church, and the Ashland Avenue
    Church.

45. Methodist Episcopal Church, Northwest Swedish District, minutes.

46. Of the persons identified in the census lists, 53.6% were be-
    tween the age of twenty and forty; 70.6% were between the ages
    of eighteen and forty-five.

47. Compendium of the Tenth Federal Census, 2:1654-58. It should
    be recognized that literacy figures may be prejudiced in this
    instance. Transients would be more likely both to be missed
    in the census and to be illiterate. Nonetheless, the hundred
    percent literacy rate for the 350 persons identified in the cen-
    sus is impressive. In Chicago in 1880, there were 59,364
    adults unable either to read or write; 39,748 of these were
    American-born. It seems safe to surmise that the high literacy
    rate of these new church members reflects a middle-class back-
    ground.

48. The term "middling classes" more accurately depicts those per-
    sons described in this study than does the more modern "middle
    class." It is used here to suggest a disparate grouping rather
    than a homogeneous whole. This group included professionals,
    shopkeepers and other trades people, independent artisans,
    some skilled workers--urban people who were neither wealthy
    nor desperately poor and who hoped to find some avenue of upward
    mobility in the expanding market of nineteenth-century
    America. Barbara Epstein, in a study of nineteenth-century
    domesticity, contends that the "middling classes" in this period
    were "as much a cultural and ideological as an economic cate-
    gory" The Politics of Domesticity [Middletown, Conn.: Wesleyan
    University Press, 1981], p. 283).

49. Ibid., pp. 67-87. Nancy F. Cott, The Bonds of Womanhood
    (New Haven: Yale University Press, 1977), p. 92, defines
    domesticity in early nineteenth-century America as "a cultural
    preference for domestic retirement and conjugal-family intimacy
    over both the 'vain' and fashionable sociability of the rich and
    the promiscuous sociability of the poor." By the 1870s this
    middle-class ideal had come to dominate American culture.

50. In this instance the percentage may be low since cases in which
    there was uncertainty as to actual blood relation between per-
    sons having the same last name were treated as unrelated.

51. New England Congregational Church, minutes, January 7, 1877.

52. A careful counting of new and old church members was done for Centenary Methodist Episcopal Church since complete addresses for all members made it more feasible to determine family connections by a factor more certain than last names alone. It was discovered that in this case 16% of the new church members had family members on the membership roll of the church who lived at the same address.

53. On the use of occupations as an index to social status, see Josef Barton, Peasants and Strangers (Cambridge: Harvard University Press, 1975), p. 91.

54. In a small number of cases, the occupation given in the census differed from that listed in the directories. Whenever this occurred, the directory listing was used due to its closer proximity in time to the revival meetings.

55. Pierce, History of Chicago, 2:150-55, discusses the number of laborers and their representation in the various economic sectors of the city.

56. This assertion, as all the generalizations offered below regarding occupational status, is based largely upon Theodore Hershberg et al., "Occupation and Ethnicity in Five Nineteenth-Century Cities: A Collaborative Inquiry," Historical Methods Newsletter (June 1974):174-216. This study is the most thorough analysis of occupational status in major urban centers of this period. For insightful comments in this regard, see also Donald Treiman, "A Standard Occupational Prestige Scale for Use with Historical Data," Journal of Interdisciplinary History 7 (Autumn 1976):283-304.

57. Pierce, History of Chicago, 3:240; Tribune, August 10, 23, 1876. I have not been able to identify the number of individuals who were unemployed. Although the census asked about employment, many respondents appear to have ignored the question. Also, unemployment in 1880 would not be proof positive of the condition in 1876. Because the data seems unreliable here, I have not included it in this assessment.

58. The psychology of success and opportunity among lower middle-class whites in American cities is explored in Richard Centers, The Psychology of Social Classes (Princeton: Princeton University Press, 1949), pp. 146-59. The popularity of the success ethic in the postwar decades is in Richard M. Huber, The American Idea of Success (New York: McGraw-Hill, 1971), chap. 3, 4; John G. Cawelti, Apostles of the Self-Made Man (Chicago: University of Chicago Press, 1965), chap. 2-4. Herbert Gutman, "The Rags-to-Riches 'Myth': The Case of the Paterson, New

Jersey, Locomotive, Iron and Machinery Manufacturers, 1830-
1880," in ed. Stephan Thernstrom and Richard Sennett Nineteenth-Century Cities, (New Haven: Yale University Press,
1969), pp. 122, observes that "so many successful manufacturers
who had begun as workers walked the streets of that city then
(1880) that it is not hard to believe that others less successful
or just starting out on the lower rungs of the occupational mobility ladder could be convinced by personal knowledge that
'hard work' resulted in spectacular material and social improvement." This observation held true to a lesser extent for 1876
Chicago.

59.   Of the heads of these families of lower-class origin, 61% were
      also foreign-born. In this study, skilled artisans are included
      as members of the middling classes. In terms of income, many
      skilled artisans earned more than clerks and bookkeepers. Ide-
      ologically most apparently embraced middle-class values and at-
      titudes. These conclusions are supported in Michael Feldberg,
      The Philadelphia Riots of 1844 (Westport, Conn.: Greenwood
      Press, 1975), p. 48, who found that "skilled, native-born crafts-
      men," disabled economically by the depression of the late 1830s,
      and hoping to stem the influx of yet more hands into an over-
      crowded labor market, "turned to both evangelical Protestant
      religion and anti-immigrant policies to make their stand against
      personal oblivion."

60.   New England Congregational Church provides a striking example
      of the inability of the revival churches to transcend ethnic
      barriers in gathering new members. This church bordered the
      largest German population in Chicago in 1876. During the re-
      vival and in the weeks immediately thereafter, 89 persons af-
      filiated with the church by profession of faith. Not one of
      these persons, however, identified himself as German-born.
      And only one listed even a single parent of German origins.

61.   The correlation between the non-Anglo-American population and
      the poor among new church communicants in this study is high.
      Of these persons 46% were unskilled workers, and another 23.1%
      were skilled artisans. On the average they were six years older
      than their Anglo-American counterparts; 64% were married, but
      almost all the unmarried adults lived as boarders apart from a
      family setting. The largest number of occupations listed were
      housewife, laborer, and servant.

62.   On Moody's desire to evangelize the lower classes, see Findlay,
      Dwight L. Moody, pp. 172-74, 323-29. In 1878 Moody altered
      his revival techniques, holding services at various city loca-
      tions and hoping better to reach the poor. He was frustrated
      in this attempt also. Subsequently, he turned to such educa-
      tional institutions as his Chicago Bible Institute to train lay
      persons to evangelize the urban poor.

63. Lenhart, "Methodist Piety," pp. 55-57.

64. Pierce, History of Chicago, 2:355.

65. Ibid., 3:425.

66. Tribune, July 30, 1877. For similar sentiment, see Standard
     19 (January 11, 1872):4; Advance 6 (October 9, 1873):5; North-
     western Christian Advocate 21 (December 31, 1873):420; Watch-
     man and Reflector 57 (June 4, 1876):6.

67. Congregationalist 55 (November 16, 1871):6.

68. Quoted in Lewis and Smith, Chicago, p. 148.

69. Pierce, History of Chicago, 3:440.

70. For an excellent study of the sympathies of the Catholic poor
     with a revival style of religion, see Jay Dolan, Catholic Re-
     vivalism: The American Experience, 1830-1900 South Bend, Ind.:
     University of Notre Dame Press, 1978). On the attitudes of
     the Catholic church toward labor, see John T. Ellis, American
     Catholicism (Chicago: University of Chicago Press, 1956), pp.
     103-6.

                        CHAPTER VII

1.   For example, Sidney Mead, The Lively Experiment: The Shap-
     ing of Christianity in America (New York: Harper & Row,
     1963), pp. 124; McLoughlin, Modern Revivalism, pp. 166-67;
     Weisberger, They Gathered at the River, pp. 177, 207-10, 217.
     Important exceptions are Findlay, Dwight L. Moody, chap. 7;
     and Gundry, Love Them In.

2.   London Daily News, March 10, 1875, quoted in Findlay, Dwight
     L. Moody, p. 227. For a similar assessment by a Chicago
     listener, see Tribune, June 5, 1876.

3.   Forty-six of Moody's Chicago sermons were collected by the
     Inter-Ocean and reprinted verbatim under the title Great Joy.
     This volume also contains a number of the less formal prayer-
     meeting talks given by Moody at Farwell Hall, several of his
     prayers, and numerous question-and-answer sessions which the
     revivalist held with clergymen during the Christian Convention.
     Several other sermons preached in Chicago but not contained
     in Great Joy are printed in New Sermons. Both volumes were
     published in 1877. The analysis offered in this and the follow-
     ing chapters relies only upon those sermons delivered in Chi-
     cago and included in these several collections.

4. D. L. Moody, Great Joy, p. 241.

5. Ibid., p. 250. Gundry's study of Moody's theology is formed around this three-part doctrinal statement. I have found this study immensely helpful in my examination of the Chicago sermons. The importance of this brief doctrinal formulation was suggested further to the author on a research trip to Northfield, Massachusetts. One of Moody's Bibles was opened by chance and it was discovered that Moody had written on the inner page these words, "This book teaches three things, Ruin, Redemption, Regeneration."

6. Daniels, Words, Works and Workers, p. 256.

7. See D. L. Moody, Great Joy, pp. 38, 105, 157, 164-65, 181, 191.

8. Ibid., pp. 183-84, 359.

9. Northwestern Christian Advocate 4 (January 30, 1856):18. See also Interior 5 (November 5, 1874):2; 7 (January 6, 1876):1.

10. New York Observer 43 (June 22, 1865):193.

11. McLoughlin, American Evangelicals, p. 14. For examples, see Interior 3 (June 20, 1872):3; 3 (July 25, 1872):4; 7 (March 2, 1876):2; 7 (March 30, 1876):4.

12. For example, D. L. Moody, Great Joy, pp. 164-65, 486-87; idem, New Sermons, pp. 156-57.

13. Cf. Kent, Holding the Fort, pp. 183-201. Kent argues that Moody's preaching was a marked departure from standard evangelical sermonizing. Kent's assertions may be correct for English theology. Moody's preaching was, however, in harmony with prevailing evangelical thought in America.

14. For an excellent discussion of Moody's premillennial views, see Gundry, Love Them In, pp. 176ff.; and Findlay, Dwight L. Moody, pp. 276-77. On American premillennialism, see Timothy Weber, Living in the Shadow of the Second Coming: American premillennialism, 1875-1925 (New York: Oxford University Press, 1979). Pessimism toward successful broad social reform did not necessarily mean that evangelicals were inactive in social concerns; see Magnuson, Salvation in the Slums; and George Marsden, Fundamentalism and American Culture: The Shaping of Twentieth-Century Evangelicalism, 1870-1925 (New York: Oxford University Press, 1980), pp. 82-85.

15. D. L. Moody, Great Joy, pp. 184, 232.

16. The doctrine of free will suggested in these statements was perhaps related to Moody's understanding of "instantaneous conversion." Salvation was a matter of decision, and a decision for God resulted in immediate regeneration. A typical remark in this regard was, "The moment you enlist in Christ's army you belong to Him." Enlistment was a choice; the results were immediate. The best explication of this thinking is in D. L. Moody, Great Joy, pp. 264, 283. It is, however, incorrect to suppose that Moody preached a wholly democratic or man-centered Gospel. Instead, his sermons reflected a tension in evangelical thought between the sovereignty of God in salvation (a Calvinist emphasis) and man's essential responsibility (an Arminian emphasis). In his preaching, Moody never resolved the tension between God's sovereignty in salvation and man's ability freely to appropriate it. Instead, he affirmed without qualification the truth of both suppositions on the ground that both were Biblically accurate. For some insightful comments in this regard, see Findlay, Dwight L. Moody, p. 243.

17. Hudson, Religion in America, pp. 178-80, says that even the Calvinism of the traditionally Calvinistic churches was becoming so diluted by Arminian conceptions as "to be unrecognizable." McLoughlin, in Revivals, Awakenings and Reform, chap. 3, finds this phenomenon to be a result of the Second Great Awakening in America.

18. D. L. Moody, Great Joy, p. 124.

19. Ibid., pp. 180, 185.

20. Ibid., pp. 281, 359.

21. Moody to sister, October 6, 1856; Moody to brother, October 19 and December 16, 1856, Powell Collection.

22. D. L. Moody, Great Joy, pp. 417, 520, 334.

23. Ibid., p. 520.

24. Ibid., p. 333. Similar sentiments are found in Northwestern Christian Advocate 17 (May 12, 1869):146; Standard 22 (December 2, 1875):4.

25. Interior 3 (July 25, 1872):4.

26. Advance 9 (February 15, 1876):2. See also Interior 3 (October 3, 1872):4. In 1877 G. Stanley Hall, a native of Massachusetts on the threshold of a prominent career in psychology and philosophy, wrote that "the American, perhaps, even more than the English Sunday might almost be called a philosophical institution. A day of rest, of family life and introspection, it not

only gives seriousness and poise to character and brings the
saving fore-, after-, and over-thought into the midst of a
hurrying objective and material life ... but it teaches self-
control, self-knowledge, self-respect, as the highest results
of every intellectual motive and aspiration" (quoted in Winton
Solberg, Redeem the Time [Cambridge: Harvard University
Press, 1977], p. 302).

27.   D. L. Moody, Great Joy, p. 334.

28.   Christopher Hill, Society and Puritanism (New York: Schocken
      Books, 1964), p. 146. See also Solberg, Redeem the Time.

29.   Interior 4 (January 16, 1874):4.

30.   C. L. Thompson, "The Workingman's Sabbath," Chicago Pulpit
      2, no. 48 (November 1872):198-200.

31.   Ibid., pp. 26-27, 338.

32.   Daniels, Words, Works, and Workers, p. 519; D. L. Moody,
      Great Joy, p. 176. For similar statements, see also Advance
      10 (February 15, 1877):454; Goodspeed, Career of Moody and
      Sankey, p. 666; D. L. Moody, Great Joy, pp. 26-28, 48. See
      also Dunn, Talks on Temperance, pp. 5-6.

33.   Not all evangelicals shared this pessimism. Frances Willard's
      comments in a letter to Moody's wife shed some light on the
      various attitudes toward social reform even among fervent Moody
      supporters. "Mr. Moody views the temperance work from the
      standpoint of a revivalist, and so emphasizes the regeneration
      of men. But to me as a woman, there are other phases of it
      almost equally important to its success, viz., saving the chil-
      dren, teaching them never to drink; showing to their mothers
      the duty of total abstinence; rousing a dead church and a tor-
      pid Sunday-school to its duty; spreading the acts concerning
      the iniquitous traffic far and wide; influencing legislation so
      that what is physically wrong and morally wrong shall not, on
      the statute books of a Christian land, be set down as legally
      right;--and to this end putting the ballot in woman's hand for
      the protection of her little ones and her home. All these ways
      of working seem to me eminently religious--thoroughly in har-
      mony with the spirit of the most devoted Christian man or wo-
      man" (Willard, Glimpses of Fifty Years, pp. 359-60).

34.   D. L. Moody, Great Joy, pp. 221-22.

35.   Ibid., pp. 48-49.

36.   See Chapter Five. See also the comments of Gusfield, Symbolic
      Crusade, p. 81.

37. Advance 5 (February 15, 1872):2; Interior 3 (January 4, 1872):
    4. Similar comments are in Advance 4 (January 2, 1871):7; 9
    (January 18, 1876):7; Interior 7 (July 13, 1876):4.

38. D. L. Moody, Great Joy, pp. 48, 51, 65, 175-76, 222, 368.

39. Gusfield, Symbolic Crusade, p. 48.

40. For example, the Congregationalist Advance 5 (February 15,
    1872):7, applauded the "Maine Law" which had abolished the
    liquor trade in that state. "Maine," said the Advance, "has
    few paupers, criminals, and vagabonds ... and her people are
    steadily increasing in thrift and wealth."

41. Gusfield, Symbolic Crusade, pp. 3, 106.

42. D. L. Moody, Great Joy, pp. 497-99.

43. Ibid., p. 417.

44. Ibid., pp. 499-501, 348, 496.

45. Great Enterprises: 100 Years of the YMCA of Metropolitan Chi-
    cago, (New York: Rand McNally, 1957), p. 60. In his first
    presidential address as head of the Chicago YMCA, Moody
    described the organization as "a heaven-born institution because
    it tended to break down barriers of sectarianism. It reached
    to all classes and ages of people. The Association gains the
    heart of the people by the aid which it furnished to them in
    distress.... The theory of the Association is to first feed and
    clothe the poor, and then pray with them" (Times, November 5,
    1866).

46. W. R. Moody, Life of Dwight L. Moody, p. 170.

47. D. L. Moody, New Sermons, Addresses and Prayers (St. Louis:
    N. D. Thompson, 1877), pp. 603-5; Northwestern Christian Ad-
    vocate 25 (January 17, 1877):5. See also Dunn, Talks on Tem-
    perance, p. 84.

48. Goodspeed, Career of Moody and Sankey, p. 695; Tribune, No-
    vember 6, 1876.

49. Goodspeed, Career of Moody and Sankey, p. 694.

50. D. L. Moody, New Sermons, p. 604; Tribune, November 29,
    1876.

51. Tribune, November 6, 29, 1876.

52. D. L. Moody, New Sermons, p. 603. See also idem, Great Joy,
    p. 49.

53. May, Churches and Industrial America, p. 91.

54. Ibid., pp. 64-72; McLoughlin, Revivals, Awakenings and Reform, p. 144.

55. Findlay, Dwight L. Moody, p. 278.

56. D. L. Moody, Great Joy, p. 16; see also pp. 140-48, 88, 171-74, 464.

57. D. L. Moody, New Sermons, p. 602; Northwestern Christian Advocate 25 (January 17, 1877):5.

CHAPTER VIII

1. See, for example, Barbara Welter, Dimity Convictions (Athens: Ohio University Press, 1976); Cott, Bonds of Womanhood; Ann Douglas, The Feminization of American Culture (New York: Alfred A. Knopf, 1977); McLoughlin, American Evangelicals.

2. Quoted in Welter, Dimity Convictions, p. 40. For similar comments issued in the revival year, see Standard 24 (January 4, 1877):1; Interior 7 (March 22, 1876):2. Ladies' Repository 35 (December 1876):494, remarked: "The influence of the mother in shaping the future destiny of the child is almost unlimited.... Industry, taste, intelligence and religion are the essential qualifications of a good mother." Her influence is "irresistible."

3. For example, Baptist Standard 24 (January 4, 1877):1, editorialized, "Christian mothers hold in their keeping, to a great degree, the interests of the future of the Christian Church." Said Interior 8 (February 19, 1877):1, "No holier office, or one of higher trust, can be bestowed upon a mortal than that of being a mother." Her influence is "boundless."

4. In this paragraph, I am indebted to the insights of Welter, Dimity Convictions, pp. 22, 104; and Cott, Bonds of Womanhood, pp. 147ff.

5. D. L. Moody, Great Joy, p. 423.

6. Ibid., p. 420.

7. Ibid., p. 475; see also pp. 381-82, 120, 464-65, 493-94.

8. Ibid., pp. 275-76.

9. Ibid., p. 66.

10. Ibid., pp. 81-82.

11. Ibid., p. 303.

12. Ibid., p. 433.

13. Idib., p. 432.

14. This manner of thinking was, of course, not unique to Moody.
    Ladies' Repository 35 (February 1876):168, described the nega-
    tive influence of an impure woman in the harshest of terms.
    "Such a woman, if she has but an ordinary share of the graces
    belonging to her sex, is far more to be dreaded than a corrupt
    and wicked man.... In the family circle she is a curse; in
    social life she is a curse; in public life she is a curse,--always,
    everywhere a curse."

15. D. L. Moody, New Sermons, pp. 21-22.

16. D. L. Moody, Great Joy, p. 29.

17. Ibid., p. 31.

18. Ibid., p. 128; see also p. 391.

19. Ibid., p. 655.

20. Ibid., pp. 412, 380-81, 274, 70, 423, 128.

21. Ibid., p. 222.

22. Ibid., p. 48.

23. Ibid., p. 421.

24. The novels of Theodore Dreiser are examples of this. In 1874,
    W. W. VanArsdale, the superintendent of the Chicago YMCA,
    gave expression to evangelical conceptions of city living. "City
    life," said VanArsdale, "holds out attractions which continually
    draw young men from their rural homes into our large cities,
    where the enemy of souls is ever on the alert to allure them
    into sin by the multitudinous devices and agencies which abound
    in the city, and which are not suspected by the unsophisticated
    until too late" (quoted in Advance 7 [September 3, 1874]:15).

25. D. L. Moody, Great Joy, p. 134.

26. Ibid., pp. 85-86, 138, 168-77.

27. Weisberger, They Gathered at the River, p. 213.

28. D. L. Moody, Great Joy, p. 221.

29. Ibid., p. 177.

30. Ibid., pp. 361-69.

31. Ibid., p. 165.

32. Ibid., pp. 65, 80, 405, 218, 165.

33. The frequency of this theme in evangelical literature in the
     nineteenth century is remarkable. For examples from a leading
     national Methodist organ, see New York Christian Advocate 48
     (September 26, 1873):310; 48 (January 8, 1874):14; 48 (June
     7, 1874):50; 51 (April 28, 1876):110.

34. D. L. Moody, Great Joy, p. 70.

35. Ibid., p. 93.

36. Although their perspectives and emphases differ significantly,
     this line of thinking is suggested by Emile Durkheim, "Search
     for a Positive Definition," in Religion, Culture and Society, ed.
     Louis Schneider (New York: Wiley, 1964), pp. 32-33. Thomas
     Luckmann, The Invisible Religion (New York: Macmillan, 1967),
     p. 45; Clifford S. Geertz, The Interpretation of Cultures (New
     York: Basic Books, 1973), p. 89; Peter L. Berger, The Sacred
     Canopy (New York: Doubleday, 1967), p. 21.

37. Berger, Sacred Canopy, pp. 35-36, 24.

38. Sunderland, Orthodoxy and Revivalism, p. 110.

                              CHAPTER IX

1. Tribune, January 17, 1877; Independent 29 (January 18, 1877):
    12.

2. Inter-Ocean, January 17, 1877.

3. Advance 10 (January 25, 1877):377.

4. Christian Register, February 17, 1877.

5. Inter-Ocean, January 17, 1877.

6. Alliance, January 20, 1877.

7. Tribune, December 31, 1876; Inter-Ocean, January 22, 1877;
    Chicago Weekly Journal, December 20, 1876; W. H. Ryder, An
    Open Letter From W. H. Ryder, D.D., of Chicago, Ill., to D. L.
    Moody, Esq., the Evangelist (Boston Universalist, 1877). For

other favorable comments of this sort, see Goodspeed, Career
of Moody and Sankey, p. 714; Advance 9 (December 21, 1876);
286; "Reminiscences of J. M. Hitchcock," in Inter-Ocean, October 27, 1907.

8. Tribune, December 1, 1876; Inter-Ocean, October 14, 1876;
New York Christian Advocate 51 (December 7, 1876):390; see
also Tribune, November 14, 1876.

9. Advance 10 (February 15, 1877):451.

10. Tribune, November 21, 1876.

11. Statements are from reports in Tribune, November 14, 21, and
December 5, 1876.

12. Advance 10 (February 8, 1877):417; 10 (January 25, 1877):377;
Interior 8 (February 8, 1877):4.

13. Inter-Ocean, January 20, 1877.

14. The Boston meetings are examined in Samuel W. Dyke, "A Study
of New England Revivals," American Journal of Sociology 15 (November 1909):361-78. The Philadelphia revival is studied by
Lefferts A. Loetscher, "Presbyterianism and Revivalism in Philadelphia since 1875," Pennsylvania Magazine of History and Biography 68 (January 1944):56-84. The results of the Philadelphia
revival for the Methodist churches are analyzed in Bell, Crusade
in the City, p. 244.

15. James F. Findlay, "Dwight L. Moody: Evangelist of the Gilded
Age" (Ph.D. diss., Northwestern University, 1961), pp. 190-95
and appendix. Also idem, Dwight L. Moody, p. 271.

16. The term "population density" refers here to the size of an
organization's membership relative to the total population of
Chicago. The statistic is useful as a measure of relative church
growth. It should be noted, however, that it is an inadequate
indicator of denominational strength in the city. Obviously the
urban population actually eligible for recruitment into the
churches was much less than the total population. Unfortunately, more precise population data are not available for Chicago
on a yearly basis for the 1870s. For helpful comments on the
use of this statistical tool, see Robert Currie et al., Churches
and Churchgoers: Patterns of Church Growth in the British
Isles since 1870 (Oxford: Clarendon Press, 1971), chap. 1.

17. From 1870 to 1880 the Chicago Presbytery reported an average
of 522 persons received into membership upon profession of
faith. In 1877 the number of such persons increased to 1,414.

18. In Chicago, for example, I was able to find complete records
    for only two of the seventeen Methodist Episcopal churches in
    the city in 1876. As one archivist suggested to me, some
    churches burned, but the majority of church records are pro-
    bably in the attics of homes once owned by church clerks or
    ministers and placed there for "safekeeping."

19. See Chapter 5 for a discussion of the churches and a rationale
    for their selection.

20. The church records list both the date of reception to member-
    ship and the cessation of that relationship, whether by trans-
    fer, dismissal, or death. Thus one is able to gain some insight,
    though limited, into subsequent church experience.

21. Goodspeed, _Career of Moody and Sankey_, p. 656; Third Presby-
    terian Church of Chicago, minutes, 1907. Although Patrick was
    not formally dismissed from the church until 1907, it is likely
    that his disaffection with Third Presbyterian may have begun
    much earlier. Interestingly, 84 of the 92 revival converts who
    were dropped from this church's membership lists were removed
    in 1907, suggesting that the church was probably taking care
    of some long overdue housekeeping of its membership lists.

22. _Inter-Ocean_, November 25, 1876; P. Sinclair to Brother Fitt,
    January 12, 1911, at Moody Bible Institute Library.

23. Dolan, _Catholic Revivalism_, pp. 140-41, offers several insight-
    ful comments on the value of the revival experience even if its
    impact was often transient. Says Dolan, "Revival religion did
    enrich and even change the lives of many people by revitalizing
    their religious sensitivity.... It was a soul-stirring event that
    presented the pious folk with an opportunity to advance further
    along the path of holiness.... To live continuously in the
    presence of God is an ideal sought by many a holy person; most
    mortals, however, do not achieve such mystical heights, nor can
    they even fathom what it means.... From a religious perspec-
    tive to have undergone this experience was good in itself, to
    prolong it was only better.... Revivalism fostered only one
    variety of the religious experience and an ephemeral one at that,
    but, like a moon eclipse, it was a unique event whose signifi-
    cance was not diminished by its transiency."

24. _Tribune_, July 8, 1877; on political economy, see Lyman Atwater,
    "The Labor Question and Its Economic and Christian Aspects,"
    Princeton Review 1 (July 1872):468-95; _Christian Union_ 6 (July
    25, 1877):62. The best modern discussion is May, _Churches
    and Industrial America_, pp. 51ff.

25. From the accounts of July 26, 1877, in _Tribune_, _Times_, and
    Chicago Post.

26. From the accounts of July 26, 27, and 28, 1877, in Tribune, Times, and Inter-Ocean; Times headline on July 26 read as follows: "TERROR'S REIGN, The Streets of Chicago Given Over to Howling Mobs of Thieves and Cut-Throats."

27. Comments from the sermons of Galusha Anderson of the Second Baptist Church, N. F. Ravlin of the Free Baptist Church, and W. W. Patton as printed in Tribune, July 30, 1877. For similar comments, see also the sermons contained in Inter-Ocean, July 30, 1877.

28. Northwestern Christian Advocate 25 (August 1, 1877):5.

29. Tribune, July 30, 1877. See also Standard 24 (August 9, 1877): 6.

30. Independent 29 (September 6, 1877):425, quoted in Northwestern Christian Advocate 25 (September 19, 1877):5. For similar comments, see Standard 24 (August 9, 1877):6. Northwestern Christian Advocate 25 (August 1, 1877):5; Tribune, July 30, 1877.

31. Pierce, History of Chicago, 3:356.

32. Standard 30 (April 12, 1883):4.

33. Pierce, History of Chicago, 3:459.

34. Ibid., 3:357-59.

35. J. A. Mayer, "Private Charities." See also Kenneth Kussmer, "The Function of Organized Charity in the Progressive Era: Chicago as a Case Study," Journal of American History 60 (December 1973):665.

36. Rev. Charles F. Goss sermon in Chicago Daily News, June 13, 1892.

37. In Chicago, George Lorimer, pastor of the First Baptist Church, provided a prophetic early evangelical voice in support of labor. Said Lorimer, "Mammonism has no conscience, no truth, it regards those whom it uses for its own advancement as having no soul. Long hours, short pay for the laborer, short hours and long pay for the capitalist, is its doctrine. It believes in the divine and exclusive right of money.... And it stupidly fails to perceive that the science of worldly interests, as now understood, is a monstrous piece of botching, as absurd as it is inhuman, and that as long as it is relied on we need not expect to see any radical abatement of evils which are perpetuating barbarism and breeding dissensions" (quoted in Pierce, History of Chicago, 3:440).

PRIMARY SOURCES

City Directories

The Lakeside Annual Directory of the City of Chicago. (Chicago, 1876-77.

Federal and State Publications

Chicago Department of Health. Report, 1881. Chicago, 1882.

_____. Report, 1882. Chicago, 1883.

Chicago Relief and Aid Society. The Sixteenth Annual Report of the Chicago Relief and Aid Society to the Common Council of the City of Chicago, 1873. Chicago, 1874.

_____. The Seventeenth Annual Report of the Chicago Relief and Aid Society to the Common Council of the City of Chicago, 1874. Chicago, 1875.

U. S. Bureau of the Census. Tenth Census of the United States, 1880: Population Schedules. Washington, U. S. National Archives, 1962.

U. S. Department of the Interior. Office of the Census. Compendium of the Tenth Census, 1880. 2 vols. Washington, 1888.

_____. Tenth Census of the United States, 1880. "Report on the Social Statistics of Cities," vol. 18. Washington, 1887.

Unpublished Papers and Records

Chicago Theological Seminary Library. New England Congregational Church. Minutes and Recordbook.

_____. Tabernacle Congregational Church. Minutes.

Garrett Theological Seminary Archives, Evanston, Ill. Centenary
Methodist Episcopal Church. Minutes.

_____. Francis Hemenway, "Lessons from the Moody Meetings."
N.d.

_____. Methodist Episcopal Church, Chicago German District.
Minutes. 1870-1880.

_____. Methodist Episcopal Church, Northwest Swedish District.
Minutes. 1870-1880.

_____. Methodist Episcopal Church, Rock River Conference.
Minutes. 1870-1880.

McCormick Theological Seminary Library. Fifth Presbyterian Church
of Chicago. Minutes and Session Book.

_____. Third Presbyterian Church, Chicago. Minutes and Ses-
sion Book.

Moody Bible Institute Library, Chicago. Moody Papers.

Moody Museum, Northfield, Mass. Powell Collection.

_____. T. R. Alexander, "Dwight L. Moody and His Contribution
to the Young Men's Christian Association." N.d.

Presbyterian Historical Society, Philadelphia, Addresses, vol. 2.
N.d.

_____. A. E. Kittridge, Historical Discourses by the Rev. A. E.
Kittridge. N.d.

Protestant Episcopal Church, New York. Church Congress. Papers,
Addresses and Debates. 1874-75.

YMCA Historical Library, Chicago. Thomas Cree Journal.

Magazines, Journals, and Periodicals
(Chicago-based)

Advance (Congregationalist). 1872-78.

Alliance (Protestant) 1872-78.

Chicago Daily Inter-Ocean. 1870-1880.

Chicago Daily News 1875-77.

Chicago Post 1872-78.

Chicago Times 1872-78.

Chicago Tribune 1872-78.

Chicago Weekly Journal 1872-78.

Interior (Presbyterian) 1872-78.

Northwestern Christian Advocate (Methodist) 1870-78

Standard (Baptist) 1872-78.

Western Brewer 1875-77.

Western Catholic 1873-78.

Workingman's Advocate 1875-77.

Books and Articles

Atwater, Lyman. "The Labor Question and Its Economic and Christian
    Aspects." Princeton Review 1 (July 1872):468-95.

Brace, Charles. The Dangerous Classes of New York. New York:
    Wynkoop & Hallenbeck, 1872.

Chicago Daily News Almanac. Chicago, 1946.

Conant, William C. "The Bible and the State." Baptist Quarterly
    5 (July 1871):276-93.

Daniels, W. H. D. L. Moody and His Work. Hartford, Conn.:
    American, 1875.

_____. Moody: His Words, Works and Workers. New York:
    Nelson and Phillips, 1877.

Dunn, James B., ed. Moody's Talks on Temperance with Anecdotes
    and Incidents. New York: National Temperance Society and
    Publishing House, 1877.

Fish, Henry C. Handbook of Revivals: For the Use of Winners of
    Souls. Boston: James H. Earle, 1874.

Goodrich, Grant. Report of the Conference Committee for the Relief
    of Methodist Institutions and Churches of Chicago. Chicago:
    Rand & McNally, 1873.

Goodspeed, E. J. A Full History of the Wonderful Career of Moody and Sankey in Great Britain and America. Cleveland: C. C. Wick, 1876.

Hawkins, Dexter. "The Anglo-Saxon Race." Methodist Quarterly 58 (January 1876):87-111.

McPherson, Edward. A Handbook of Politics for 1876: Being a Record of Important Political Action, National and State from July 15, 1874, to July 15, 1876. Washington: Solomons & Chapman, 1876.

McQuaid, Bernard. The Public School Question. Boston, 1876.

Moody, Dwight L. Glad Tidings: Comprising Sermons and Prayer-Meeting Talks Delivered at the New York Hippodrome. New York: E. B. Treat, 1876.

_____. Great Joy: Comprising Sermons and Prayer-Meeting Talks. New York: E. B. Treat, 1877.

_____. Great Redemption; or, Gospel Light, under the labors of Moody and Sankey. Chicago: Century Book & Paper. 1889.

_____. New Sermons, Addresses and Prayers. St. Louis: N. D. Thompson, 1877.

Mueller, Michael. Public School Education. New York, 1873.

_____. "A Revival at Frogtown." Catholic World 22 (February 1876):699-707.

Richmond, J. F. "The Dangerous Classes, and Their Treatment." Methodist Quarterly 55 (July 1873):455-74.

Ryder, W. H. An Open Letter from W. H. Ryder, D.D., of Chicago, Ill., to D. L. Moody, Esq., the Evangelist. Boston: Universalist, 1877.

Sheahan, J. W. "Chicago." Scribner's Monthly 11 (September 1875): 529-51.

Sturdevant, J. M. "Church and State." Congregational Quarterly 15 (October 1873):508-35.

Sunderland, J. T. Orthodoxy and Revivalism. New York: James Miller, 1876.

Thompson, C. L. Times of Refreshing. Chicago: L. T. Palmer Co., 1877.

_____. "The Workingman's Sabbath." Chicago Pulpit 2, No. 48
(November 1872):198-200.

                        SECONDARY SOURCES

                              Books

Abell, Aaron I. The Urban Impact on American Protestantism, 1865-
1900. London: Archon Press, 1962.

Ahlstrom, Sydney E. A Religious History of the American People.
New Haven: Yale University Press, 1972.

Andreas, A. T. A History of Chicago from the Earliest Period to
the Present Time. 3 vols. Chicago: A. T. Andreas, 1884-86.

Andrews, Wayne. Battle for Chicago. New York: Harcourt, Brace
& Co., 1946.

Baird, Robert. Religion in America. 1856. Reprint. New York:
Harper Torchbooks, 1970.

Barton, Josef J. Peasants and Strangers. Cambridge, Harvard University Press, 1975.

Bell, Marion. Crusade in the City. Philadelphia: Temple University Press, 1978.

Berger, Peter L. The Sacred Canopy. New York: Doubleday,
1967.

Berthoff, Rowland. An Unsettled People. New York: Harper &
Row, 1971.

Billington, Ray Allen. The Protestant Crusade, 1880-1860: A Study
of the Origins of the American Nativism. New York: Atheneum
Press, 1938.

Bradford, Gamaliel. D. L. Moody: A Worker in Souls. New York:
George H. Doran Co., 1927.

Carter, Paul A. The Spiritual Crisis of the Gilded Age. Dekalb:
Northern Illinois University Press, 1971.

Cawelti, John G. Apostles of the Self-Made Man. Chicago: University of Chicago Press, 1965.

Centers, Richard. The Psychology of Social Classes. Princeton:
Princeton University Press, 1949.

Chamberlain, Everett. Chicago and Her Suburbs. Chicago, 1874.

Chapman, J. Wilbur. The Life and Work of Dwight L. Moody. Philadelphia: International, 1900.

Chartier, Myron Raymond. The Social Views of Dwight L. Moody and Their Relation to the Workingman of 1860-1900. Hays, Kans.: Fort Hays State University, 1969.

Chicago. Department of Development and Planning. Historic Chicago: The Settlement of Chicago. Chicago, 1976.

_____. The People of Chicago. Chicago, 1976.

Chicago Tribune Company. A Century of Tribune Editorials, 1847-1947. Chicago, 1947.

Chicago Young Men's Christian Association. Fifty-Five Years: The Young Men's Christian Association of Chicago, 1858-1913. Chicago, 1913.

Churches of Chicago. Chicago: Lakeside Press, 1878.

Cook, Charles T., and Houghton, William H. Tell Me about Moody. London: Marshall, Morgan & Scott, 1936.

Cook, Frederick F. Bygone Days in Chicago: Recollections of the "Garden City" of the Sixties. Chicago: A. C. McClurg, 1910.

Cott, Nancy F. The Bonds of Womanhood. New Haven: Yale University Press, 1977.

Cross, Robert D. The Church and the City, 1865-1910. New York: Bobbs-Merrill Co., 1967.

_____. The Emergence of Liberal Catholicism in America. Chicago: Quadrangle Books, 1968.

Currie, Robert; Gilbert, Alan; and Horsly, Lee. Churches and Churchgoers: Patterns of Church Growth in the British Isles since 1870. Oxford: Clarendon Press, 1971.

Curtis, Richard K. They Called Him Mister Moody. New York: Doubleday, 1962.

Dedmond, Emmett. Fabulous Chicago. New York: Random House, 1953.

Devins, R. M. American Progress; or, The Great Events of the Greatest Century, Also Life Delineations of Our Most Noted Men. 6 vols. Chicago: Hugh Heron, 1882.

Dolan, Jay. Catholic Revivalism: The American Experience, 1830-1900 South Bend, Ind.: University of Notre Dame Press, 1978.

Douglas, Ann. The Feminization of American Culture. New York: Alfred A. Knopf, 1977.

Durkheim, Emile. "Search for a Positive Definition." In Religion, Culture and Society, Louis Schneider, pp. 27-35. New York: Wiley, 1964.

Eliade, Mircea. Myths and Reality. New York: Harper & Row, 1963.

_____. Myths, Dreams and Mysteries. New York: Harper & Row, 1960.

Ellis, John T. American Catholicism. Chicago: University of Chicago Press, 1956.

Epstein, Barbara. The Politics of Domesticity. Middletown, Conn.: Wesleyan University Press, 1981.

Farr, Finis. Chicago: A Personal History of America's Most American City. New Rochelle, N.Y.: Arlington House, 1973.

Farwell, John V. Early Recollections of Dwight L. Moody. Chicago: Winona Press, 1907.

Feldberg, Michael. The Philadelphia Riots of 1844. Westport, Conn.: Greenwood Press, 1975.

Ferry, Abby Farwell. Reminiscences of John V. Farwell by His Eldest Daughter. 2 vols. Chicago: R. F. Seymour, 1928.

Findlay, James F. Dwight L. Moody: American Evangelist, 1837-1899. Chicago: University of Chicago Press, 1969.

Formisano, Ronald. The Birth of Mass Political Parties: Michigan, 1827-1861. Princeton: Princeton University Press, 1971.

Garrison, Winfred. The March of Faith: The Story of Religion in America since 1865. New York: Harper & Bros., 1933.

Geertz, Clifford. The Interpretation of Cultures. New York: Basic Books, 1973.

Great Enterprises; 100 years of the YMCA of Metropolitan Chicago. New York: Rand McNally, 1957.

Griffin, Clifford S. Their Brother's Keepers: Moral Stewardship in the United States, 1800-1865. New Brunswick, N.J.: Rutgers University Press, 1960.

Gundry, Stanley N. Love Them In: The Proclamation Theology of
    D. L. Moody. Chicago: Moody Press, 1976.

Gusfield, Joseph. Symbolic Crusade: Status Politics and the Ameri-
    can Temperance Movement. Urbana: University of Illinois Press,
    1963.

Hammond, John L. The Politics of Benevolence: Revival Religion and
    American Voting Behavior. Norwood, N.J.: Ablex Publishing
    House, 1979.

Handy, Robert T. A Christian America: Protestant Hopes and His-
    torical Realities. New York: Oxford University Press, 1971.

Higham, John. Strangers in the Land: Patterns of American Na-
    tivism, 1860-1925. New Brunswick, N.J.: Rutgers University
    Press, 1955.

Hill, Christopher. Society and Puritanism. New York: Schocken
    Books, 1964.

Hopkins, C. Howard. History of the YMCA in North America. New
    York: Association Press, 1951.

Howe, Daniel W., ed. Victorian America. Philadelphia: University
    of Pennsylvania Press, 1976.

Hoyt, Homer. One Hundred Years of Land Values in Chicago, 1830-
    1930. Chicago: University of Chicago Press, 1933.

Huber, Richard M. The American Idea of Success. New York:
    McGraw-Hill, 1971.

Hudson, Winthrop. Religion in America. 3rd ed. New York:
    Charles Scribner's Sons, 1965.

Hutchinson, William. The Modernist Impulse in American Protestant-
    ism. Cambridge: Harvard University Press, 1976.

Jewell, Frank. Annotated Bibliography of Chicago History. Chicago,
    1979.

Johnson, Paul. A Shopkeeper's Millennium. New York: Hill &
    Wang, 1978.

Kane, J. S. Catholic-Protestant Conflicts in America. Chicago:
    Regency Press, 1965.

Kent, John. Holding the Fort. London: Epworth Press, 1978.

Kirkland, Edward C. Dream and Thought in the Business Community,
    1860-1900. Ithaca: Cornell University Press, 1956.

Kogan, Herman. Lords of the Levee. Indianapolis: Bobbs-Merrill Co., 1943.

_____, and Wendt, Lloyd. Chicago: A Pictorial History. New York: Dutton, 1958.

Lewis, Lloyd, and Smith, Henry J. Chicago: The History of Its Reputation. New York: Harcourt, Brace & Co., 1929.

Luckmann, Thomas. The Invisible Religion. New York: Macmillan, 1967.

McKinnon, Mrs. J. Recollections of D. L. Moody and His Work in Britain, 1874-1892. London, 1901.

McLoughlin, William G. The American Evangelicals, 1800-1900. New York: Harper Torchbooks, 1968.

_____. Modern Revivalism: Charles Gradison Finney to Billy Graham. New York: Ronald Press, 1959.

_____. Revivals, Awakenings and Reform. Chicago: University of Chicago Press, 1978.

Magnuson, Norris. Salvation in the Slums: Evangelical Social Work, 1865-1920. Metuchen, N.J.: Scarecrow Press and the ATLA, 1977.

Maguire, John Francis. The Irish in America. 1873. Reprint. New York: Arno, 1969.

Marsden, George. Fundamentalism and American Culture: The Shaping of Twentieth-Century Evangelicalism, 1870-1925. New York: Oxford University Press, 1980.

May, Henry F. The Protestant Churches and Industrial America. New York: Harper & Bros., 1949.

Mayer, Harold M., and Wade, Richard C. Chicago: Growth of a Metropolis. Chicago: University of Chicago Press, 1969.

Mead, Sidney. The Lively Experiment: The Shaping of Christianity in America. New York: Harper & Row, 1963.

Miyakawa, T. Scott. Protestants and Pioneers. Chicago: University of Chicago Press, 1964.

Moody, Paul. My Father: An Intimate Portrait of Dwight Moody. Boston: Little, Brown & Co., 1938.

Moody, William R. The Life of D. L. Moody. New York: Revell, 1900.

O'Dea, Thomas. Sociology and the Study of Religion. New York: Basic Books, 1970.

Orr, J. Edwin. The Second Evangelical Awakening in America. London: Marshall, Morgan & Scott, 1952.

Parot, Joseph John. Polish Catholics in Chicago, 1850-1920. DeKalb: Northern Illinois University Press, 1981.

Pierce, Bessie L. As Others See Chicago: Impressions of Visitors, 1673-1933. Chicago: University of Chicago Press, 1933.

_____. A History of Chicago. 3 vols. New York: Alfred A. Knopf, 1937-57.

Pollock, John C. Moody: A Biographical Portrait of the Pacesetter in Modern Mass Evangelism. New York: Macmillan Press, 1963.

Rischin, Moses. The American Gospel of Success. Chicago: Quadrangle Books, 1965.

Sandburg, Carl. Chicago Poems. New York: Henry Holt & Co., 1916.

Sankey, Ira D. My Life and the Story of the Gospel Hymns. New York: Harper & Bros., 1907.

Sennett, Richard. Families Against the City: Middle-Class Homes of Industrial Chicago, 1872-1890. Cambridge: Harvard University Press, 1970.

Shanabruck, Charles. Chicago's Catholics. South Bend, Ind.: University of Notre Dame Press, 1980.

Shea, John. Stories of God. Chicago: Thomas More Press, 1978.

Sirjamaki, John. The Sociology of Cities. New York: Random House, 1964.

Sizer, Sandra S. Gospel Hymns and Social Religion. Philadelphia: Temple University Press, 1978.

Smith, Timothy. Revivalism and Social Reform in Mid-Nineteenth Century America. New York: Abingdon Press, 1957.

Smith, Wilbur, comp. An Annotated Bibliography of D. L. Moody. Chicago: Moody Press, 1948.

Solberg, Winton. Redeem the Time. Cambridge: Harvard University Press, 1977.

Stebbins, George C. Reminiscences and Gospel Hymn Stories. 1924. Reprint. New York: AMS, 1971.

Thernstrom, Stephan. The Other Bostonians. Cambridge: Harvard University Press, 1973.

Tremmel, William. Religion: What Is It? New York: Holt, Rinehart & Winston, 1976.

Wade, Louise C. Graham Taylor: Pioneer for Social Justice, 1851-1938. Chicago: University of Chicago Press, 1964.

Weber, Timothy. Living in the Shadow of the Second Coming: American Premillennialism, 1875-1925. New York: Oxford University Press, 1979.

Weisberger, Bernard. They Gathered at the River. Boston: Little, Brown & Co., 1958.

Welter, Barbara. Dimity Convictions. Athens: Ohio University Press, 1976.

Wiebe, Robert W. The Search for Order, 1877-1920. New York: Hill & Wang, 1967.

Willard, Frances. Glimpses of Fifty Years: The Autobiography of an American Woman. Chicago: Women's Temperance Publication Association, 1889.

Articles

Banner, Lois. "Religion and Reform in the Early Republic: The Role of Youth." American Quarterly 23 (December 1971):677-95.

Cott, Nancy F. "Young Women in the Second Great Awakening." Feminist Studies 3 (Fall):15-29.

Dunn, F. Roger. "Formative Years of the Chicago YMCA: A Study in Urban History." Journal of the Illinois State Historical Society 37 (December 1944):342-45.

Dyke, Samuel W. "A Study of New England Revivals." American Journal of Sociology 15 (November 1909):361-78.

Gutman, Herbert. "The Rags-to-Riches 'Myth': The Case of the Paterson, New Jersey, Locomotive, Iron and Machinery Manufacturers, 1830-1880." In Nineteenth-Century Cities, ed. Stephan Thernstrom and Richard Sennet, pp. 98-124. New Haven: Yale University Press, 1969.

Hershberg, Theodore; Katz, Michael; Blumin, Stuart; Glasco, Law-
rence; and Griffin, Clyde. "Occupation and Ethnicity in Five
Nineteenth-Century Cities: A Collaborative Inquiry." Historical
Methods Newsletter (June 1974):174-216.

Kett, Joseph F. "Growing Up in Rural New England, 1800-1840."
In Anonymous Americans: Explorations in Nineteen-Century So-
cial History ed. Tamara K. Haraven, pp. 1-17. Englewood Cliffs,
N.J.: Prentice-Hall, 1971.

Kussmer, Kenneth. "The Function of Organized Charity in the
Progressive Era: Chicago as a Case Study." Journal of American History 60 (December 1973):657-78.

Loetscher, Lefferts A. "Presbyterianism and Revivals in Philadelphia
since 1875." Pennsylvania Magazine of History and Biography 68
(January 1944):54-92.

Sizer, Sandra. "Politics and Apolitical Religion: The Great Urban
Revivals of the Late Nineteenth Century." Church History 48
(March 1979):81-98.

Treiman, Donald. "A Standard Occupational Prestige Scale for Use
with Historical Data." Journal of Interdisciplinary History 7
(Autumn 1976):283-304.

                    Dissertations and Theses

Findlay, James F. "Dwight L. Moody: Evangelist of the Gilded
Age." Ph.D. diss., Northwestern University, 1961.

Huber, Robert B. "Dwight L. Moody: Salesman of Salvation--A
Case Study in Audience Psychology." Ph.D. diss., University
of Wisconsin, 1942.

Lenhart, Thomas. "Methodist Piety in an Industrializing Society,
Chicago, 1860-1914." Ph.D. diss., Northwestern University,
1981.

Lunsford, Rowan. "The Evangelistic Campaigns of Dwight L. Moody."
M.A. thesis, University of Redlands, 1945.

Mayer, John. "Private Charities in Chicago from 1871 to 1915."
Ph.D. diss., University of Minnesota, 1978.

Olenik, Dennis L. "The Social Philosophy of Dwight L. Moody."
M.A. thesis, Northern Illinois University, 1964.

Quimby, Rollin W. "Dwight L. Moody: An Examination of the Historical
Conditions Which Contributed to His Effectiveness as a Speaker."
Ph.D. diss., University of Michigan, 1951.